Wordsworth and the Beginnings of Modern Poetry

ROBERT REHDER

CROOM HELM LONDON

BARNES & NOBLE BOOKS
TOTOWA, NEW JERSEY

© 1981 Robert Rehder
Croom Helm Ltd, 2 – 10 St John's Road, London SW11

British Library Cataloguing in Publication Data

Rehder, Robert M
  ˙Wordsworth and the beginnings of modern poetry.
  1. Wordsworth, William — Criticism and interpretation
  I. Title
  821'.7   PR5888

ISBN 0 – 85664 – 368 – 8

First published in the USA 1981 by
BARNES & NOBLE BOOKS
81 ADAMS DRIVE,
TOTOWA, New Jersey, 07512
ISBN: 0 – 389 – 20209 – 6

Acknowledgements: The author and publisher are grateful to Faber and Faber Ltd for permission to reprint 'Of Modern Poetry' by Wallace Stevens from *The Collected Poems of Wallace Stevens* and to Alfred A. Knopf, Inc., Random House, Inc., for permission to reprint 'of Modern Poetry' from *The Palm at the End of the Mind: Selected Poems and a Play*, edited by Holly Stevens, © 1967, 1969, 1971.

Printed and bound in Great Britain by
Biddles Ltd, Guildford and King's Lynn

Contents

TO CAROLINE WITH LOVE

Notes

Except for works mentioned in the List of Abbreviations, a full reference is given the first time that a work is cited, after which a shorter form is used. All the English books were published in London and all the French books in Paris except where another place is specified. All translations are mine unless otherwise noted.

Unless otherwise indicated, all citations of Wordsworth's poems are from Hayden's edition (Poems), Wordsworth's letters from de Selincourt's edition, revised in part by various hands (WL) and those of Coleridge from Griggs's edition (CL). Citations from these sources have generally not been noted, as the poems can be found easily through the index of titles and the letters through the dates. The references to Wordsworth's autobiographical poem are given in the text. The Roman numerals denote the books, the Arabic, the lines. All references are to the 1805 text as revised by Gill (PG), unless they include the date, 1850, in which case the text is that of the de Selincourt-Darbishire edition.

The Shavers' *Wordsworth's Library* and Butler's edition of *The Ruined Cottage and The Pedlar* appeared as I was preparing my MS for the publisher so I have only been able to make very limited use of them.

Abbreviations

Works by Wordsworth

PTV   *Wordsworth, Poems, in Two Volumes*, 1807, ed. Helen Darbishire (Oxford, 1914)

P   *The Prelude*, ed. Ernest de Selincourt and Helen Darbishire (Oxford, 1965)

PW   *The Poetical Works of William Wordsworth*, ed. Ernest de Selincourt and Helen Darbishire (Oxford), I (1967), II (1969), III (1968), IV (1970), V (1966)

WL   *The Letters of William and Dorothy Wordsworth*: I, *The Early Years 1787–1805*, ed. Ernest de Selincourt and C.L. Shaver (Oxford, 1967); II, *The Middle Years, Part 1, 1806–1811*, ed. Ernest de Selincourt and Mary Moorman (Oxford, 1969); III, *The Middle Years, Part 2, 1812–1820*, ed. Ernest de Selincourt, Mary Moorman and A.G. Hill (Oxford, 1970); IV–VI, *The Later Years 1821–1850*, ed. Ernest de Selincourt (Oxford, 1939)

PG   *The Prelude*, ed. Ernest de Selincourt, corrected by Stephen Gill (Oxford, 1970)

LB   *Wordsworth and Coleridge, Lyrical Ballads, 1798*, ed. W.J. Owen (Oxford, 1971)

Prose   *The Prose Works of William Wordsworth*, ed. W.J. Owen and J.W. Smyser, 3 vols. (Oxford, 1974)

PM   *The Prelude*, ed. J.C. Maxwell (Harmondsworth, 1975)

SP   *The Salisbury Plain Poems of William Wordsworth*, ed. Stephen Gill (Ithaca, 1975)

HG   *Home at Grasmere, Part First, Book First of the Recluse*, ed. Beth Darlington (Ithaca, 1977)

Poems   *The Poems*, ed. J.O. Hayden, 2 vols. (Harmondsworth, 1977)

PP   *The Prelude 1798–1799*, ed. Stephen Parrish (Ithaca, 1977)

RCP   *The Ruined Cottage and The Pedlar*, ed. James Butler (Ithaca, 1979)

Works by Coleridge

CP   *The Complete Poetical Works of Samuel Taylor Coleridge*, ed. E.H. Coleridge, 2 vols. (Oxford, 1912)

CS   *Selected Poetry and Prose of Coleridge*, ed. D.A. Stauffer (New York, 1951)

CN   *The Notebooks of Samuel Taylor Coleridge*, ed. Kathleen Coburn, 3 vols. (New York and London, 1957 – 1973)

CL   *Collected Letters of Samuel Taylor Coleridge*, ed. E.L. Griggs, 6 vols. (Oxford, 1966 – 1971)

CC   *The Collected Works of Samuel Taylor Coleridge*, ed. Kathleen Coburn, 16 vols. (London and New York, 1969 –)

Other Works

CLRM   *Catalogue of the Varied and Valuable Historical, Poetical, Theological, and Miscellaneous Library of the Late Venerated Poet-Laureate, William Wordsworth, D.C.L., Last, Not Least of the Line of Lake Minstrels;. . .*(the sale catalogue of the 'nearly three thousand volumes' sold by auction by John Burton at Rydal Mount on 19 – 21 July 1859)

Moorman Moorman, Mary, *William Wordsworth, A Biography*, 2 vols. (Oxford, 1967)

Shaver   Shaver, C.L., and A.C. Shaver, *Wordsworth's Library* (New York, 1979)

Reed I   Reed, M.L., *Wordsworth, The Chronology of the Early Years 1770 – 1799* (Cambridge, Mass., 1967)

Reed II ＿＿＿, *Wordsworth, The Chronology of the Middle Years, 1800 – 1815* (Cambridge, Mass., 1975)

Memoirs Wordsworth, Christopher, *Memoirs of William Wordsworth*, 2 vols. (London, 1851)

JDW   Wordsworth, Dorothy, *Journals of Dorothy Wordsworth*, ed. Mary Moorman (Oxford, 1971)

Music   Wordsworth, Jonathan, *The Music of Humanity* (London, 1969)

BWS   ＿＿＿, ed., *Bicentenary Wordsworth Studies in Memory of John Alban Finch* (Ithaca, 1970)

Other Abbreviations

DC   Dove Cottage
OED   *The Oxford English Dictionary*, 13 vols. (Oxford, 1933)

Preface

This is a work of hypotheses. The ideas put forward here are tentative. Their starting-point was an observation of the difference between the styles of Pope and Wordsworth. Even though the connection between them was clear and the development from one to the other could be traced through the poetry of Thomson, Gray, Collins, Goldsmith, Cowper, Blake and Burns, the difference seemed to me greater than that between any other two successive, great English poets, and Wordsworth's poetry, this development notwithstanding, radically unlike that of any poet before him. Subsequent poets, however, share so many of his poetic assumptions, beliefs and concerns that the history of the poetry of the last two hundred years seemed most easily comprehensible when considered as a whole and interpreted as beginning with Wordsworth. This book, then, is an attempt to understand the change that takes place in poetry with Wordsworth and the nature of Wordsworth's achievement.

My concern throughout is with Wordsworth's poetry itself. There are two important, related subjects that are only touched upon: the great change in European sensibility of which Wordsworth's work is a part and the effect of his work on other authors. Both are beyond the scope of this book; either would demand a history of *European thought* on the model of Fernand Braudel's *La Méditerranée et le monde méditerranéen à 1 'époque de Philippe II*. Occasionally I have used *modern* as a short way of denoting all the poetry (or literature) from Wordsworth to the present. I have done so in the interests of economy and simplicity without any wish to establish it as a period. The disadvantage of all period terms is that they impose upon the continuous process of change that is the life of every culture a spurious definiteness, and inevitably shift our attention from a particular author or work to the hypostatised period, so that the terminology becomes the reality instead of the literature. As much as possible (and perhaps it is not always possible) we need to make our summary statements in terms of particular authors and works, because this is the only method of making those statements more precise.

Like everyone who is interested in Wordsworth I am indebted to the Herculean labours of Ernest de Selincourt and to those who have revised his editions: Helen Darbishire, Chester Shaver, Mary Moorman and Alan Hill, and I have made extensive use of the work of Beth Darlington, John Finch, Stephen Gill, W.J. Owen, Stephen Parrish, Mark Reed, Jane Smyser and Jonathan Wordsworth on Wordsworth's texts, relying in matters of chronology, in most cases, on Reed's indispensable two volumes. The ideas in this book were originally worked out in the course in poetics that I gave at the University of Wisconsin (1968 – 1973) and then in my undergraduate seminars at the University of Stirling (1973 – 1980). I am indebted to all the students who participated in those courses for what they have taught me and grateful to all those with whom I have discussed this work for everything that they have contributed, in particular, my colleagues at the University of Stirling. I would like to thank the staffs of Stirling University Library (especially Nora Glasgow and Douglas Mack), Edinburgh University Library, the British Library, and Peter Laver and Elizabeth Corey of the Wordsworth Library at Grasmere, and to express my gratitude to the Trustees of Dove Cottage for the pleasure and excitement of working in the Wordsworth Library and for permission to print manuscript material, and to Stephen Gill for his kind assistance. My thanks go to: Neil Keeble, Alasdair Macrae, Ian McGowan and Felicity Riddy for helping with particular points; T.A. Dunn and A.N. Jeffares for their support; Katherine McKenzie, Olwen Peel and Margaret Prentice, who with care and patience typed the final copy as well as some inscrutable rough draft; and Catherine Gray who checked most of my French translations and saved me from a number of mistakes. In addition, I want to mention Arthur Gold to whom I have been talking about literature on and off for more than twenty-five years — inevitably some of his ideas will be found here; David Croom, who asked me to write this book and who has waited for it with great patience; and R.P. Blackmur, from whose teaching I discover every year that I have learned something more. My greatest debt is to Caroline Rehder, the best proof-reader, editor and wife that an author could have. She has improved every page and contributed some of the best ideas.

1
Self-consciousness and English Poetry

The continuity of poetry is more important than any division we make of it, but if we want to speak about modern poetry, we need to begin with Wordsworth. He is the first great modern poet.

Modern poetry is, more than anything else, a poetry of self-analysis, of the exploration of consciousness. That is, the exploration of consciousness is both its explicit and implicit subject. It is a poetry that tries to bring more and more of the life of the mind to consciousness. Thus it becomes a poetry interested in the exploration or representation of the unconscious.

The history of English literature — and English poetry — has been put together in an *ad hoc* manner. Each generation has added its contribution without troubling very much about the structure as a whole or about the relation of English literature to European culture. English literature, however, is not simply a native growth and its development is unintelligible except in the context of European culture. Wordsworth's work is part of the continuous European struggle to come to terms with consciousness.

Development is the pattern of change when change has a pattern, the perception of a direction or drift in events. This is a problematical subject because we tend to project the processes of our own development on to whatever we study. This is inevitable as the forms of our thought grow out of our experience (notably the idea of development itself) and what we are depends on what we have been. And yet this means that we are always going away from our subjects and unconsciously returning to ourselves. When we discover successive golden, silver and iron ages, or a progress from the primitive to the sophisticated, or from renaissance to decadence, we are affirming that children grow up and that men grow old. There is, moreover, a difficulty in distinguishing development from progress, in finding patterns of change that do not depend upon judgements of good and bad. The distinction is important because there is no progress in art.

Michelangelo is not superseded by Rembrandt. Tolstoy cannot take the place of Balzac. Each great writer and each great work is unique.

Wordsworth may be the first great modern poet and a great inno-vator, but he does not create modern poetry single-handed. His work is part of an immense continuum. To understand his achievement it is necessary not only to think of his poetry in the context of European culture, but also to consider European culture as the record of an increasing consciousness. Wordsworth is radically more self-conscious than any poet before him. His greatest poem is on the growth of his mind. This is the long poem for which he never found a title and which Mary Wordsworth published as *The Prelude*.[1] What could be more self-conscious than to write the history of your own consciousness?

The more or less steady but very irregular increase in consciousness is a distinguishing characteristic, and perhaps a principle, of the development of European culture for over three thousand years. Wordsorth is the heir (as we all are) of this tradition — and an impor-tant contributor to it. The exact workings of this increasing conscious-ness are not clear, although it appears to come about as part of a change in the nature of the feeling of group solidarity, a shift from kinship to individual awareness. According to Bloch, the most striking transformation in the agrarian life of Europe is that which occurs in most of England between about 1500 and 1800: 'that vast movement of the *enclosures* whose essentials can be defined under its double form (enclosure of common land, enclosure of tillage) as: the disappearance of collective servitudes, individualisation of cultivation.'[2] My assumption is that changes in ways of life are related to changes in states of mind. (There is no doubt that the enclosures made an imagi-native appeal to that deeply searching autobiographer Rousseau: 'The first man who having enclosed a piece of land said to himself: *This is mine. . .*was the true founder of civil society.'[3]) Namier identifies 'the triumph of linguistic nationality' as the basic factor in European political history during the period 1815 – 1919.[4] This involved the creation of a new form of group solidarity: the nation of all those who speak the same language. Thus, the idea of a society of individuals comes to replace the old, vanishing sense of a community of house-holds.[5]

The complexity of the development of self-consciousness in Europe can only be hinted at here, and the interpretations can be no more than suggestions. To provide a glimpse of this vast subject, I have considered briefly a number of phenomena: confession and mirrors, self-portraits and words formed with the prefix *self*, and introduced in turn: Dante, Dürer, Petrarch, Luther, Montaigne and Shakespeare. Their work reveals in the process of formation some of the stylistic modes that can be seen in Wordsworth's poetry.

The history of confession is of a growing self-awareness. Confession is one way of coping with the inner voice, and its continuing practice is a demonstration of how hard it is for us to take our guilt into ourselves and be responsible for it. If the private confession of sins by a believer to a priest existed in the early church, it was extremely rare. Confession and penance were public, and made to God and the group of other believers, as with Augustine's *Confessiones* (398). Private confession, as more than an occasional occurrence, seems to begin in the fifth century, after Leo I in 459 forbids the custom of reading confessions before the congregation. The first evidence of confessors stationed in churches is the statement that Simplicius in 470 set aside a week in each of three Roman churches in which priests were to be present to receive penitents and administer baptism, but this is an isolated case.

The arguments of Peter Lombard (d.1160) and Richard of St Victor (d.1173) that penitence is a sacrament and that confession is necessary to secure pardon for sin are made at a time when confession was becoming more popular, but they were not given any legal form, although the inviolability of the seal of confession was fixed in canon law in the twelfth century. The Latern Council (1216) ordered every Christian to make an annual confession of sins on pain of being denied entrance to church and a Christian burial. Until this decree confession had been voluntary. This established it as an institution. The Council of Florence (1493) made penitence (including confession) a sacrament and empowered the confessor to grant absolution. The first manual for confessors dates from about 1230, but it is the Council of Trent (1563) that required priests to be specially trained as confessors.[6]

During this time confession was usually heard in the open church, between sunrise and sunset, in a place visible from all sides, and if the penitent was a woman there was to be someone else in the church and the confessor was instructed not to look at her face. The idea of the confessional did not occur to anyone until after Luther's death. The earliest reference to it is an order for installation of confessionals by the Council of Valencia (1565). The Roman Ritual of 1614 directs that confessionals should be used in all churches.[7] The new arrangement, where neither penitent nor confessor sees the face of the other, recognises the inwardness of the transaction: the priest hidden in the confessional becomes the voice of conscience.

The psychoanalyst, like the confessor, is only a voice. Compare Freud's description of his technique: 'I hold to the plan of getting the patient to lie on a sofa, while I sit behind him out of his sight.'[8] Both are forms of dialogue used to promote self-knowledge. Authors employ a variation of this technique when they address the unseen reader. This address is not very common before Dante, and when it does occur it is usually brief and casual. Auerbach states that Dante's address to the reader in the *Commedia* is 'a new creation although some of its features appear in earlier texts.' He argues that it constitutes 'a special and independent development of the apostrophe' and marks, by its intensity and seriousness, 'a new relationship between reader and poet.'[9]

Dante writes an autobiography before beginning his greatest work. The title, *La Vita nuova*, stands for his belief that he could change his life. His great poem is also autobiographical and he appears to be the first poet to make his own life in any way the subject of a long poem. As its plot, he uses, like so many autobiographers, including Wordsworth, the metaphor of a journey. Dante makes himself the protagonist of the *Commedia*, and the poem is about his struggle for a new life, it is a poem of change and development.

Dante finds the form of his poem in Christian philosophy. Wordsworth's poem is without any such form. He interprets his experiences as much as possible in their own terms. Dante's great originality lies in the way he uses the world to think with. For his symbolic purposes he employs real people in all their historicity and treats imaginary people as if they were real. He fuses allegory and history. We do not meet Everyman or the Redcrosse Knight in the *Commedia*, but Ugolino della Gherardesca, Guido Guincelli and Dante's great-great-grandfather. The *Commedia* is full of individuals.[10] The power of Dante's conception, of seeing the world in the totality of its history as composed of individuals, is such that it informs one of the greatest achievements in the history of the novel, Balzac's *La Comédie humaine*. (Balzac died four months after Wordsworth.)

Dante is a master of observed detail. The characters in the *Commedia* are described by unique, personal traits and described in action. There is a moment in the twilight of the *Inferno* when he and Virgil meet a group of souls who 'sharpen their brows' at them in the way that an old tailor looks at the eye of his needle. Dante studies everything with this meticulous scrutiny. He is one of the creators of a new consciousness. He notes the texture of a landslide 'that on the flank, on this side of Trent, struck the Adige' and how, when a green stick is burning, sap oozes and air hisses from the end that is not in the fire. He is alive to the slight movement of Farinata degli Uberti's eyebrows and to the time in a summer evening when 'the fly gives way to the gnat,' and he looks at his own feelings as carefully as he looks at other people's faces.[11] The *Commedia* is the first of many works to show that self-consciousness and world-consciousness are interdependent: they increase together.

This increase in Dante is connected with his increased intimacy with his reader. Wordsworth develops this technique still further. To compose the long poem about his life and deepest feelings, like the pentitent and the patient, he addresses a specific person. This work was commonly referred to in his household as 'the poem to Coleridge' and the title page of MS B makes it clear that this shaped Wordsworth's conception of the work: 'Poem Title not yet fixed upon by•William Wordsworth Addressed to S.T. Coleridge.'[12]

The feeling of communication depends on the belief that someone is listening. Thus the mirror is an agent of self-communication. The method of quicksilvering glass that makes possible better mirrors was perfected in Venice in the early sixteenth century, when glass mirrors were first produced in large numbers. Before this they were made of polished metal. The Venetian mirror makers formed a guild in 1564, the year before the Council of Valencia ordered the installation of confessionals.[13] The new mirrors provided people with a clearer, sharper and more realistic self-image. They made possible an exchange of glances between the individual and himself; every man could now study his own face.

The appeal that the mirror makes to the imagination is shown by a silver point drawing of a thirteen-year-old boy inscribed in the upper right hand corner: 'I drew myself out of the mirror in the year 1484, when I was still a child. Albrecht Dürer.' This drawing is the first of many pictures that Dürer made of himself. His first painted self-portraits are dated 1493 and 1498. They, like the drawing, show the artist from the waist up, which suggests that he used a large mirror, therefore one of glass, not of metal. The second painting, now in the Prado, is inscribed: 'This I painted after my image, I was six-and-twenty years old. Albrecht Dürer.' Of this painting, Panofsky says that it 'was painted without any ulterior purpose and is thus perhaps the first independent self-portrait ever produced' and that it could have been painted

only by an artist become 'self-conscious' — in every possible sense of the word — through his providential encounter with the Italian *rinascimento*. There is undeniably an element of vanity and pride in Dürer's attitude. . . But this personal element is outweighed by the gravity of a more than personal problem — the problem of the 'modern' artist as such.[14]

What is remarkable is that the problem of the modern artist could be posed and answered by a self-portrait.

It is, moreover, the inwardly preoccupied Dürer who paints the remarkable *Large Piece of Turf*, a microscopically detailed portrait of grasses and weeds. All the intensity of the artist is lavished on a piece of earth chosen for its ordinariness. The accuracy and freedom of Dürer's studies of plants and animals are matched only by the scientific drawings of the very self-aware Leonardo da Vinci, and Dürer's landscapes are done with such loving precision that they seem forever of the present, as if looking into the mirror gives him a new vision of the world. His work, like that of Dante, demonstrates the mutuality of seeing the world and seeing one's self.

Gusdorf observes: 'Certain Flemish or Dutch paintings of interiors show on the wall a small mirror where the picture repeats itself a second time; the image in the mirror not only redoubles the scene, it adds a new dimension, a perspective of flight.'[15] This dissolving perspective is like a representation of the passage of time, together with a demonstration that every image has another side. The artists enjoyed painting rooms into which they often painted pictures, or a view framed in a window, like the corner of landscape Dürer included in his 1498 self-portrait. The mirror in the picture and the picture in the picture, like the play within a play, testify to the self-consciousness of the artist and they disclose that these pictures are *about* that consciousness. Similarly, the actor who tells us in the midst of a play that all the world is a stage, or that we are but poor players, reminds us, as do prologues and epilogues, that we are participating in an illusion, as perhaps they remind the playwright that, with all his phantasies, he is participating in reality.

Thus, the mirror leads to the self-portrait and daily self-scrutiny, while confession and self-portrait, voice and image, merge in autobiography — the form of Wordsworth's poem to Coleridge. The proximity of their dates suggests that they are part of the same complex process: Dürer's first painted self-portraits, 1493 and 1498; cheaper and better mirrors, after 1500; the Council of Valencia's order for the installation of confessionals, 1565. The first English autobiography of any length was composed by Thomas Whythorne about 1576, the first English self-portrait is a miniature painted by Nicholas Hilliard in 1577.[16] During this time a new vocabulary also comes into being. The *Oxford English Dictionary (OED)* states:

> *self-* first appears as a living formative element about the middle of the 16th cent., . . . The number of *self-* compounds was greatly agumented towards the middle of the 17th cent., when many new words appeared in theological and philosophical writing, some of which had apparently a restricted currency of about 50 years (e.g. 1645 – 1690), while a large proportion became established and have a continuous history down to the present time.

Barfield concludes:

> Self-consciousness, as we know it, seems to have first dawned faintly on Europe at about the time of the Reformation, and it was not till the seventeenth century that the new light really began to spread and brighten. One of the surest signs that an idea or feeling is coming to the surface of consciousness — surer than the appearance of one or two new words — is the tendency of an old one to form compounds and derivatives. After the Reformation we notice growing up in our language a whole crop of words hyphened with *self*; such are *self-conceit, self-liking, self-love,* and others at the end of the sixteenth century, and *self-confidence, self-command, self-contempt, self-esteem, self-knowledge, self-pity*. . .in the next. . .Locke adopts the new (1632) word *consciousness*, defining it as 'perception of what passes in a man's own mind', and at the same time impresses on the still newer *self-consciousness* its distinctive modern meaning.[17]

The crucial period then — if any time can be said to be more crucial than another — in the development of self-consciousness in Europe seems to be that which runs more or less from Dante (1265 – 1321) and Petrarch (1304 – 1374) to Montaigne (1533 – 1592) and Milton (1608 – 1672), with the earlier dates applying to Italy and the later to northern Europe. These approximations constitute the accuracy of cultural history. This is the time of the Renaissance and Reformation. These terms are perhaps best understood not as events, but as denoting a process of psychological change in which men created a new freedom such that they felt that they were offering themselves a new life. Both terms suggest regeneration. There emerged a feeling for the human life as a unit of form that disappeared from *poetry* after Shakespeare and is re-invented by Wordsworth. This way of feeling is a function of a new sense of time: the writing of history after the example of the Greeks and the forging of the tools of historical scholarship began again with Bruni (1444) and Biondo (1483) after several hundred years of chronicles.[18] The individual acquires a history by defining himself in time and thus learns to feel himself changing.

Petrarch is the first Christian thinker to separate himself from the past. He introduces a new view of history and produces a new poetry. He is a great lyric poet who determines the nature of European lyric poetry for some three hundred years and who helps to make it a poetry of self-analysis. Cassirer's comment on Petrarch's lyrics that 'The lyrical mood does not see in nature the opposite of psychical reality; rather it feels everywhere in nature the traces and the echo of the soul. For Petrarch, landscape becomes the living mirror of the Ego' is equally true of Wordsworth.[19]

On 30 November 1341, Petrarch writes to Giovanni Colonna of the pleasure he had had walking about Rome with him, and of how, when they were tired of walking, they had often climbed on to the roof of the ruined Baths of Diocletian to rest in its solitude and to continue their talk:

> As we walked over the walls of the shattered city or sat there, the fragments of the ruins were under our very eyes. Our conversation often turned on history which we appeared to have divided up between us in such a fashion that in modern history you, in ancient history I, seemed to be more expert; and ancient were called those events which took place before the name of Christ was celebrated in Rome and adored by the Roman emperors, modern, however, the events from that time to the present.

Petrarch thinks of the time of Greek and Roman culture as a period of glory, and of the time from the adoption of Christianity by the Roman Emperors (337) to himself as a period of darkness, but he feels that a new dawn is near. This is the metaphor that he uses at the close of his long poem, *Africa*: 'This sleep of forgetfulness will not last for ever. When the darkness has been dispersed, our descendants can come again in the former pure radiance.' The notions of the Dark Ages and the Middle Ages are derived from this distinction of Petrarch, as apparently is the designation of the whole ancient past by the collective noun, *antiquity*.[20]

For Petrarch this separation of the present from the past is part of his effort at self-definition. He finds himself in history and hopes to find the knowledge that will rebuild the ruins of Rome. His major historical work, *De viris illustribus*, is a sequence of biographies. He writes history so that others can know themselves. In the same letter to Giovanni Colonna, he complains that the Romans know nothing about Rome: 'Who can doubt that Rome would rise up again if she but began to know herself?'

This sense of living in a new time that is a distinctive feature of Petrarch's work becomes a European mood after Petrarch, a mood intimately connected with the creation of new art and new knowledge. Lorenzo Valla recognises a change without being able to explain it. He states in the preface to his *Elegantiae linguae latinae* (composed between 1435 and 1444):

> I do not know why the arts most closely approaching the liberal arts — painting, sculpture in stone and bronze, and architecture — had been in so long and so deep a decline and almost died out together with literature itself; nor why they have come to be aroused and come to life again in this age; nor why there is now such a rich harvest of good artists and good writers. Happy these, our times, in which if we endeavor a little more. . .all learning will be restored.

Machiavelli sees (1520) 'the perfection' that has been achieved in 'poetry, painting, and writing' as proof that Providence is now given over 'to reviving [*risuscitare*] dead things.'[21] Dürer refers (1523) to the new growing-up (*Wiedererwachsung*) of art that he dates from about 1375 and Rabelais in *Gargantua et Pantagruel* (1542) speaks of 'la restitution des bonnes lettres.'[22] Vasari makes the rebirth of art (*la rinascita*) and the progress of this rebirth (*il progresso della sua rinascita*) the subject of his *Le Vite de' piu eccellenti pittori, scultori e architettori* (1550), and his dates for the start of this new art (which he sees as going from Cimabue and Giotto to Michelangelo) agree with those of Petrarch and Dürer.[23] That Vasari's history is a series of biographies of artists is evidence of a new conception of man as a conscious individual. Pierre Belon combines (1553) the metaphors of awakening and springtime to describe this rebirth:

> From that it has followed that men's minds, which before were as if dormant and lulled in a profound sleep of ancient ignorance, have

begun to rouse themselves and to leave the shadows where for such a long time they remained buried, and in leaving they have thrown off and put forth all kinds of good disciplines, which at their so happy and desirable *renaissance* are just as new plants after the season of winter which recover their vigour in the heat of the sun and are soothed by the softness of the spring.[24]

The feeling of being reborn is expressed in art as well as in writing. At perhaps no other time in European history are there so many images of mother and baby together — especially of the baby held or nursing at the mother's breast — as there appear to be between Giotto (1267 – 1337) and Murillo (1617 – 1682). Each child builds up its notion of reality on its idea of its mother's breast and finds its identity in the mutual recognition of mother and child. The baby looks at the mother and sees its self. Wordsworth sees this exchange of glances as forming the bond that connects the child to the world, and the 'Poetic spirit' (II.237 – 280). The images of Madonna and Child are symbols of the creation of identity. After Giotto the figures of the Madonna and Child become larger and more realistic, and as part of this realism they show more feeling. They become a subject in their own right, and the child grows up. The child in Leonardo's *The Virgin and St Anne* (1510?) glances over its shoulder at its mother as if about to go its own way. The two children in Raphael's *Madonna of the Goldfinch* (1547) are both standing and seem to be leaning against their mother only for the moment. When the Council of Trent (1563) forbids 'undue nudity' in the representation of sacred figures (from an unconscious feeling that the human body is essentially secular?), the nursing Madonna, 'the most ancient type of Virgin and Child,' disappears.[25]

The far-reaching and thoroughgoing nature of this waking up to the world is shown by the fact that much of Europe changed its religion after 1517. The creation of new consciousness necessitated rebuilding the old structures of belief. *Reformation* means a change of form. A change in religion means a change in our unconscious phantasies about our parents and this, I would hazard, was what was reformed. Certainly the relation between father and son at the centre of Christinity was completely re-interpreted by Luther, and it may perhaps be said that new parents are required for a new birth. The Protestant religions offered to Christians the possibility of conversion, the chance to be born again, the experience that had distinguished Christinity (and Judaism) from the other religions of the Roman Empire. Even those who remained with the old religion were changed, because they were forced to choose to remain, and because, in many places, they had to confront large numbers of people like themselves who believed something other than what they believed. They had self-examination thrust upon them willy-nilly. The depth of this change is demonstrated by the number of people who were prepared to kill in the name of their beliefs, by the persecutions, murders and wars that followed from it.

Luther insists on the independence of God and denounces all mediation between God and man. 'Let God be God' is his phrase.[26] Each man is surrendering to this God has to assume the responsibility for his own life. There are to be no religious communities or persons who live apart from the world. Each person faces his God, his self and the world with a new immediacy. This brought about an explosion of religious feeling.

Luther's notion of justification by faith means that your religion depends upon what you feel, that our *raison d'être* must come from within. He was a careful student, like Petrarch, of Augustine's *Confessiones* and a member of the Augustinian order, and he made extensive use of confession in the re-forming of his own inner life. Upon his entry into the monastery at Wittenberg, he 'confessed frequently, often daily, and for as long as six hours on a single occasion.'[27] The emphasis on the individual conscience by the early Protestants and the later Puritans was at once an emphasis on the individual, on his private thoughts (that which is between a man and himself) and on his inner relation to God, and reminds us that *consciousness* is related etymologically to *conscience*. Luther opened the door to introspection. He caused men to confess to themselves. The variety and number of Protestant sects is proof of how many different inner voices were being heard.

The proliferation of voices occurred in poetry as well as in Protestantism. The gradual appreciation of the individuality of each person made possible the wide range of styles that characterises European poetry after Wordsworth, a variety that is a consequence of writers enlarging their scope with a vision of their inner world and becoming able in their work to bring the outer and inner world together knowingly. Valéry, viewing what he names the crisis of intelligence in the Europe of 1914, makes this variety the basis of his definition of his own time. The current disorder of Europe consists:

Of the free coexistence in all cultivated minds of the most dissimilar ideas, of the most opposed principles of life and knowledge. This is

> what characterises a *modern* epoch. . . Now on the immense
> terrace of an Elsinore that extends from Basel to Cologne, that
> touches the Nieuport sands, the Somme marshes, the Champagne
> chalks and the Alsace granites — the European Hamlet gazes on
> millions of ghosts.[28]

The reference to Hamlet indicates his understanding that introspection is the motor of this new diversity.

There appears to exist between Wordsworth, his contemporaries
and his successors, and the artists of the period from Giotto to
Shakespeare a certain community of feeling that does not seem to
depend upon any direct historical connections, a shared set of
responses, as if each was exploring for himself the same psychological
mechanisms. This resemblance must not be exaggerated, but both
appear to be times in which there was a basic rethinking of the
processes of the creation of identity. If the Madonna and Child represents the earlier period, then the landscape without any (or only very
small) human figures and the abstraction without realistic forms can
stand for the later. There are other differences — a growing preoccupation of modern artists of all kinds with the twilights of the mind.
Starting with Wordsworth, most of the best poems are about
separation and loneliness. The sonnets of Baudelaire are more melancholy than those of Shakespeare; the optimism of *The Bridge* is darker
than that of *Paradise Lost*. There is, however, an analogous concern
with rebirth — to 'make it new.'[29] As this new poetry is an autobiographical poetry, perhaps it can be said that every autobiographer re-
forms his life in the hope of being reborn. An observation by Blackmur
suggests that the popularity of the novel, the most popular of all
modern literary forms, may be an expression of this hope. He notes
'that the European novels of greatest stature seem to follow, not the
conceptual pattern of Greek tragedy but the pattern of Christian
rebirth, conversion or change of heart.'[30]

Certainly an interest in the Renaissance is one of the signs of this
concern with self-renewal. The re-discovery of the Reaissance as a
decisive period of rebirth is a modern phenomenon. The idea is
suggested by Jules Michelet (1798–1874) in the seventh volume of his
Histoire de France, subtitled *La Renaissance* and published five years
after *The Prelude*. He calls the Renaissance a revolution and states
that two things belong to that age more than to all its predecessors:

> the discovery of the world, the discovery of man.

The sixteenth century in its large and legitimate extension goes from Columbus to Copernicus, from Copernicus to Galileo, from the discovery of the earth to that of the sky.

Man has found himself again. While Vesalius and Servetius have revealed life to him, by Luther and by Calvin, by Dumoulin and Cujas, by Rabelais, Montaigne, Shakespeare, Cervantes, he has been imbued with its moral mystery. He has sounded the deep foundations of his nature.[31]

Michelet does not say that the world and man were unknown before the Renaissance, but that during the Renaissance they became known in a new way, with a feeling of discovery. He sees the time in terms of individuals, and for him, Luther and Calvin belong to the Renaissance. The discovery, as he states it, is a question of degree, not something that can be fixed as happening at a particular date or with any one event. The history of feeling is a matter of approximations.

Michelet interestingly found this idea only after he had spent ten years (1843–1853) working on one of the decisive events of modern history. He interrupted his work on the *Histoire de France*, having completed six volumes (1833–1844), to write his *Histoire de la révolution française*, and only then did he resume, beginning with the notion of the Renaissance, the *Histoire de France*. This thought was developed by Jacob Burckhardt, and our idea of the Renaissance is his creation, set forth in his *Die Kultur der Renaissance in Italien* (1860).

The Italian of the Renaissance, he declares, is 'the first-born among the sons of Europe.' This expression of kinship shows the desire to find a definite point for the beginning of one's own history. Burckhardt expresses his view of the radical change in European culture in this often-cited passage:

In the Middle Ages both sides of consciousness — that which was turned to the world as that which was turned within — lay dreaming or half awake beneath a common veil. The veil was woven of faith, childish prepossession and illusion, through which the world and history were seen clad in strange hues. Man was conscious of himself only as a member of a race, people, party, corporation or family — only through some general category. In Italy this veil first melted into air; an objective treatment and consideration of the state and of all the things of this world became possible. The subjective side at the same time asserted itself with corresponding emphasis; man became an intellectual individual, and recognized himself as such.[32]

Even if the distinction between objective and subjective states is unacceptable, it is clear that Burckhardt understands the history of culture as, more than anything else, the history of consciousness, and that the Renaissance exists for him as the time of self-recognition and self-awareness. The metaphor of waking from sleep is that of Petrarch and Belon, and it is a primary metaphor of poets beginning with Wordsworth. They, with the discovery of the world and the discovery of man, suffer both Coleridge's 'pains of sleep' and Keats's 'wakeful anguish.' This twilight world is the world of the edge of consciousness. The attraction of modern writers to the work of this much earlier time is the affinity they feel for their own experience, their recognition of themselves, as in a mirror.

Wordsworth told Henry Crabb Robinson that when he considered his future as a poet, he was convinced that there were only 'four English poets whom I must have continually before me as examples — Chaucer, Shakespeare, Spenser and Milton' and that he 'need not think of the rest.'[33] Three of these four names, and easily the most important ones for him, belong to the new beginning of English literature. Wordsworth is the first of many poets to return to the period between Spenser and Milton. After Wordsworth, Shelley, Keats, Tennyson and Yeats turn again and again to Spenser. They experiment with the dream world of *The Fairie Queene* as well as essaying its stanza. Keats takes the trouble to mark 'the most beautiful passages' for Fanny Brawne and Yeats praises the lines in Spenser's stanza as 'like bars of gold thrown ringing one upon another.'[34] As Jespersen points out:

Modern archaizing poetry owes its vocabulary more to Edmund Spenser than to any other poet. Pope and his contemporaries made a very sparing use of archaisms, but when poets in the middle of the eighteenth century turned from his rationalistic and matter-of-fact poetry and were eager to take their romantic flight away from everyday realities, Spenser became the poet of their heart, and they adopted a great many of his words which had long been forgotten. Their success was so great that many words which they had to explain to their readers are now perfectly familiar to every educated man and woman.[35]

This archaising is a mimetic remembering whose purpose is the symbolic reconstruction of primitive experiences. Each of these poets is trying to gain access to his own past.

Modern writers, perhaps because each is striving for a personal renaissance, feel that they are undergoing experiences analogous to those of the authors of the period from Spenser to Milton, and that these older writers can help them with the interpretation of their new material. Hart Crane writes to Gorham Munson (26.11.1921):

> I can see myself from now rapidly joining Josephson in a kind of Elizabethan fanaticism. You have doubtless known my long-standing friendship with Donne, Webster, and Marlowe. Now I have another Mermaid 'conjugal' to strengthen the tie. [Jonson] The fact is, I can find nothing in modern work to come up to the verbal richness, irony and emotions of these folks, and I would like to let them influence me as much as they can in the interpretation of modern moods.[36]

Although there are many differences in emphasis, it is significant that in this return to the past the chronology is maintained in that a taste for Spenser is succeeded by a taste for Donne. As phantasy comes before reality, emotion precedes the effort to master it. This is the order of the Burckhardt citation: the dreaming melts into 'all the things of this world.' This suggests that cultural forms may embody stages of human development and that, consequently, different times and different cultures can repeat the same forms for more or less the same reasons.

The importance that these two, in many ways disparate, times attach to metaphors of rebirth and awakening is one example of the resemblance between them, and the work of Petrarch offers another.

Francesco Dionigi had given Petrarch his copy of Augustine's *Confessiones*. On 26 April 1336 Petrarch wrote to him a long letter describing how he had, that very day, climbed Mount Ventoux in Provence. Petrarch, who had spent most of his childhood in the region, says that the mountain had always loomed large on his horizon: 'this mountain, visible far and wide from everywhere, is always in your view.'[37] 'For years,' he tells Dionigi, 'I have been intending to make this expedition,' but he did not want to make the ascent alone. At last he and his only brother, accompanied by a servant each, set off before dawn. They found the ascent difficult and Petrarch, repeatedly succumbing to the temptation to take a longer and easier way, says that he often discovered himself going down instead of up. He makes this experience into a metaphor. He compares his wanderings to the difficulties that men have in 'making their way toward the blessed life' in a passage reminiscent of Dante's attempt to climb the mountain of happiness at the beginning of the *Commedia*, and of his ascent of the mountain of purgatory.

Finally they reached the summit.

> At first I stood there almost benumbed, overwhelmed by a gale such as I had never felt before and by the unusually open and wide view. I looked around me: clouds were gathering below my feet, and Athos and Olympus grew less incredible. . . From there I turned my eyes in the direction of Italy, for which my mind is so fervently yearning. The Alps were frozen stiff and covered with snow. . . They looked as if they were quite near me, though they are far, far away. I was longing, I must confess, for Italian air, which appeared rather to my mind than my eyes. [Again he moves from the visible scene inward and then reviews his whole recent life.] I revolved in my thoughts the history of the last decade. . . In this manner I seemed to have somehow forgotten the place I had come to and why. . .I had better look around and see what I had intended to see in coming here. The time to leave was approaching, they said. The sun was already setting, and the shadow of the mountain was growing longer and longer. Like a man aroused from sleep, I turned back and looked toward the west.

Petrarch sees distinctly the mountains of Lyon and 'the waves that break against Aigues Mortes,' but yet again the vast vistas and the remote, blue landscapes cause him to look within.

> I admired every detail, now relishing earthly enjoyment, now lifting up my mind to higher spheres after the example of my body, and I thought it fit to look into the volume of Augustine's *Confessions* which I owe to your loving kindness and preserve carefully, keeping it always in my hands. . . Where I fixed my eyes first, it was written: 'And men go to admire the high mountains, the vast floods of the sea, the huge streams of the rivers, the circumference of the ocean, the revolutions of the stars — and desert themselves.'

He declares that he was 'stunned' and 'turned my inner eye toward myself.' Petrarch states that he did not speak at all during the descent.

The rest of the letter records his meditations on Augustine's words. He resolves to try to control his passions and to mend his life.

This letter has been used many times to document the beginnings of those feelings about nature that are fully stated in the works of Rousseau and Wordsworth. This is correct. The mere fact that Petrarch climbed a mountain in order 'to see its conspicuous height' demonstrates a new feeling of the relation between man and the world, and there is nothing comparable to his account until Thomas Gray's letters of 1739 about his journey over the Alps.[38] Petrarch shows us how the contemplation of nature merges with that of human nature and the *Confessiones* are his gate to the inner world. Augustine's work remains one of the greatest autobiographies, but when Petrarch was writing it was the only book of its kind, and his recognition of its value is part of his greatness. He follows Augustine as Dante follows Virgil. His self-examination, the *Secretum* (probably composed in 1343), is presented as the record of three days of dialogue with Augustine in which Augustine acts as his confessor.[39] Petrarch is sometimes thought to have turned away from the world in turning to Augustine on top of Mount Ventoux and in reading a book instead of looking at the scenery, but if we read what he says carefully, we find that it is looking at the scenery that causes him to look within. This reflex is modern.

Throughout his reworking of the long poem on the story of his own life, Wordsworth reserves one episode for the conclusion: his ascent of Snowdon in June 1791. This is the event that for him sums up his work. Even when he thinks of the poem as consisting of five books, he plans to end with the climbing of Snowdon.[40] Wordsworth gives only a brief account of the ascent and none of the descent. What holds his attention is how, when he was on the cloud-enclosed summit, the clouds opened, the moon appeared and he found himself 'on the shore. . .of a huge sea of mist' with a panorama over the ocean of clouds to 'the real Sea,': a perfect image of how phantasy is continuous with the world. Like Petrarch, he turns inward and his self-consciousness is such that he imagines that what he has seen is the mind thinking about itself:

> A meditation rose in me that night
> Upon the lonely Mountain when the scene
> Had pass'd away, and it appear'd to me
> The perfect image of a mighty Mind,
> Of one that feeds upon infinity,
> That is exalted by an underpresence,

> The sense of God, or whatsoe'er is dim
> Or vast in its own being. . .

                                                              (XIII.66 – 73)

Coleridge had not seen Mount Blanc when he writes his 'Hymn Before Sun-Rise, In the Vale of Chamouni,' but he does have in mind his ascent of Scafell, 5 August 1802. When he looks up at the mountain, he declares:

> O dread and silent Mount! I gazed upon thee,
> Till thou, still present to the bodily sense,
> Didst vanish from my thought: entranced in prayer
> I worshipped the Invisible alone.[41]

Shelley had seen the mountain when he writes 'Mount Blanc, July 23, 1816.' He begins with an image of the continuity of thought with the 'universe of things.' Phantasy is a hidden spring welling up within the mind's perception of the world:

> The everlasting universe of things
> Flows through the mind, and rolls its rapid waves —
> Now dark, now glittering, now reflecting gloom,
> Now lending splendour where, from secret springs,
> The source of human thought its tribute brings
> Of waters. . .

As he looks on Mount Blanc and its streams, he, too, is aware of drifting into a consideration of his own consciousness:

> . . .And, when I gaze on thee,
> I seem as in a trance sublime and strange
> To muse on my own separate fantasy,
> My own, my human mind. . .[42]

Keats composed 'On First Looking into Chapman's Homer' in October 1816. When he read Chapman's translation of the *Odyssey*, he felt himself to be looking into a poet's mind, gazing on a vast landscape of the imagination, and, as his final metaphor, he chooses to compare himself to an explorer who has just climbed a mountain:

> Or like stout Cortez when with eagle eyes

He stared at the Pacific — and all his men
Looked at each other with a wild surmise —
Silent, upon a peak in Darien.[43]

'The time of true revolutions,' Braudel says, 'is also the time in which
the roses bloom.'[44] This image of the slow maturation of great
changes, of the vegetable life of cultures, can also serve to remind us of
the concurrent action in every culture of many, varying rates of
change and development, and that our sense of time itself is not a
constant. After the true revolution of the reform of Christianity, men
seem keenly aware of the world as subject to time in a new way. The
feeling of discovery is the wonder of seeing the Pacific or one's own
mind or anything as if for the first time, as if newly created (or reborn),
and is a consequence of the perceiver being conscious that he and what
he is seeing are changing as he perceives them. Experience, which is
the stuff of modern literature, is perception of this kind.

Montaigne (and Wordsworth) perceive the world in this way.
Montaigne is all but overwhelmed by his awareness of time and
change, and this results in his style of continuous qualification:

> I cannot fix my object; it keeps tottering and reeling by a natural
> drunkenness. I take it as it is at the instant I am occupied with it. I
> do not paint its being. I paint its passage: not a passage from one
> age to another, or, as the people say, from seven years to seven
> years, but from day to day, from minute to minute. I must accom-
> modate my history to the hour.[45]

Truth is a narrative of the process of metamorphosis; being is a story or
history. He says: 'je recite l'homme.' There is no great author who uses
less form than Montaigne. He follows, like Shakespeare in so many of
his speeches, the logic of his free associations. The tentativeness and
formlessness of his *Essais* are in themselves the revelation of what he is
one of the first to call *experience*. The preference of modern authors
for commodious and indeterminate forms derives from an understanding of the nature of experience that is much the same as that of
Montaigne. *De l'Experience* is Montaigne's concluding essay,
probably composed in 1587. According to the *OED*, *experience* as a
verb meaning *to test, try* or *to make experiment of* enters English in
1533. The first occurrence of its use in the sense of *to find by
experience* is dated 1580; and of *to have experience of, to feel, suffer*,
or *undergo*, 1588. The first occurrence noted of its use as a noun

meaning personal knowledge is 1553.

This new sensibility exemplified by Montaigne enables him to present himself as more of an individual than anyone since Augustine, but unlike Augustine and like Rousseau, he recounts the mundane and intimate details of his life. He states that most of his best ideas come to him on horseback and that he cannot remember the names of the people who work for him, that he prefers bread without salt, possesses a tender and sensitive skin, defecates upon rising and is too sudden in the act of love.[46] 'I desire that men should see me in my simple, natural, and ordinary fashion, without straining or artifice: for it is myself that I portray,' he tells his reader. He wishes to show himself completely. Total honesty is his ideal and the self-portrait his metaphor:

> Had I belonged to one of those nations which are still said to live in the sweet liberty of nature's first laws, I assure you that I should very gladly have painted myself at full length and in all my nakedness.[47]

His self-knowledge and world knowledge feed each other. Everything can claim his interest for a moment, and every subject brings Montaigne back to himself.

For Montaigne the theoretical or scientific value of his enterprise depends upon presenting himself with all his idiosyncrasies.[48] He writes: 'Others form man; I describe him, and portray a particular one. . . Every man carries in himself the entire form of the human condition.' He stresses even more the importance of his separate and distinct existence by calling himself by name: 'Authors communicate themselves to people by some special and extrinsic mark; I, the first by my universal being, as Michel de Montaigne, not as a grammarian, a poet, or a lawyer.'[49] Here the most particular becomes the most universal

Shakespeare shares Montaigne's sense of being in time. This is demonstrated by his ability to show his characters making up their minds or changing them in a single speech or brief dialogue, and by his invention of the history play. Especially remarkable is his beginning with three history plays about Henry VI. As F.P. Wilson indicates: 'There is no certain evidence that any popular dramatist before Shakespeare wrote a play based on English history.'[50] Shakespeare did not simply write on isolated historical subjects, but composed series of plays. He appreciated history as a sequence of events, was interested in problems of succession and development, and wrote his great tragedies only after he had explored the history of his own country, after he had written all but one of his history plays. Shakespeare was the only contemporary playwright to make extensive use of historical chronicles, which he used for both his histories and his tragedies.

Shakespeare, like Dante before him, imagines history in terms of individuals. His plots are episodes from life histories, and his characters are neither Biblical nor allegorical figures, but men and women with proper names. By contrast Chaucer's pilgrims are types rather than individuals. Few have names. They are the Pardoner, the Merchant and the Man of Law, even to each other. All Shakespeare's histories and all his tragedies have as their titles the names of individuals. The soliloquy, at once a public confession and a technique of admitting the audience to the inner world of the character, is a distinctive feature of these plays.

Shakespeare in his sonnets (published in 1609) may be the first English poet to make great poetry out of directly representing his self-consciousness. This is how his sonnets differ from all other sequences of the time and why we feel they have a plot. He is concerned to devise a new language for selfhood (a word that the OED records as being first used in 1649). When we consider all Shakespeare's plays and poems together we see that the sonnets represent a *tertium quid* of his experience: they satisfy a craving not satisfied anywhere else. Shakespeare had a need to speak for himself in the first person singular.

This need was felt by many others. That many believers wanted to confess when they were alone and to commune by themselves with their inner worlds is demonstrated by the popularity of the books of meditation. They were very much a European phenomenon. The most important were probably the *Imitatio Christi* (c.1418), Ignatius Loyola's *Ejercicios espirituales* (1548), Luis de Granada's *Libro de la oracion y meditacion* (1554), *Il Combattimento spirituale* (1589), attributed to Lorenzo Scupoli, and François de Sales's *Introduction à la vie dévote* (1601). All were translated into English soon after their publication, and there were many other works of this kind. The *Imitatio Christi* and *Il Combattimento spirituale* were the most popular in Europe as a whole, with the former issued in thirty editions in France alone between 1550 and 1610. The *Book of Prayer and Meditation* was the most popular meditative work in England at the beginning of the seventeenth century. There were over forty French editions of *Introduction à la vie dévote* by 1620 and by 1656 it was published in seventeen different languages.[51]

These books offer a discipline for the inner voice, a method of inner change and a closer, more intimate contact with God. They are paradigms of identity, models of Christian character that are similar to those embodied in the religious autobiograhies that are a somewhat later development. The manuals of meditation share with the peotry of Southwell, Donne, Herbert, Crashaw, Traherne and Vaughan essentially the same approach to religious experience and self-examination, and seem to have contributed to the shaping of this poetry.[52]

Histories, biographies and autobiographies — in that order — appeared along with the books of meditation. As history is separated from chronicle, biography is separated from history and autobiography from biography. This involved men detaching themselves from events, other persons and their own memories. Bacon in *The Advancement of Learning* (1605) calls for a specifically English modern history and finds it strange that there are so few biographies.[53]

The first English biographies are: Thomas Moore's *Life of John Picus* (1505), the anonymous *Life of Henry V* (1513) and Moore's *History of Richard III* (1513). The earliest extant scholarly biography that is the first attempt to write a complete and detailed historical account of another person's life is Nicholas Harpsfield's *Life of Sir Thomas More* (1557?).[54] For a short time the writing of history and biography was accompanied by the writing of characters, short prose summaries of individuals, each like the nucleus of an essay, on the pattern of the *Characters* of Theophrastus. They began with Causabon's translation of Theophrastus (1592), Nicholas Breton's *Fantastics* (1604?) and Joseph Hall's *Characters of Virtues and Vices* (1608). Unlike the lives of the saints, which often seem almost random collections of brief anecdotes, usually of the saint performing some action, the characters are static and self-contained, and yet give the impression of concentrated energy where the lives of the saints feel diffuse. This diffusion results from the absence of any theory of character. The characters show personality perceived as a unity. Clarendon, one of the best writers of characters, fills his history and his autobiography with his portraits, and his passion for portraits extended to choosing to live surrounded by them as if he thereby established the continuity of the past with the present. When, on 20 December 1668, 'after an excellent advent sermon,' John Evelyn dined at Clarendon's London residence, his collection was in place, although he was in exile:

dined with *my Lord Cornbury* at *Clarendon house*, now bravely

furnish'd; especially with the Pictures of most of our Antient &
Modern *Witts, Poets, Philosophers*, famous & Learned Englishmen, which collection of my L: Chancelors, I much commended,
and gave his Lordship a Catalogue of more to be added.[55]

The year after Evelyn's dinner saw the death of one of the greatest
painters of portraits, Rembrandt (1606 – 1669), who never stopped
looking at himself. His work makes plain the relation of self-knowledge to the knowledge of others — a relation which also emerges in
the work of Wordsworth. Rembrandt did more than a hundred self-
portraits. His later pictures are usually dark, illuminated only by the
light on the faces of his subjects, which stand out against the obscure
black, brown and red-brown backgrounds even when they are still half
in the shadows. The face is the focus of his meditation, but the people
in the paintings do not return the artist's scrutiny. They neither smile
nor frown, but wait, shrouded in an interior twilight, without any
definite expression, pensive and intangibly sad. Their faces show the
effects of time: wisdom and mortality.

The sense of the individual as a historical being develops slowly. 'In
Holinshed's *Chronicles* (1578) a small number of woodcuts, used time
after time in rotation, suffices to give the portraits of all England's
monarchs from legendary times to the sixteenth century,' implying
that kings are interchangeable, and that to the biographers of the time
men looked much the same from the inside as from the outside.
Stauffer observes that 'the distinction between biography and autobiography before 1700 is slight' and comments on 'the objective quality of
early autobiographers, their *unconscious neglect* of those oppor-
tunities for self-analysis' (my italics).[56] There were no English autobiographies before the establishment of the new religion. There were very
few until after 1600, but nearly 200 exist that were composed between
1600 and 1700.[57] The bulk of these are religious autobiographies
which concentrate on the author's experience of conversion or rebirth.
Most of them are written by members of sects who rejected confession
and they seem to emerge as a special form with its own conventions
somewhere about 1640.

This soul-searching was a cause of the English Civil War that lasted
from 1642 to 1651. The war, one in the series of religious wars that
swept Europe after Luther, can be seen as a consequence of the failure
of institutions to adapt themselves to the reformed consciousness and
the urge for freedom that it embodied. Clarendon calls the Civil War
'The Great Rebellion.' All the theatres in Britain were closed by law

from 1642 until about 1660 — not long after one of the greatest periods of the drama in the history of the world. Criticised and attacked from the beginning, now they were shut in what appears as an act of atonement. The only reigning king in British history to be tried and executed died on 30 January 1649. To kill a king, as every reader of *Oedipus Tyrannus* (a play that many people refer to as *Oedipus Rex*) or *The Golden Bough* knows, is an event of the greatest psychological significance.

Over a hundred years elapsed before similar events occurred elsewhere: the Americans formally rejected their king in 1776 and the French did not execute theirs until 1793. Both these events happened in Wordsworth's lifetime and his reaction to the French Revolution:

> Bliss was it in that dawn to be alive,
> But to be young was very heaven. . .

(X.692–693)

are among his most frequently quoted lines. Wordsworth describes the result of this change in language that is reminiscent of Burckhardt. The French Revolution, he says, pushed people into the world. They were called upon to 'exercise their skill, / Not in Utopia. . .' nor in any phantasy world,

> But in the very world which is the world
> Of all of us, the place on which, in the end,
> We find our happiness, or not at all.

(X.722–723; 725–727)

Montaigne and Shakespeare appear to have assumed easily the responsibility for the freedom that they enjoyed after Luther, Wordsworth seems to just manage to accept the responsibility for the freedom that he gained after the French Revolution, but the poets between Milton and Wordsworth give the impression of not being able to free themselves.

In his book *The Growth of Political Stability in England 1675–1725*, Plumb states:

By 1688 conspiracy and rebellion, treason and plot, were a part of the history and experience of at least three generations of Englishmen. Indeed, for centuries the country had scarcely been free from turbulence for more than a decade at a time. How to achieve political stability had haunted men of affairs since the death of Cecil.[58]

His book is an attempt to describe how an unusually stable political system came to be established in Britain. I would suggest that the turbulence was not merely political and that something analogous to the politics of stability takes place in English poetry. Poets live their lives in the same world as men of affairs, only poetry, like all art, is primarily a response to the conditions of the inner rather than the outer life. Poetry is a way of accommodating the changes that take place within us.

It is as if the freedom and the richness of the work done by poets from Spenser to Milton is intolerable to the poets who follow them, as if it is more than their successors can work through or take into themselves. Perhaps we might say that they respond to it as if it is forcing them to change in ways they cannot cope with. What happens after Shakespeare and after Donne is not a dissociation of sensibility, but a repression of feeling. No one poet can be said to be a turning-point. This repression can be observed in Ben Jonson and Sam Johnson, as well as in Donne, Marvell and Milton, but it seems to be a primary characteristic of most of the poetry written between *Paradise Lost* (1674) and *Lyrical Ballads* (1798). The poetry of Dryden and Pope represents a turning away from the personal, a substitution of the radically abstract for the actual, an imposition of order at the cost of emotion. They are either unable or unwilling to confront their own experiences.

When Coleridge writes in the *Biographia Literaria* (1817) about his early reaction to 'the writings of Mr Pope and his followers,' he says: 'the matter and the diction seemed to me characterized not so much by poetic thoughts, as by thoughts *translated* into the language of poetry.'[59] This is a way of saying at what a remove Pope's poetry is from anything genuine and from the thought that leads to discovery. The poems are not informed by all the things that we do not understand about ourselves, by the ayenbite of inwyt or what Blackmur in a poem refers to as the hugger mugger inside us. The poetry of Pope is the poetry of a static world. Pope appears to do his thinking or feeling somewhere else, separate from his poetry. The vital transactions do not take place in the poems. This is why the poems seem empty and hollow, or translated. They are at a certain point false. Poetry is a mode of thought in which honesty may not be enough, but anything but honesty fails.

The poetry of Pope (1688 – 1744) is the most extreme case of the repression of feeling. The series of Pope's couplets might be said to approximate the movement of forms without content, if such a thing were possible. As Coleridge reminds us, in *On Poesy or Art* (1818?), 'there is a difference between form as proceeding, and shape as super-induced; — the latter is either the death or the imprisonment of the thing; — the former is its self-witnessing and self-effected sphere of agency.'[60] Poets search in their poems for the form of their experiences, but Pope works with a limited repertory of apparently ready-made forms. Pope demands so much order, and always the same order, for all his experiences. Everything must be under control. His poems are all certainties and judgements, neither the world nor phantasy seem to impinge on him. He is a great creator of types, of behaviour that belongs to no one in particular. He does not look at the landscape, not even that of London. The result is a poetry virtually without mystery, with almost nothing living or authentic, except the hate and the craftmanship. His *saeva Indignatio* saves him. The simplicity of his style, his directness and his control are qualities that I think mattered to Wordsworth, but wit in his poems seems so often a deprivation of intelligence and wisdom is reduced to epigrams.

The greatest change in English poetry after Shakespeare takes place with Wordsworth. To say this is in no way to deny the continuity of development between Pope and Wordsworth or Wordsworth's debt to Pope. The degree to which feeling had been repressed is shown by the energy and detail with which poets after Wordsworth insist on telling us how they feel. The effort is to put as much emotion as possible into the poems, but, at the same time, in different ways, to analyse it. Perhaps this analysis may be said to be a way of adding other emotions or of intensifying the feeling. Poets are especially concerned with the borderland between sleeping and waking, with night dreams and day dreams. Their emphasis is on moments and moods.

The most important work of philosophy written after the death of Aristotle is an autobiography. The *Discours de la méthode* (1637) contains the history of its author and of its own composition. Descartes effects a revolution by beginning with himself. He takes his own feelings as his point of departure. He is unable to tell of his discoveries without telling how he has made them. This is a key part of his heuristic method. Descartes is also revolutionary in that he did not want simply to codify, but to provide a way of making more discoveries. Wordsworth more than any other poet before him succeeds in writing directly and fully about his experience. His achievement is analogous to that of Descartes (and he borrows one of Descartes's dreams for his autobiographical poem).[61] His revolutionary decision is to write about himself. Wordsworth is the first of many poets to attempt in his poetry to take full possession of his own life.

2
Wordsworth Chooses Himself

Wordsworth's decision to make himself the subject of a long poem is one of the most important events in the history of poetry. He was fully aware of what he was doing. As he writes to Sir George Beaumont (1.5.1805):

> I turned my thoughts again to the Poem on my own life. . . It will be not less than 9,000 lines, not hundred but thousand lines, long; an amazing length! and a thing unprecedented in Literary history that a man should talk so much about himself.

The decision did not happen all at once, and even when it was made part of him resisted the idea. That Wordsworth was unable to find a title for the poem — which was not a difficulty he had with any of his other works — was one form of this resistance, another was his decision not to publish the poem during his life. His inability to name the poem, however, was also a recognition that the work was *sui generis*.

Wordsworth never thought of himself as only a lyric poet. This is evident in his choice of Chaucer, Shakespeare, Spenser and Milton as the authors he seeks to equal. He always kept before him the idea of a major work, and the ambition of writing a great long poem seems to have been present in his thoughts virtually from the beginning of his career as a poet. Wordsworth probably composed his first poem in 1784 when he was fourteen, and over the next thirteen years he attempted five long poems one after another: *The Vale of Esthwaite* (1787), *An Evening Walk* (1788 – 1789), *Descriptive Sketches* (1791 – 1792), *Salisbury Plain* (begun 1793) and *The Ruined Cottage* (begun 1797), before he made the first drafts for the poem on his own life in 1798.[1]

The Vale of Esthwaite, a work of around a thousand lines, only parts of which survive, represents the first tentative movement towards

an autobiographical poem.[2] It is set on Wordsworth's home ground.
Esthwaite Water is immediately south-east of Hawkshead where
Wordsworth lived from 1779 to 1787 and attended the Hawkshead
Grammar School. The work wavers between observation of nature
and a lurid and disjointed account of ruins, ghosts, a 'Gothic mansion'
and a 'haunted Castle.' The seventeen-year-old Wordsworth had
already started to work back and forth between the outer world and
the inner, and the all-pervasive twilight is the borderland uniting
them. There can be no question of *The Vale of Esthwaite's* relation to
the 'Poem on my own life,' as it contains the earliest version of one of
the 'spots of time' (see XI.345 – 389):

> One Evening when the wintry blast
> Through the sharp Hawthorn whistling pass'd
> And the poor flocks, all pinch'd with cold
> Sad-drooping sought the mountain fold
> Long, long, upon yon naked rock
> Alone, I bore the bitter shock;
> Long, long, my swimming eyes did roam
> For little Horse to bear me home,
> To bear me — what avails my tear?
> To sorrow o'er a Father's bier.
> Flow on, in vain thou hast not flow'd,
> But eased me of a heavy load;
> For much it gives my heart relief
> To pay the mighty debt of grief,
> With sighs repeated o'er and o'er,
> I mourn because I mourned no more.
>
>   (427 – 433)

and, in place of the addresses to Coleridge, there are passages praising
his schoolfellow, John Fleming, as the 'Friend of my soul.'[3]

An Evening Walk and *Descriptive Sketches* were issued on the same
day: 29 January 1793, and except for a pseudonymous poem in the
European Magazine (1787), they were Wordsworth's first published
work. Discussing *An Evening Walk* with Isabella Fenwick in 1843,
Wordsworth is very aware of how during his career he moved from
idealised to particular landscapes and of how in this poem he is still in
the world of daydreams:

the plan of it has not been confined to a particular walk or an individual place; a proof (of which I was unconscious at the time) of my unwillingness to submit the poetic spirit to the chains of fact and real circumstance. The country is idealized rather than described in any one of its local aspects.

He is, nevertheless, emphatic that every moment in the poem is part of his personal history: 'There is not an image in it which I have not observed; and now, in my seventy-third year, I recollect the time and place where most of them were noticed.'[4] *Descriptive Sketches* is 'confined to a particular walk' and explicitly autobiographical, it is a record of Wordsworth's walk over the Alps with Robert Jones in 1790 that he describes afresh in the autobiographical poem.

These three poems are composed in couplets and in all of them the poet speaks about what he feels in the first person. They are reports of experience rather than attempts to tell a story. There are many echoes of Pope and the poems show in many ways Wordsworth's debt to the poets who are his immediate predecessors. They also show that Wordsworth's syntactic instincts and his whole way of feeling are much too complicated to fit with couplets. Each of the next two long poems that he attempted was a new beginning in terms of form, and each time he decided to work in larger units: *Salisbury Plain* is in Spenserian stanzas and *The Ruined Cottage* in blank verse. He completes two versions of *Salisbury Plain* and then abandons the poem (until 1841).[5] He abandons *The Ruined Cottage* without finishing it, but it is this poem, in the freest form, that contains the best work and that leads directly to the autobiographical poem.

The Vale of Esthwaite, An Evening Walk and *Descriptive Sketches* are no more than sets of images presented in the order in which they occur to the poet, and the poet, as is usually the case in Wordsworth's poetry, is a man walking through a landscape. He is an observer who is himself in motion (in space and time), taking in a scene that shifts as his point of view changes and as a result of the everlasting movement of light and shadow — and yet possesses an underlying permanence. That Wordsworth thinks of himself as being like a landscape painter and of his poems as sequences of images is clear from the terms in which he speaks of *An Evening Walk*: he *observed* every *image in it*, he can recall 'where most of *them* were *noticed*' — and from the title: *Descriptive Sketches. In Verse. Taken During a Pedestrian Tour. . .* He can perhaps be said to have preferred to write about rustic life because it enabled him to isolate one person or a few in a landscape. Almost from the start Wordsworth's poems are composed of images of changing landscapes that reflect changing moods, like the description of the sunset in *The Vale of Esthwaite*:

> While in the west the robe of day
> Fades, slowly fades, from gold to gray,
> The oak its boughs and foliage twines
> Mark'd to the view in stronger lines,
> Appears with foliage marked to view,
> In lines of stronger browner hue,
> While, every darkening leaf between,
> The sky distinct and clear is seen.
> But now a thicker blacker veil
> Is thrown o'er all the wavering dale. . .   (95 – 104)
> Now holy Melancholy throws
> Soft o'er the soul a still repose,
> Save where we start as from a sleep
> Recoiling from a gloom too deep.
> Now too, while o'er the heart we feel
> A tender twilight softly steal,
> Sweet Pity gives her forms array'd
> In tenderer tints and softer shade;
> The heart, when pass'd the Vision by,
> Dissolves, nor knows for whom nor why.
>
>   (121 – 130)

In the version of *An Evening Walk* that Wordsworth published in 1849, the oak against the sky is condensed to:

> And, fronting the bright west, yon oak entwines
> Its darkening boughs and leaves, in stronger lines;
>
>   (214 – 215)

He quotes this version to Isabella Fenwick, but his memory is of his perception of the scene in the time before he had finished *The Vale of Esthwaite*:

> This is feebly and imperfectly expressed, but I recollect distinctly the very spot where this first struck me. It was in the way between Hawkshead and Ambleside, and gave me extreme pleasure. The moment was important in my poetical history; for I date from it my

consciousness of the infinite variety of natural appearances which had been unnoticed by the poets of any age or country, so far as I was acquainted with them; and I made a resolution to supply in some degree, the deficiency. I could not have been at the time above 14 years of age.[6]

These remarks illustrate Wordsworth's consciousness of his own poetic development, showing the craftsman's detailed grasp of his own techniques, a type of self-knowledge that is *excluded* from the autobiographical poem. Like his comment to Sir George Beaumont that it is 'a thing unprecedented in literary history that a man should talk so much about himself,' they reveal his ambition to be original and his decision as to the nature of his originality. 'Of any age or country' proves that he is looking beyond English literature.

The apprehension of 'the infinite variety of natural appearances' tends to fragmentation and this is what happens in *The Vale of Esthwaite, An Evening Walk* and *Descriptive Sketches*. They are collections of moments. There is greater integration in *Salisbury Plain* and *The Ruined Cottage*. They are put together so that much of the narrative is in the first person, although only occasionally is it the poet speaking about himself. The emphasis on moments of vision remains, moods are defined in terms of landscape and events often take place at night or twilight, but the plots are not overwhelmed, as in the earlier poems, by sheer perception. Instead Wordsworth works with the life histories of his characters, of the soldier and his wife in *Salisbury Plain*, of Margaret and the pedlar in *The Ruined Cottage* — this seems to be the unit of form that makes the integration possible.

The best evidence of the ongoing nature of Wordsworth's efforts to write a great long poem is the way in which he transfers sections of one poem to another. He tells Isabella Fenwick that most of the 'thoughts and images' of *The Vale of Esthwaite* 'have been dispersed through my other writings.' De Selincourt conjectures that the pages missing from MS A of this work contained material that was worked into *An Evening Walk*.[7] Phrases in *An Evening Walk* are picked up again in *Descriptive Sketches*, episodes from *The Vale of Esthwaite* and *Descriptive Sketches* are re-described in the autobiographical poem, and four of these five poems demonstrate Wordsworth's obsessive concern with the image of the homeless (sometimes mad) mother and her children.[8] He refers to his own orphaned state in *The Vale of Esthwaite* (434–435, 514–517) and there is a mad woman in the poem. The stories of the homeless mother in *An Evening Walk*, the soldier's wife in *Salisbury Plain* and Margaret, another soldier's wife, in *The Ruined Cottage* seem three solutions to this problem, that might be said to be resolved in the description of the mother and nursing infant in the poem on his own life (II.237 – 341). These stories are about himself only at a remove, but the biography of the pedlar in *The Ruined Cottage* is a first sketch for his autobiography. Gradually he discovered that only his own life history was enough to integrate the fragments of his multitudinous perceptions.

Wordsworth was, of course, not exclusively preoccupied with long poems in this period and wrote many short poems, as he did at all periods when he was composing, and the short cannot be separated from the long when considering his development. *Lyrical Ballads*, for example, can be seen as a set of experiments in writing life histories: *The Female Vagrant*, *The Thorn*, *Simon Lee*, *the Old Huntsman*, *The Last of the Flock*, *The Mad Mother* and *Lines written a few miles above Tintern Abbey* (the first completely autobiographical poem that Wordsworth published) are all attempts to understand character through seeing its development in time. One of these, *Simon Lee, the Old Huntsman*, shows Wordsworth changing the form as he uses it and making the changes in order to make the poem more personal. The poem starts as an imitation ballad (this is the 1798 text):

> In the sweet shire of Cardigan,
> Not far from pleasant Ivor-hall,
> An old man dwells, a little man,
> I've heard he once was tall.
> Of years he has upon his back,
> No doubt, a burthen weighty;
> He says he is three score and ten,
> But others say he's eighty.
>
> A long blue livery-coat has he,
> That's fair behind, and fair before;
> Yet, meet him where you will, you see
> At once that he is poor.
> Full five and twenty years he lived
> A running huntsman merry;
> And, though he has but one eye left,
> His cheek is like a cherry.
>
> No man like him the horn could sound,

> And no man was so full of glee;
> To say the least, four counties round
> Had heard of Simon Lee;
> His master's dead, and no one now
> Dwells in the hall of Ivor;
> Men, dogs, and horses, all are dead;
> He is the sole survivor.[9]

The next five stanzas portray how the old huntsman lives with Old Ruth, his wife, in 'their moss-grown hut of clay' on a scrap of poor heathland. Throughout, Wordsworth insists upon Simon Lee's bodily weakness. Then, abruptly, in the middle of the ninth stanza, he addresses the reader directly with the same aggressiveness that characterises the 'Advertisement' and the 'Preface' to *Lyrical Ballads*. The immediacy of this address is increased by 'As he to you will tell,' making it seem as if Simon Lee is about to speak for himself; instead Wordsworth interrupts the ballad. He speaks to destroy all the poem's conventions and to make us aware of the poem as a poem:

> Few months of life has he in store,
> As he to you will tell,
> For still, the more he works, the more
> His poor old ancles swell.
> My gentle reader, I perceive
> 10   How patiently you've waited,
> And I'm afraid that you expect
> Some tale will be related.

> O reader! had you in your mind
> Such stores as silent thought can bring,
> O gentle reader! you would find
> A tale in every thing.
> What more I have to say is short,
> I hope you'll kindly take it;
> It is no tale; but should you think,
> 80   Perhaps a tale you'll make it.

After this Wordsworth proceeds as if it is the story of his life. He relates an anecdote that can stand as a poem by itself. The amount of detail increases as he concentrates on a single moment:

One summer-day I chanced to see
This old man doing all he could
About the root of an old tree,
A stump of rotten wood.
The mattock totter'd in his hand;
So vain was his endeavour
That at the root of the old tree
He might have worked for ever.

'You're overtasked, good Simon Lee,
90   Give me your tool' to him I said;
And at the word right gladly he
Received my proffer'd aid.
I struck, and with a single blow
The tangled root I sever'd,
At which the poor old man so long
And vainly had endeavour'd.

The tears into his eyes were brought,
And thanks and praises seemed to run
So fast out of his heart, I thought
100   They never would have done.
    — I've heard of hearts unkind, kind deeds
With coldness still returning.
Alas! the gratitude of men
Has oftner left me mourning.

The conclusion is syntactically awkward and the more difficult to understand because the poet has previously acted as if he was with-holding the meaning (69 – 72 and 77 – 80). The way in which this conclusion forces us to re-interpret the first eight stanzas is a function of Wordsworth intruding himself into the poem. The nature of the work is changed by the address to the reader and by the poet making himself a character in the poem.

There is another history of how Wordsworth comes to write the poem on his own life besides the one obtained by reading in chronological order all his work up to 1798. Wordsworth not only chooses to write about himself, but he chooses to make an account of how he wrote his poem part of the poem. This account constitutes the first 271 lines of Book I (1805).

This radical step (which it is possible to see as adumbrated in the way he breaks into *Simon Lee, the Old Huntsman* and in the way he moves between present and past thoughts in the *Lines written a few miles above Tintern Abbey*) has the effect of making his long poem more informal, more loosely ordered — and it reveals Wordsworth's deep concern with origins. As a result, the boundary between the poem and the poet's experience all but ceases to exist. The poem cannot be a thing apart from its author if it is to be a complete record of his introspection, of him becoming what he is. One reason why Wordsworth keeps allowing the present into the poem is so that he and the reader are immediately in touch with the quick of his thoughts at the moment of composition, or, at least, have the illusion of instantaneous communication. Wordsworth traces the processes of thinking and of the poet fulfilling his vocation by describing the poet thinking about his poem. Poetry after Wordsworth is characterised by a very large number of poems about poetry and by the way in which the poet includes himself in his poem.

Finding a place to begin was not easy for Wordsworth. He was unable to approach his subject directly and eventually solved the problem, after many drafts and re-arrangements, by starting with his uncertainties. The more he worked on the poem the more complicated it became. He completed in 1799 a version in two parts. Between 24 January and 7 February 1804, he writes to Francis Wrangham: 'At present I am engaged in a Poem on my own earlier life which will take five parts or books to complete, three of which are nearly finished;' however, the work that he completed in 1805 is in thirteen books, and sometime, probably in 1804, he altered the opening.[10]

The beginning of the autobiographical poem from 1798 until probably 1804 was developed from these lines, scrawled on the next to the last page of one of his pocket notebooks in 1798:

>   was it for this
> That one, the fairest of all rivers,
>   loved
> To blend his murmurs with my nurse's song
> And from his alder shades and rocky falls
> And from his fords and shallows sent
>   a voice
> To intertwine my dreams. . .[11]

A simple chronological order is obviously not what he wants. Even in this relatively short space he produces an involved, compressed and oblique statement, starting from a half-conscious state in which the babble of the river helps to provide a voice for his dreams. The river murmur, the nurse's song and the dreams *intertwine* and merge. The voice orders the chaos. Wordsworth seeks to record the movement from the first stirrings of thought to speech: the moment of creation. This is a movement from the unconscious to the conscious. The continuous murmur of barely heard voices is like a pulse beating in the memory, the river is the stream of consciousness. The resulting passage is finally rejected, but only as the opening. Wordsworth did not delete it from the poem; instead he wrote a second beginning (I.1–71) that is even more indirect and joined it to the first (which became I.271–285).

On the last page of the same notebook, he had roughed out, also in 1798, twenty or so lines about 'a mild creative breeze' turning into a storm.[12] These lines, rejected in 1798 and dormant in his mind since then, Wordsworth worked into a new beginning that incorporated the old. He wrote in effect more of the same. The abrupt question of the river was muffled in equally involved descriptions of other moments in which the amorphous is given form or takes shape. They precede the narrative of his childhood as if they were phantasies of his conception. It is as if he understands that through this work he is re-creating himself.

Chaucer, Spenser and Milton begin their major long poems in straightforward, matter-of-fact ways. Milton states his subject in the first six lines of *Paradise Lost*. This is how Wordsworth starts in 1805:

Oh there is blessing in this gentle breeze
That blows from the green fields and from the clouds
And from the sky: it beats against my cheek,
And seems half-conscious of the joy it gives.
O welcome Messenger! O welcome Friend!
A captive greets thee, coming from a house
Of bondage, from yon City's walls set free,
A prison where he hath been long immured.
Now I am free, enfranchis'd and at large,
May fix my habitation where I will.
What dwelling shall receive me? In what Vale
Shall be my harbour? Underneath what grove
Shall I take up my home, and what sweet stream
Shall with its murmurs lull me to my rest?
The earth is all before me: with a heart

Joyous, nor scar'd at its own liberty
I look about, and should the guide I chuse
Be nothing better than a wandering cloud,
I cannot miss my way. I breathe again;
Trances of thought and mountings of the mind
Come fast upon me: it is shaken off,
As by miraculous gift 'tis shaken off,
That burthen of my own unnatural self,
The heavy weight of many a weary day
Not mine, and such as were not made for me.
Long months of peace (if such bold word accord
With any promises of human life),
Long months of ease and undisturb'd delight
Are mine in prospect; whither shall I turn
By road or pathway or through open field,
Or shall a twig or any floating thing
Upon the river, point me out my course?

                                                                    (I.1 – 32)

He opens abruptly and it is only after 271 lines that it is possible to see
where the poem is going. Then and only then does Wordsworth adopt
the chronological order that he follows to the end. He starts with the
history of his poem instead of that of his life. At the beginning we are
plunged straight into a particular moment. It seems to be an important one, but very little is made precise except what the poet feels. He is
walking into the country, away from the city. We are told neither the
time nor the place, nor the name of the city. Only at lines 74 – 76 do we
learn that it is two o'clock on an autumn afternoon, but not the month
or year. There is a lack of particularity. The first proper name to occur
is *Eolian* (104), the second *British* (179), and only after this do proper
names occur in any number. The poet declares that 'the earth is all
before him' and that he looks about; nevertheless, he does not seem to
see the landscape, which is described in the most general terms: 'green
fields,' 'azure sky.' The passage is full of questions, uncertainties. The
existence of the things referred to in the questions is problematic. We
cannot be certain whether there is a stream or river nearby, whether
the poet can see a road or pathway, or whether they are metaphors.
The poet is free and without roots. He is alone and does not belong
anywhere. He has no fixed purpose. Any action he might perform
appears arbitrary. When he contemplates his freedom he confronts
an emptiness. The absence of specifics is perhaps necessary to the

description of indeterminate states. His questions are like the spinning and trembling of a compass needle before it finds the north.

For hundreds of years poets begin their poems with an invocation to the muse. Here Wordsworth adapts this invocation. His beginning is literally about inspiration: 'I breathe again; / Trances of thought and mountings of the mind / Come fast upon me.' The 'gentle breeze' is like an external breath, as if the muse wooes him. He welcomes the breeze like a messenger from another world, but it is the sacred, inner world of the imagination:

> For I, methought, while the sweet breath of Heaven
> Was blowing on my body, felt within
> A corresponding mild creative breeze,
> A vital breeze which travell'd gently on
> O'er things which it had made. . .
>
> (I.41 − 45)

The poet is on the frontier between the external and internal land-scape. Composing poetry for him is a process of self-knowledge, of shaking off the 'burthen of my own unnatural self' and being his true self. He, too, is *half-conscious*. This is conveyed by 'trances of thought': a trance is unconscious, thought is conscious.

Wordsworth is seeking to communicate, as in the address to the river Derwent, how consciousness works. Having described in the present tense his new freedom and energy, he shifts tenses and stands outside his mood:

> Thus far, O Friend! did I, not used to make
> A present joy the matter of my Song,
> Pour out, that day, my soul in measur'd strains,
> Even in the very words which I have here
> Recorded. . .
>
> (I.55-59)

He then, in a manner characteristic of the entire work, sums up, abstracts and interprets what has gone before, aware of himself and his poem as existing in time, aware, moreover, of what lies outside of consciousness: he listens both to his own voice and to 'the mind's / Internal echo of the imperfect sound' (I.64 − 65). With this 'internal echo' that apparently denotes the accord of the unconscious, poetry sounds the depths of his being. This is what causes Wordsworth to believe that poetry is a 'miraculous gift' whose sources are beyond his knowledge and whose power is beyond his control.

Wordsworth throughout his career felt that there was something awful (in the full sense of that word) about his ability. He felt driven. He was a man possessed by his genius and sometimes speaks of it as of a burden. Now when walking through the 'splendid evening' 'towards the Vale' he tests his ability to compose. Finding first that he can and then that he cannot, he decides not to persevere, with the words:

> So like a Peasant I pursued my road
> Beneath the evening sun, nor had one wish
> Again to bend the sabbath of that time
> To a servile yoke.

> (I.110—113)

The interaction of the external and the corresponding internal breeze is the interaction of the unconscious and the conscious mind. Inspiration is breathing in and breathing out. This rhythm — the rhythm of the coming and going of poetic energy — dominates the poet. The beginning of the poem is a description of these constant alterations, a tug of war between tension and relaxation. Wordsworth contrasts 'the mountings of the mind' with his 'slackening' thoughts (I.72), and this occurs throughout the poem: after the apostrophe to imagination in the Alps, there follows a 'dull and heavy slackening' (VI.549). Here his enjoyment of 'happiness entire' is overtaken without warning by a longing to take up the slack: 'To brace myself to some determin'd aim' (I.116—133). He prefers, he says, the voluptuousness of 'vacant musing' to the bafflement of a mind:

> that every hour
> Turns recreant to her task, takes heart again,
> Then feels immediately some hollow thought
> Hang like an interdict upon her hopes.

> (I.259—262)

The voluptuousness of vacancy indicates the anguish of following the vocation of poetry. Wordsworth knows as well as Eliot that 'anyone who has ever been visited by the Muse is thenceforth haunted.'[13] The first 271 lines are about the difficulty of writing poetry, about how the potency of the poet comes and goes, and how he struggles with this particular poem. The whole is a sustained analysis of an intensity and a psychological precision that is unlike anything composed before it and that foreshadows innumerable poems on the torments of poetic work. Wordsworth opens up a new subject for writers of all kinds in making the failure of the power to create serve as a source for inspiration.

The genesis of the poem in the final form of the opening is literally presented in the metaphor of seed being sown. Wordsworth tells how after walking he stops to rest, 'Passing through many thoughts, yet mainly such / As to myself pertain'd.' There he makes a decision:

> I made a choice
> Of one sweet Vale whither my steps should turn
> And saw, methought, the very house and fields
> Present before my eyes: nor did I fail
> To add, meanwhile, assurance of some work
> Of glory, there forthwith to be begun,
> Perhaps, too, there perform'd. Thus long I lay
> Chear'd by the genial pillow of the earth
> Beneath my head, sooth'd by a sense of touch
> From the warm ground, that balanced me, else lost
> Entirely, seeing nought, nought hearing, save
> When here and there, about the grove of Oaks
> Where was my bed, an acorn from the trees
> Fell audibly, and with a startling sound.
>
> (I.81−94)

The work of glory is to be an oak among poems. Imagining its vague beginnings, the poet passes from indistinct thoughts to the particular and actual sound of dropping acorns.

The choice of a new dwelling place, to him vivid in all its particularity, 'the very house and fields / Present before my eyes,' leads the poet to think more definitely about a long poem. The fixity of the poet is a prerequisite for fixing its subject. The movement is towards form:

> I had hopes
> Still higher, that with a frame of outward life,
> I might endue, might fix in a visible home
> Some portion of those phantomns of conceit
> That had been floating loose about so long,

> And to such Beings temperately deal forth
> The many feelings that oppress'd my heart.

> (I.127 – 133)

Here Wordsworth specifies what is at stake for him in the poem. He desires to free himself from oppressive phantasies, to lay the ghosts in his heart.

Thus he passes from his freedom to his home at Grasmere, from aimlessness to a settled purpose. Even so, Wordsworth still does not begin, he continues to think about beginning. The prolonged and meandering start is not yet concluded:

> When, as becomes a man who would prepare
> For such a glorious work, I through myself
> Make rigorous inquisition, the report
> Is often chearing; for I neither seem
> To lack, that first great gift! the vital soul,
> Nor general truths which are themselves a sort
> Of Elements and Agents, Under-Powers,
> Subordinate helpers of the living mind.
> Nor am I naked in external things,
> Forms, images; nor numerous other aids
> Of less regard, though won perhaps with toil,
> And needful to build up a Poet's praise.
> Time, place, and manners; these I seek, and these
> I find in plenteous store; but nowhere such
> As may be singled out with steady choice;
> No little Band of yet remember'd names
> Whom I, in perfect confidence, might hope
> To summon back from lonesome banishment
> And make them inmates in the hearts of men
> Now living, or to live in times to come.

> (I.157 – 176)

His reflexes are clear: his first movement is to look within. He wonders who he is and starts with an inventory of himself. Throughout the whole passage he feels the burden of his hopes and he makes us feel, as he does everywhere in the poem, what a struggle it is for him to find his meaning. The poem he seeks is not a spontaneous work, but one that needs careful preparation. Starting in this way Wordsworth shows us that he wants a fully conscious poetry and that he believes he can only do what he wants if he knows what he is doing. The harshness of his self-examination is conveyed in both *rigorous* and *inquisition*, and he later changes *glorious* to *arduous* (I.147; 1850).

Wordsworth very briefly thinks of himself as naked, as Montaigne does in the note to the reader that he placed at the head of the *Essais*. It is for both an image of their honesty and of the autobiographical nature of their enterprises. Wordsworth is trying to strip himself to the essentials. He begins with an analysis of 'the living mind' in very abstract terms: 'vital soul', 'general truths,' 'Elements and Agents, Under-Powers.' He does not want to leave anything out. He is abstract in order to be comprehensive and because he is trying to come to terms with the many ghostly intangibles of mental life.

Wordsworth's analysis discloses his feeling that the mind is composed of many diverse parts. This inventory is traditional. Dryden makes a similar one when he proposes an epic poem on the book of Daniel and the philosophy of Plato 'as it is now accomodated to Christian use' in *A Discourse Concerning the Original and Progress of Satire* (1693). He recommends the subject to any man

> who to his natural endowments of a large invention, a ripe judgement, and a strong memory, has joined the knowledge of the liberal arts and sciences, and particularly moral philosophy, the mathematics, geography, and history, and with all these qualifications is born a poet; knows, and can practise the variety of numbers, and is the master of the language in which he writes. . .[14]

Wordsworth's list is more a model of the mind than an enumeration of knowledge and skills. Dryden is imagining someone else standing in front of him, Wordsworth's attention is turned inward. He is closer to Freud than he is to Dryden.

Wordsworth's use of *Under-Powers* together with *subordinate* is especially revealing in this context. As de Selincourt shows, Wordsworth forms a number of compounds with the prefix *under*. He lists: *Under-Powers* (I.163), *under soul* (III.540), *under-countenance* (VI.236) and *under-thirst* (VI.489). Of these only *Under-Powers* is in the *OED*, with this example from Wordsworth, and *under-soul* is given with no example earlier than 1868. De Selincourt's observation is made as a gloss on another passage (XIII.69 – 73):

The perfect image of a mighty Mind,

> Of one that feeds upon infinity,
> That is exalted by an underpresence,
> The sense of God, or whatsoe'er is dim
> Or vast in its own being. . .

Wordsworth when revising this passage in both MSS A and B deletes *underpresence* (MS B: *under-presence*) and substitutes *under-consciousness*, which is also not in the *OED*.[15] He creates new words in order to record new discoveries and these words show him trying to go beneath the surface of consciousness. This is confirmed by his referring to 'Forms, images' as 'external things.' They are not outside the mind. They are external only in relation to the under-consciousness.

Wordsworth revised the passage in Book XIII so that it reads in the 1850 text:

> There I beheld the emblem of a mind
> That feeds upon infinity, that broods
> Over the dark abyss. . .

> (XIV.70 – 72; 1850)

He had already used this image, a reworking of *Paradise Lost* (I.21) and reminiscent of the first chapter of Genesis, in Book I, where he speaks of the poet's 'distress' at his own 'unmanageable thoughts' and adds:

> The mind itself
> The meditative mind, best pleased, perhaps,
> While she, as duteous as the Mother Dove,
> Sits brooding. . .

> (I.149 – 152)

In both instances, the under-words follow thoughts on the nature of poetic meditation. For Wordsworth the unconscious is a dark under-world, and much of the fear and the awe in the poem issues from this abyss. It is not an accident that this image of the brooding mind precedes his inventory of his powers. He looks into the abyss in order to begin his poem.

Wordsworth, when he has satisfied himself that he has the powers to undertake 'a glorious work,' speaks almost as if any time, any place and any manners would do, as if they are external to his major purposes. This is not the language of the born story-teller to whom the particulars of his story are everything. There is something frantic about Wordsworth's willingness to consider anything, and if anything will do, it is not surprising that nothing is truly satisfying. It is worth noting that he expects the poem to kindle from a 'little Band of yet remember'd names,' to emerge from language itself, and that 'these names are to be summoned back from 'lonesome banishment,' to be found in loneliness at the edge of memory. A story-teller in one of the old story-telling traditions would not hesitate to tell us again of what happened when Adam and Eve lived in the garden or how Odysseus came home from the war. He would enjoy repeating himself in the same way that children insist on the identical story being told over and over. Shakespeare borrowed all his plots; Wordsworth wants to tell us something new. This is a modern wish.

After this self-examination, there follows a very long and strange passage, unique in the history of literature, where Wordsworth enumerates all the subjects that he entertained and rejected. He mentions the poems that he considered possible before he settled to work out his own history. The rough drafts of his thoughts are included in the finished work, and we see that this is a poem in which it is vital to the poet to represent the apparently random movements of his mind, vital because that is what makes the poem go:

> Sometimes, mistaking vainly, as I fear,
> Proud spring-tide swellings for a regular sea,
> I settle on some British theme, some old
> Romantic tale, by Milton left unsung;
> More often resting at some gentle place
> Within the groves of Chivalry, I pipe
> Among the Shepherds, with reposing Knights
> Sit by a Fountain-side, and hear their tales.
> Sometimes, more sternly mov'd, I would relate
> How vanquish'd Mithridates northward pass'd,
> And, hidden in the cloud of years, became
> That Odin, Father of a Race, by whom
> Perish'd the Roman Empire: how the Friends
> And Followers of Sertorius, out of Spain
> Flying, found shelter in the Fortunate Isles;
> And left their usages, their arts, and laws,
> To disappear by a slow gradual death;

To dwindle and to perish one by one
Starved in those narrow bounds: but not the Soul
Of Liberty, which fifteen hundred years
Surviv'd, and, when the European came.
With skill and power that could not be withstood,
Did, like a pestilence, maintain its hold,
And wasted down by glorious death that Race
Of natural Heroes: or I would record
How in tyrannic times some unknown man,
Unheard of in the Chronicles of Kings,
Suffer'd in silence for the love of truth;
How that one Frenchman, through continued force
Of meditation on the inhuman deeds
Of the first Conquerors of the Indian Isles,
Went single in his ministry across
The Ocean, not to comfort the Oppress'd,
But, like a thirsty wind, to roam about,
Withering the Oppressor: how Gustavus found
Help at his need in Dalecarlia's Mines:
How Wallace fought for Scotland, left the name
Of Wallace to be found like a wild flower,
All over his dear Country, left the deeds
Of Wallace, like a family of Ghosts,
To people the steep rocks and river banks,
Her natural sanctuaries, with a local soul
Of independence and stern liberty.
Sometimes it suits me better to shape out
Some Tale from my own heart, more near akin
To my own passions and habitual thoughts,
Some variegated story, in the main
Lofty, with interchange of gentler things.
But deadening admonitions will succeed
And the whole beauteous Fabric seems to lack
Foundation, and, withal, appears throughout
Shadowy and unsubstantial. Then, last wish,
My last and favourite aspiration! then
I yearn towards some philosophic Song
Of Truth that cherishes our daily life;
With meditations passionate from deep
Recesses in man's heart, immortal verse
Thoughtfully fitted to the Orphean lyre;

But from this awful burthen I full soon
Take refuge, and beguile myself with trust
That mellower years will bring a riper mind
And clearer insight.

(I.177—238)

Although Wordsworth begins by naming Milton and alluding to
Spenser, his list of subjects does not show us the true literary genealogy
of the work. There is no reference to the four more or less recent poems
that he probably had in mind when thinking about a new long poem:
Thomson's *The Seasons* (1730), Akenside's *The Pleasures of the
Imagination* (1744), Beattie's *The Minstrel* (1777) and Cowper's *The
Task* (1785).[16] Most of his subjects are not in any sense conventional
and, perhaps more important, most of them are not literary. Milton
opens Book IX of *Paradise Lost* with a passage in some ways comparable to this one.[17] He declares that his is a new heroic subject, but
he defines it in exclusively literary terms, and makes specific and traditional references to the Homeric poems and to the *Aeneid*. There
are no such references in Wordsworth's list; he ignores the Greek and
Latin heritage of English poetry.

Poetry involves the transmission of a tradition. Every poet learns
what poetry is from the poems of his predecessors, and makes his own
evaluation of the work of the past. The poets from Wordsworth to the
present exhibit a greater desire to analyse the past because they have a
greater desire to be original. The poet who can accept the work of his
immediate predecessors and who is prepared to go on with it feels no
need to rethink the tradition. Wordsworth is doing here, and in the
other passages in which he discusses his poetic vocation (notably
III.276—293, VI.55—109), what Yeats, Pound and Eliot do in their
criticism, and it is probably significant that poets after Wordsworth
have written more criticism than earlier poets. When every poet is
attempting to do something new, and when the culture he possesses is
not only different from that of his predecessors, but also from that of
his contemporaries, then it is not only more difficult to put the work of
the past in order, but the need to do so is greater. The poet, in order to
know who he is, has had to find out where he is in time, and as a consequence each modern poet creates his own history of poetry.

Searching for a subject for a long poem, Wordsworth does not
linger on literary matters; he knows the tradition, but does not follow
it. Six of his ten subjects are historical — as is the subject that he at last
chooses. His impulse is to describe things which have actually

happened, his desire is to match events in the mind with events in the world. Both his list and his final choice represent a radical break with tradition, and he contemplates subjects that no poet has considered before or since:

(1) 'some old / Romantic tale, by Milton left unsung'
(2) tales of knights and 'the groves of Chivalry'
(3) how Mithridates became Odin
(4) how the followers of Sertorius struggled to maintain their liberty
(5) the suffering of some unknown man
(6) how one Frenchman roamed 'Withering the Oppressor'
(7) Gustavus I of Sweden
(8) William Wallace
(9) 'a tale from my own heart'
(10) 'some philosophic Song'.[18]

They are as oddly assorted and as idiosyncratic as the literary and historical references in *The Waste Land* and *The Cantos*. These subjects are strange enough to be worth examining in detail.

(1) Wordsworth begins by electing to stay on his native ground. His story will be British, and romantic — moving in the direction of dreams — and it will be one 'by Milton left unsung.'[19] He immediately locates himself in the history of English poetry. He chooses Milton as his hero and affiliates himself to him in the most definite way: he thinks of finishing Milton's work for him, he will not simply be his successor, but his continuator, as if he is choosing as his subject one that Milton had already chosen before him. Wordsworth in taking Milton as his model passes over all his own immediate predecessors, and, after naming Milton, he does not come forward, but goes further back. He does not consider Pope or Dryden.

(2) Wordsworth next entertains the possibility of retelling some chivalric tales. That *tales* is plural suggests that the poem is to contain more than one story, but the poet's thoughts are of the *locus amoenus* rather than of action.[20] Although Wordsworth locates his poem after the Fall, he is always nostalgic for Paradise. When he says at the very beginning: 'The earth is all before me (I.15), he is echoing the conclusion of *Paradise Lost* (XII.646 – 647) and making his predicament resemble that of Adam and Eve:

> The world was all before them, where to choose
> Their place of rest. . .

Perhaps it can be said that every landscape reminds Wordsworth in some way of the Eden he has lost. He thinks now of 'some gentle place,' the groves and the fountain-side, not of romance, war or adventure. The slackness and static nature of this brief description are remarkable.[21] That Wordsworth is aware of this is indicated by his transition to the following subject: 'Sometimes, more sternly mov'd. . .'

(3) The history of Mithridates, the king of Parthia, is scattered through Plutarch's *Parallel Lives*.[22] Plutarch reports that Mithridates, after his defeat by Pompey, fled over the Caucasus to 'the shores of the Maeotian Sea' and that, gathering the local tribes together there, he planned to march on around the Black Sea into Italy.[23] It is Gibbon who connects Mithridates and Odin. He makes Odin a local barbarian chief who, after the fall of Mithridates, was so angry with the Romans that he conducted his tribe to Sweden:

> with the great design of forming, in that inaccessible retreat of freedom, a religion and a people which, in some remote age, might be subservient to his immortal revenge; when his invincible Goths, armed with martial fanaticism, should issue in numerous swarms from the neighbourhood of the Polar circle, to chastise the oppressors of mankind.[24]

Thus Odin is vaguely associated with Gustavus as a Swedish chief, and with Gustavus and Wallace as a northern champion of liberty. The story might well appeal to Wordsworth, himself a northerner who retreated into the mountain fastness of the Lake District to free himself from 'The many feelings that oppress'd' his heart. Certainly the six subjects that are neither literary nor personal all concern men who struggled for the liberty that the poet possesses in such superabundance at the start of the poem.

Gibbon proposes Odin as the matter of a long poem: 'This wonderful expedition of Odin, which, by deducing the enmity of the Goths and Romans, from so memorable a cause, might supply the noble groundwork of an epic poem, cannot safely be received as authentic history,' so that here, too, Wordsworth is considering a subject marked out by someone else, although there is no more remote or curious corner of the epic tradition than this footnote in Gibbon,[25] but Wordsworth's metamorphosis of Mithridates, 'Rome's ancient and inveterate enemy,' as Plutarch calls him, into Odin, the gloomy Norse god of war, is a strange, mythic act and very much his own.[26] Thereby he turns the vanquished into the victor. Wordsworth's sources make them both unrelenting enemies of the greatest empire Europe has ever known. It is perhaps equally strange to find Wordsworth wanting to celebrate the destruction of the Roman Empire. Gibbon's words provide the necessary clue: Odin stands not only for irresistible anger and revenge, but also for freedom and the chastisement of 'the oppressors of mankind.'[27] His words are as if echoed in the description of 'one Frenchman. . .Withering the Oppressor.'

Hannibal did lead an army across the Alps into Italy and win a great victory against the Roman legions, fulfilling, in part, the plan that Gibbon ascribes to Odin. Wordsworth, who had in his turn walked over the Alps, also identifies himself with this famous enemy of Rome:

> The predecessors of an original Genius of a high order will have smoothed the way for all that he has in common with them; — and much he will have in common; but, for what is peculiarly his own, he will be called upon to clear and often shape his own road: — he will be in the condition of Hannibal among the Alps.[28]

This image of Wordsworth's awareness of his own originality suggests that these stories of embattled men stand for the poet's war to make his own way.

(4) Sertorius had one eye (as did Odin and Simon Lee), and it is with this detail that Plutarch starts to tell of the events of his life. Sertorius was banished from Rome. During the rest of his life, he commanded only armies of strangers, barbarians, and fought against the Senate for eight years, supported by Mithridates. Plutarch describes the islands where Sertorius sailed to escape his enemies as a Paradise 'so abundantly fruitful that it produces spontaneously an abundance of delicate fruits, sufficient to feed the inhabitants, who may here enjoy all things without trouble or labour.'[29] As this passage from Plutarch makes clear, Wordsworth is again attracted to a *locus amoenus*. Curiously, he discards his hero and concentrates on the story of the destruction of the inhabitants of this Eden. The poem is not to be

concerned with Sertorius, but with his 'Friends / And Followers.' As he metamorphosed Mithridates and Odin, he joins Sertorius to the people dwelling in the Canary Islands in the fifteenth century and creates a 'Race of natural Heroes.' The previous subject combines the historic and the mythic, this one, ancient and modern history. It is as if in both cases Wordsworth is healing a split. His interest in continuity over a long period of time is obvious in 'with fifteen hundred years / Surviv'd.' The first four subjects demonstrate this, and throughout the poem on his own life, Wordsworth works to bring together the remote past and the present.

(5) No one in Wordsworth's list of subjects is more obscure than the 'unknown man', and nothing enables us to place him in history. The statement:

> I would record
> How in tyrannic times some unknown man,
> Unheard of in the Chronicles of Kings,
> Suffer'd in silence for the love of truth

is like an algebraic expression of subjects (3), (4), (6), (7) and (8). Their common denominator is that they involve struggles to preserve the 'Soul of Liberty.' Eliot suggests that in *Hamlet* Shakespeare confronts intractable material and that this crisis opened the way for his great tragedies.[30] The 'poem on his own life' opens the way for most of Wordsworth's best poetry. Wordsworth's anonymous man, however, does not kill a king or even fight. The death of Robespierre in Wordsworth's poem is more important than the death of Louis XVI.[31] The phrasing is such that this unknown man is opposed directly neither to tyranny nor to any individual king. His resistance is passive; he suffers in silence and the poet proposes to end that silence.

(6) The poem then moves from this passive suffering to its opposite. 'That one Frenchman' is obscure enough to be provided with a footnote by Wordsworth. The 1850 edition describes him as: 'Dominique de Gourges, a French gentleman who went to Florida to avenge the massacre of French by the Spaniards there.' He organised a private expedition especially to execute vengeance for the death of a friend when Charles IX would do nothing, and it was a fierce and merciless revenge. This incident is even less significant as history than the conquest of the Canary Islands, but it stands for what one man

alone can do and the power of thought. De Gourges succeeds 'through continued force / of *meditation*' (my italics). Florida, like the Canaries, is a new world. As in the preceding subject, the Spanish are the enemy, described as 'the first Conquerors of the Indian Isles,' so that in the poem Wordsworth makes it appear as if their 'inhuman deeds' were against the aboriginal inhabitants. Less than a hundred lines further on Wordsworth thinks of himself as an American Indian:

> . . .as if I had been born
> On Indian Plains, and from my Mother's hut
> Had run abroad in wantonness, to sport,
> A naked Savage, in the thunder shower.

(I.301 – 304)

De Gourges, 'like a thirsty wind,' is in every respect the counterpart of the 'reposing Knights' by the 'Fountain-side.'

(7 – 8) With Gustavus and Wallace, Wordsworth continues to range on the periphery of Europe and of history (showing, in choosing the conquest of the Fortunate Isles, his 'one Frenchman' and Gustavus, an unexpected preference for the sixteenth century). The obscurity of this repertory of subjects is a measure of Wordsworth's desire to be original and, perhaps, of his need to test his powers. Certainly they are all names that would have to be summoned back 'from lonesome banishment.' As a young man Gustavus I (1496 – 1560) freed Sweden from Denmark. He is the first modern, independent Swedish king and a national hero. With Wallace, Wordsworth returns to British history and to a country adjoining his own ground. Wallace (*c*.1272 – 1305) resembles Gustavus in that he is a young leader fighting for independence against tyranny. As in the case of the people of the Fortunate Isles, Wordsworth identifies with the autochthonous inhabitants of a land, and it is the land, with its wild flowers, 'steep rocks' and 'river banks,' with its 'local soul,' that claims his attention — more than in any of the other subjects. The landscape, as it is throughout the poem, is inhabited by memories. When he introduces the story of Mithridates the poet is 'more sternly mov'd.' This, the last of the historical subjects and the last that concerns liberty, closes in the same severe mood, liberty is *stern*, the result of struggle and resistance.

(9) Wordsworth now shifts from the external to the internal world:

Sometimes it suits me better to shape out
Some Tale from my own heart, more near akin
To my own passions and habitual thoughts,
Some variegated story, in the main
Lofty, with interchange of gentler things.
But deadening admonitions will succeed
And the whole beauteous Fabric seems to lack
Foundation, and, withal, appears throughout
Shadowy and unsubstantial.

(I.220−228)

He decides to trust his imagination. He goes to the heart as the centre of feeling in order to get close to 'my own passions and habitual thoughts.' He seeks something that will embody or represent his mental life, although he does not say so outright. His 'more near akin' insists on proximity without specifying any particular relation. To accomplish his purpose, he forsakes fact for fiction, history for 'Some Tale.'

The most important characteristic of this tale, in addition to being 'from my own heart' is that it should be *variegated*. It is all of piece, a *Fabric*, but it must vary in its quality or tone and be of different elements interchanged. The meaning of this is made clear in another passage where Wordsworth uses *interchange*:

From nature doth emotion come, and moods
Of calmness equally are nature's gift,
This is her glory. . .Hence it is,
That Genius which exists by interchange
Of peace and excitation, finds in her
His best and purest Friend. . .

(XII.1−3, 7−10)

Lofty and *gentle* in Book I correspond to *emotion* and *calmness* in Book XII. The metaphor of the two breezes also describes this basic interchange. To express the gamut of nature and the essence of genius, Wordsworth's tale must convey the 'happy stillness of the mind' (XII.13) as well as its restless, striving energy. This is why the 'philosophic Song / Of Truth' must cherish 'our daily life,' an uncommon demand on the Orphic lyre. The high in Wordsworth's view does not exist without the low. As he makes clear in the 'Preface' to *Lyrical Ballads*, the 'incidents of common life' are interesting to him because he can trace in them 'the primary laws of our nature.'[32]

The ordinary — 'habitual thoughts,' 'our daily life' — soothes Wordsworth. Gentleness belongs with cherishing. Moreover, the ordinary is a source of power. This is true in Wordsworth's poetry as a whole, and especially in his best work, and it is true even in these extraordinary stories. The race of Odin emerges from obscurity to overthrow the Roman Empire. 'Some unknown man' suffers for truth and 'one Frenchman' brings a whole nation to judgement. Gustavus and Wallace draw their strength from the low and the poor. Gustavus goes into the earth, into the mines of Dalecarlia, in order to emerge victorious, while the deeds of Wallace merge him with the countryside, Wordsworth repeating his name three times in four lines to make this point.

Wordsworth's plan for a long poem on an imaginary subject of his own devising fails for him because it 'seems to lack / Foundation' and is 'throughout / shadowy and unsubstantial.' It does not touch the earth, is not sufficiently grounded in reality, or the ordinary. How unlike Pope is this desire to grasp the real, to tell true stories. This is the need that causes Wordsworth to entertain so many historical subjects and to yearn for a 'song / Of Truth that cherishes our daily life.' His poem, he feels, cannot be true if it is not about the world. The imagination by itself is not enough. Wordsworth's great descriptions of the imaginative powers all grow out of accounts of particular happenings in his own life.

How seriously Wordsworth pursued most of these ten subjects is not known, but before starting on the story of his own life, he did attempt several long narrative poems. What he says here can be taken as referring to *Salisbury Plain*, *The Ruined Cottage* and some fragments of narratives in blank verse and Spenserian stanzas (such as 'The Road extended o'er a heath', 'No spade for leagues had won a rood of earth' and 'Along a precipice they wound their way') that may or may not belong to these works.[33] *The Borderers*, Wordsworth's only verse play, can also be called a tale from his own heart.

His MSS show that Wordsworth's mind was full of stories, but none that offered the possibility of a sustained development. He experimented with various forms, shaped and reshaped the material without being able to satisfy himself. He completed *The Borderers* in 1797, but left the other narratives unfinished. This rejection of fiction was only temporary. Many of his poems are tales from his own heart, but most of them came after a substantial amount of the autobiographical poem had been composed, and even then he stresses the truth of his fictions and takes pains to point out their relation to reality. Only after he wrote about himself could he concentrate on the stories of others. From 1787 to 1798 he worked through a tangle of narratives, from which, with a sure instinct, he slowly unravelled the thread of his own life.

The transition from fiction to fact can be observed in Wordsworth's transformation of *The Ruined Cottage*.[34] He probably started on this work between March and June 1797 and then put it aside until early 1798. Some of the material that was later included in the poem to Coleridge was drafted between January and March 1798, but 'the first substantial work toward an autobiographical poem' was done after his arrival in Goslar in Germany, between October 1798 and February 1799.[35] When Wordsworth began *The Ruined Cottage*, Margaret was its centre. Then his interest moved to the pedlar who in the poem tells the poet the story of Margaret. The shift is from the narrative to the narrator. When Wordsworth returned to his work-sheets in 1798, he enlarged upon the description of what the pedlar feels and the whole was made more personal. Wordsworth was no longer thinking primarily about the story. 'The entries at this stage are random and do not suggest work towards a single poem.'[36] With many of the fragments it is difficult to decide whether they concern the pedlar or Wordsworth himself. There is another very significant change: Wordsworth has the poet give a prolonged account of the pedlar's life, with the emphasis on his childhood and the development of his character. We know from what Wordsworth later says that he saw himself in the character of the pedlar.[37] This is confirmed by the subsequent transfer of passages about the pedlar to the poem on his own life as he became dissatisfied with the notion of creating a persona and decided to stand before us in his own person.

(10) The last subject that Wordsworth considers he calls his 'favourite aspiration':

> some philosophic Song
> Of Truth that cherishes our daily life.

The *some* reveals that his ideas on this subject are still in a formless state. The song is a *wish*, an *aspiration* towards which he *yearns*. His words suggest that it is an elusive ideal and one perhaps that could never be realised, as *unsubstantial* as the previous subject. Wordsworth was neither a philosopher nor very interested in philosophy and it is not surprising that he felt this enterprise to be alien to him. Coleridge urged Wordsworth to write a philosophical poem and it was his profound, lifelong respect for Coleridge that kept the notion alive as much as anything else. Here Wordsworth shrinks from the idea as an 'awful burthen' and his inventory of subjects is concluded.

These ten subjects represent a break with tradition, and at the same time offer a new way of defining or creating tradition. Through them Wordsworth puts himself in touch with Milton and Spenser, and links himself to both the history of English poetry and to the history of Europe. Through them he furnishes his poem with a group of ancestors and its own individual past, a past that because of their idiosyncratic and eclectic nature is as unique as any person's genealogy. These subjects reveal a great concern for history as a form, and Wordsworth in this poem becomes a historian. He returns in them to memories of paradise, to the beginnings of time, to what is far away and obscure in himself, and seeks to establish a continuum of distant past and present. His heroes are lonely men struggling against the odds to be free, men who oppose tyranny and empire. They are mythic shadows of the poet who at the start escapes from the bondage of the city. The whole opening is a celebration of liberty. Wordsworth's sympathies are with aboriginal inhabitants, with those people who belong to the land and whose being is anchored in the landscape. For him the principal virtue in the struggle for freedom seems to be endurance. Strong emotions of despair, anger and revenge are mentioned, but the action is abstract. Aggression is very deeply buried.

This review of possible subjects is part of Wordsworth's description of the poetic imagination. It exemplifies the imagination's infinite capacity to re-shape. In addition, the list seems to ask, what subject shall receive me? thereby repeating, 'What dwelling shall receive me?' which appear to be two forms of the question: who am I? After these speculations on possible subjects, Wordsworth is still lost in dreams of the future, making plans that continually melt away and unable to choose what is workable. He recognises without being able to help himself that he is his own enemy. This recognition is the result of discriminating between nuances of feeling, naming each impulse. The poem is again a record of his exasperation and excruciation:

> Thus from day to day
> I live, a mockery of the brotherhood
> Of vice and virtue, with no skill to part

Vague longing that is bred by want of power
From paramount impulse not to be withstood,
A timorous capacity from prudence;
From circumspection, infinite delay.
Humility and modest awe themselves
Betray me, serving often for a cloak
To a more subtle selfishness, that now
Doth lock my functions up in blank reserve,
Now dupes me by an over-anxious eye
That with a false activity beats off
Simplicity and self-presented truth.

(I.238–251)

Vice, *virtue* and *selfishness* sound the moral note of his self-criticism.
'Self-presented truth' is the direction and goal.

Wordsworth elaborates on his 'listlessness' and 'vain perplexity' and
then says that he is:

Unprofitably travelling towards the grave,
Like a false steward who hath much received
And renders nothing back. — Was it for this
That one, the fairest of all Rivers, lov'd
To blend his murmurs with my Nurse's song,
And from his alder shades and rocky falls,
And from his fords and shallows, sent a voice
That flow'd along my dreams? For this, didst Thou,
O Derwent! travelling over the green Plains
Near my 'sweet Birthplace', didst thou, beauteous Stream,
Make ceaseless music through the night and day
Which with its steady cadence, tempering
Our human waywardness, compos'd my thoughts
To more than infant softness, giving me,
Among the fretful dwellings of mankind,
A knowledge, a dim earnest, of the calm
Which Nature breathes among the hills and groves.

(I.269-285)

This thought of his approaching death together with that of his selfishness is a turning-point. His sense of his guilt is decisive. When he sees
himself as 'a false steward' existing because of the generosity of others,

he is suddenly able to give in return. His work is to be an act of reparation. The change over takes place in the middle of a line. The gears mesh and the poem is under way.

Wordsworth dispenses with any further preliminaries and begins the story of his life. Up to this point he has blocked himself from pouring out his 'soul in measur'd, strains,' but now a river of poetry begins to flow. Creation is understood as a form of generosity. 'Travelling towards the grave' shows his awareness of being in time. At this point Wordsworth adopts the chronological order that he follows to the end of the poem. He is an 'infant' (I.282), 'a five years' Child' (I.291) and then has seen 'Nine summers' (I.311). He does not, however, keep to a strict chronological sequence but works from moment to moment and from experience to experience. He is too conscious to forget that every present moment contains the whole past.

*

Stendhal, writing an autobiography in 1835, declares:

> What consoles me a little for the impertinence of writing *I* and *me* so often is that I assume that many very ordinary people of this nineteenth century are doing as I do. We will then be inundated by memoirs towards 1880, and with my *Is* and *mes*, I will only be like every one else.[38]

More important, perhaps, is that after about 1760 an increasing number of the best writers write autobiographies and that more good autobiographies are composed of which the greatest are Rousseau's *Les Confessions* and Wordsworth's 'Poem, Title not yet fixed upon.'

Rousseau (1712 – 1778) began *Les Confessions* in 1766 and finished them in 1770, the year that Wordsworth was born. The first part was published in 1782 and the whole in 1789. He also writes *Rousseau, juge de Jean Jacques* (1772), *Les Rêveries du promeneur solitaire* (1776 – 1778) and a variety of autobiographical fragments. Among Wordsworth's books was a copy of *Émile* and an edition of the first part of *Les Confessions* bound with *Les Rêveries du promeneur solitaire*, and one of the two specific references he makes to Rousseau is to his 'paradoxical reveries.'[39] There is not enough evidence to be able to estimate with any precision the effect of Rousseau upon Wordsworth, but together their work constitutes a revolution in the understanding of the self.

It is interesting to note that there are no English autobiographies of any particular literary merit published between 1700 and 1800, unless we count Boswell's *The Journal of a Tour to the Hebrides* (1785) or his great biography-autobiography, *The Life of Samuel Johnson* (1791), or *The Autobiography of Benjamin Franklin* (1793), all published in Wordsworth's lifetime. Gibbon wrote six drafts of an autobiography in 1796, but they remained unknown until 1894 and unpublished until 1896.[40]

Samuel Johnson is a biographer of genius. He tells Boswell that 'the biographical part of literature. . .is what I love the most' and affirms that: 'No one is so fit to be a man's biographer as the man himself.' And yet he never wrote an autobiography.[41] He jotted down many notes, but burnt most of them a few days before he died.[42] The quality of his self-interest is very different from that of Rousseau or Wordsworth or Stendhal. He is less analytical. Although we do not know if he read any of *Les Confessions*, he hated Rousseau: 'Rousseau, Sir, is a very bad man. I would sooner sign a sentence for his transportation, than that of any felon who has gone from the Old Bailey these many years.'[43] Johnson's remarks on 'the *inward light*, to which some methodists pretended' — the starting-point of so many English autobiographies — show him as sceptical of the value and communicability of inner states:

If a man (said he) pretends to a principle of action of which I can know nothing, nay, not so much as that he has it, but only that he pretends to it; how can I tell what that person may be prompted to do? When a person professes to be governed by a written ascertained law, I can then know where to find him.[44]

Discussing with Boswell the review of a spiritual diary, Johnson agreed with the reviewer that: 'There are few writers who have gained any reputation by recording their own actions.'[45] Johnson satisfied his autobiographical impulses by encouraging Boswell and confiding in him. Boswell, of the next generation, expresses the new self-interest: 'in reality, a man is of more importance to himself than all other things or persons can be' and 'Sometimes it has occurred to me that a man should not live more than he can record. . .'[46]

There is a similar contrast of views between Reynolds and Goethe. On 10 December 1774 Reynolds addressed the students of the Royal Academy on the importance of studying the great works of the past. 'The mind,' he told them, 'is but a barren soil; a soil which is soon exhausted, and will produce no crop, or only one, unless it be continually fertilized and enriched with foreign matter.'

The greatest natural genius cannot subsist on its own stock: he who resolves never to ransack any mind but his own, will be soon reduced, from mere barrenness, to the poorest of imitations; he will be obliged to imitate himself, and to repeat what he has before often repeated.[47]

Goethe, on the other hand, observes: 'To record everything that went through my mind I would have needed an army of secretaries.'[48] Before Rousseau no one would have put such a value on unformed thoughts, on the free flow of consciousness, or have thought of the mind as an inexhaustible source. Seeing his own life in this way enabled Goethe to write what is commonly regarded as the first *Bildungsroman, Wilhelm Meisters Lehrjahren* (1795–1796), in which the events that pass through the mind are interpreted as a development and in which self-development becomes a conscious goal. Wilhelm confides to Werner in Book V (Chapter 3) that 'to develop myself, just as I am, that was the wish and aim I was obscurely aware of from my youth upwards.'[49] This 'just as I am' (*ganz wie ich da bin*), however, becomes an increasingly complex matter in European poetry and fiction.

The belief in the virtually unlimited possibilities of the mind creates its own uncertainties, fears and mysteries. Sterne in volume seven (1765) of *The Life and Opinions of Tristam Shandy, Gentleman* recounts this exchange between a citizen of Lyon and his hero:

— My good friend, quoth I — as sure as I am I — and you are you —
— And who are you? said he. — Don't puzzle me; said I.[50]

Who am I? becomes a problem when the mind is conceived of as in a state of flux. Not felt as a problem by the generation of Johnson (b.1709) and Reynolds (b.1723), it begins to become a matter of all-absorbing interest with the generation of Boswell (b.1740) and Goethe (b.1749). Wordsworth ransacks his own mind in order to answer the question of his identity: the long poem on his own life is his solution to the puzzle.

After the publication of *Les Confessions* there was a great burst of autobiographical writing. Wordsworth began his untitled poem in 1798, completed the first version in 1799 and another much longer version in 1805. Chateaubriand started to compose his memoirs in 1803, but did not finish until 1847. Scott began in 1808 an autobiography that he never finished. He kept a journal from 1825 to 1832. Goethe wrote *Dichtung und Wahrheit* between 1811 and 1832. Coleridge published his *Biographia Literaria* in 1817. Byron kept a journal intermittently between 1813 and 1823, and he wrote his memoirs between 1818 and 1821. (The MS was burned after his death.)[51] The autobiography of Keats's friend, Benjamin Haydon, covers the years 1786 – 1820 and his journals continue until his death in 1846. De Quincey published the instalments of the *Confessions of an English Opium Eater*, the first of his many autobiographical pieces, in 1821. Hazlitt's essays began to appear in 1813 and Lamb's in 1821. James Hogg's *The Private Memoirs and Confessions of a Justified Sinner* was published in 1824.

Stendhal, like Rousseau, was not content with one autobiography and drafted several, all of which he left unfinished: a journal (1801 – 1823), some autobiographical sketches (1822 – 1837), *Souvenirs d'égotisme* (1832) and *Vie de Henry Brulard* (1835 – 1836). Galt's novels, *The Member: An Autobiography* and *The Radical: An Autobiography*, and Disraeli's *Contarini Fleming: a psychological autobiography* were published in 1832, and Galt's *Autobiography* in 1833. *Jane Eyre: an autobiography* was issued in 1847. *The Bildungsroman* was identified as a form in the early 1820s and in 1847 Dostoevsky remarked that all novelists are writing confessions.[52] The first of Borrow's autobiographical volumes, *The Bible in Spain*, came out in 1843. *Mémoires d'outre-tomb* was published 1849 – 1850, *The Prelude* and Leigh Hunt's *Autobiography* in 1850. The complete title of Wordsworth's poem as it appears on the title page of the 1850 edition is rarely given: *The Prelude, or Growth of a Poet's Mind; An Autobiographical Poem*. The first part of Tolstoy's *Childhood, Boyhood and Youth* appeared in 1852 and the first part of Herzen's *My Past and Thoughts* in 1854. The first edition of *Leaves of Grass* was in 1855.

Rousseau believed that his confessions were unique in their honesty. He claimed that as they were without precedent, they would be without imitators. 'Here is,' he writes, 'the only portrait of a man painted exactly after nature and completely truthful that exists, and that probably will ever exist.'[53] Within sixty years of the publication of Rousseau's book, Poe maintained the impossibility of writing a truthful autobiography. He does, however, recognise that such a work would mark a revolution in thought:

If any ambitious man have a fancy to revolutionize, at one effort, the universal world of human thought, human opinion, and human sentiment, the opportunity is his own — the road to immortal renown lies straight, open, and unencumbered before him. All that he has to do is to write and publish a very little book. Its title should be simple — a few plain words — 'My Heart Laid Bare.' But — this little book must be *true to its title*. . . To *write*, I say. . . — there is the rub. No man dare write it. No man ever will dare write it. No man *could* write it, even if he dared. The paper would shrivel and blaze at every touch of the fiery pen.[54]

One writer, at least, is known to have responded to this challenge: among Baudelaire's papers was found a group of scattered notes entitled: *Mon Coeur mis à nu*.[55] Poe's comments, especially when compared with Reynold's, indicate the change in ideas about the mind, and how these many autobiographies served only to make the self and its experiences seem ever more indeterminate.

The word *autobiography* was introduced at this time. When Isaac D'Israeli devotes a chapter of his *Miscellanies or Literary Recreations* (1796) to 'Some observations on diaries, self-biography and self-characters,' his reviewer in the *Monthly Review* (XXIV.375; 1797) is doubtful whether *self-biography* 'be legitimate. . .yet *autobiography* would have seemed pedantic.'[56] On 4 January 1804 Coleridge writes in one of his notebooks: 'Wordsworth read to me the second Part of his divine Self-biography — .'[57] George Burnett in *Specimens of English Prose-Writers* (1807) says that: '*Autobiography* was begun by lord Herbert of Cherbury. . .' and Wordsworth's neighbour, Robert Southey, employs the term in 1809.[58] (Neither *self-biography* nor *self-character* are in the *OED*.) Isaac D'Israeli writing in the *Quarterly Review* (May 1809), like Stendhal, sees autobiography as a phenomenon of the future. He fears 'an epidemical rage for autobiography' 'more wide in its influence and more pernicious in its tendency than the strange madness of the Abderites, so accurately described by Lucian.'[59]

The proliferation of autobiographies is the clearest indication of a radical increase in consciousness and of a new habit of self-analysis. During Wordsworth's lifetime it becomes ordinary for a writer to compose an autobiography. John Stuart Mill identifies self-consciousness as a modern characteristic: 'self-consciousness, that demon of men of our time from Wordsworth to Byron, from Goethe to Chateaubriand, and to which this age owes so much both of its cheerful and mournful wisdom.'[60] He states in his *Autobiography* (1873) that

Wordsworth's poems are a medicine that cured him of habitual depression and made it possible for him to face himself: 'And the delight which these poems gave me, proved. . .there was nothing to dread from the most confirmed habit of analysis.'[61]

Wordsworth is the first great English author to write an autobiography that is neither perfunctory nor fragmentary. Before Wordsworth the only poets of any stature who do so are Lord Herbert of Cherbury (1643?; published 1764) and William Cowper (1766 or 1767; published 1816).[62] He is followed by Coleridge, Yeats, Hardy and Williams, but Wordsworth is the only major autobiographer to write in verse. Whitman in *Leaves of Grass* and Eliot in *Four Quartets* approach autobiography, but their poems are not life histories. That Wordsworth's autobiography is a poem is very important in determining its character.

Rousseau, the prose writer, is direct where Wordsworth is indirect. Rousseau is interested in his relation to other people, while Wordsworth is preoccupied with his relations with himself. The most important moments in the poem are when he is alone or somehow isolated from his surroundings or companions. Rousseau recounts his entire history to the present and attempts to integrate the whole of his life. Wordsworth stops more or less with the events of his twenty-seventh year (although he works on the poem until he is fifty-nine). He only dwells on particular 'spots of time' and his earliest years are what is most important to him. Rousseau is full of anecdotes; he re-enacts the drama of his life and plays to the audience. Wordsworth attempts to re-live certain feelings and he is most concerned with what is most amorphous. He seeks to recover lost parts of himself. Both writers wrestle with the emotion of memory.

Rousseau thinks of his work as a confession. Wordsworth is only able to get started when he sees himself as 'a false steward. . .who renders nothing back.' This suggests that autobiography as a form is a response to guilt. Rousseau makes a point, near the beginning of *Les Confessions*, of telling how he only receives sexual satisfaction from being beaten by a woman. This had tormented him his whole life, but until now, he says, he has always kept silent. As soon as he finishes talking about it in his autobiography, he writes:

I have taken the first and the most painful step in the obscure and filthy labyrinth of my confessions. . . From now on I am sure of myself, after what I have just dared to say nothing can stop me.[63]

Wordsworth confesses to three thefts: of woodcocks (I.309–332), birds' eggs (333–350) and a skiff (372–427). He places these episodes at the very beginning of his chronological account. They seem to stand for more primitive guilt, and indicate perhaps some discontinuity in his earliest years, that there is something missing within that he seeks to restore by taking from without.

For both authors writing their lives is equivalent to being born again, which means freeing themselves from what they imagine as past crimes. The relief is not in any explanation or apology, but simply in the saying. Rousseau's self-justifications are more elaborate than Wordsworth's but his work is less moral in its tone. Wordsworth's moralising is a continuous process of self-judgement. The fear that is so often the subject of his poem can be understood, in part, as the fear of punishment. Beyond this, Rousseau feels persecuted and Wordsworth fears disintegration. As a poet he is better able to go to the sources of being. Poetry is a unique form of statemment, a way of saying what cannot be said any other way and of laying hold of otherwise inaccessible experience. Perhaps it is the case that less can be said in poetry than in prose, but that more can be communicated.

3
Wordsworth's Long Sentences

Synge once remarked to Yeats: 'Is not style born out of the shock of new material?'[1] Wordsworth's new style is the result of his discovering new subjects for poetry, the new material of his own life. This is a matter of increased sensitivity to feeling. As Eliot puts it: 'every vital development in language is a development of feeling as well.'[2] Wordsworth's style can be best seen by analysing some passages of his greatest poem, the work in which he first finds himself.

Wordsworth's history of the growth of his mind is a sequence of episodes, of which this is one of the most beautiful — and one of seven sections that Wordsworth published during his life (in the version of 1850):

> There was a Boy: ye knew him well, ye cliffs
> And islands of Winander! — many a time
> At evening, when the earliest stars began
> To move along the edges of the hills,
> Rising or setting, would he stand alone
> Beneath the trees or by the glimmering lake,
> And there, with fingers interwoven, both hands
> Pressed closely palm to palm, and to his mouth
> Uplifted, he, as through an instrument,
> Blew mimic hootings to the silent owls,
> That they might answer him; and they would shout
> Across the water vale, and shout again,
> Responsive to his call, with quivering peals,
> And long halloos and screams, and echoes loud,
> Redoubled and redoubled, concourse wild
> Of jocund din; and, when a lengthened pause
> Of silence came and baffled his best skill,
> Then sometimes, in that silence while he hung
> Listening, a gentle shock of mild surprise

Has carried far into his heart the voice
Of mountain torrents; or the visible scene
Would enter unawares into his mind,
With all its solemn imagery, its rocks,
Its woods, and that uncertain heaven, received
Into the bosom of the steady lake.

This Boy was taken from his mates, and died
In childhood, ere he was full twelve years old.
Fair is the spot, most beautiful the vale
Where he was born; the grassy churchyard hangs
Upon a slope above the village school,
And through that churchyard when my way has led
On summer evenings, I believe that there
A long half hour together I have stood
Mute, looking at the grave in which he lies!

(V.364 – 397; 1850)

The description of the boy making 'mimic hootings' is remarkable for being one very long sentence. The dash and the absence of a capital letter after *Winander* indicate that there is no stop at the exclamation mark. On three occasions, after *answer him*, *jocund din* and *mountain torrents*, the opportunity to put a full stop and begin again is rejected.[3] Thus, Wordsworth deliberately prolongs his sentences, the experience determines its own form.

The rhythm of the passage depends on the tension between the blank verse and the long sentences. Milton does not rhyme *Paradise Lost*, but he thinks it necessary to explain why and he justifies his decision as a return to tradition:

The measure is *English* Heroic Verse without Rime, as that of *Homer* in *Greek*, and of *Virgil* in *Latin*; Rime being no necessary Adjunct of true Ornament of Poem or good Verse, in longer Works especially, but the Invention of a barbarous Age, to set off wretched matter and lame Meter; grac't indeed since by the use of some famous modern Poets, carried away by Custom, but much to their own vexation, hindrance, and constraint to express many things otherwise, and for the most part worse than else they would have exprest them.[4]

A poet writing after Wordsworth might have justified such a decision as being an innovation and closer to experience. Although he does not reject rhyme, Verlaine in *Art poétique* calls for

> De la musique avant toute chose,
> Et pour cela préfère l'Impair. . .[5]
> (Music before everything
> And for that prefer the Uneven. . .)

and Pound instructs poets 'to compose in the sequence of the musical phrase, not in the sequence of a metronome.' Pound states:

> Don't chop up your stuff into separate *iambs*. Don't make each line stop dead at the end, and then begin every next line with a heave. Let the beginning of the next line catch the rise of the rhythm wave, unless you want a definite longish pause.[6]

Milton, too, strives for 'true musical delight,' and for him this 'consists only in apt Numbers, fit quantity of Syllables, and the sense variously drawn out from one Verse into another, not in the jingling sound of like endings. . .'[7]

Wordsworth decides not to rhyme in order to obtain greater syntactical freedom. He has two units of thought: the sentence and the line. He is concerned that 'the sense' is 'variously drawn out from one Verse to another,' and works *with iambs* to create the less obvious music that results from uneven, unrhymed undulations of 'the rhythm wave' through a whole passage. The sentence about the boy and the owls overflows the line again and again. Some of the enjambments are very radical. Wordsworth separates the elements of a verb: 'stars began / To move,' and actor and action: 'both hands / Pressed.' There are some very abrupt stops and starts: 'and to his mouth / Uplifted, he, as through an instrument.' He seems to want in this case the full value of the pause at the end of the line *and* the enjambment. He runs on the line only to pause again after *Uplifted* and *he*. Sometimes, as with 'the edges of the hills,' we expect a pause because it is the end of the syntactical unit and the line, as well as being marked with a comma, but instead there is the adverbial phrase, *Rising or setting*, which refers back to *stars began*. The sentence is so extended that a number of pronouns and modifiers refer back over a considerable distance.

Wordsworth's sentences are not periodic like those of Pope and Johnson where one clause balances another and where the elements usually come in pairs. This sentence about the boy mimicking the owls, unbalanced, asymmetrical and irregular, is characteristic of Wordsworth's poetry. There is no neat pattern. The variety of the syntax can be seen by reading as a list the words with which the lines begin. Wordsworth uses three techniques to expand the sentence: he adds, modifies and repeats. He joins his words and his experiences together in the simplest way: and. . .and. . .and. . . Experience for him, however, is never simple. There is a constant need to emphasise and define: it is at evening *when* the stars *began* to move; they are the *earliest* stars, rising *and* setting. The sound of the owls is described eight different ways. They *answer, shout* and *shout again* with *quivering peals, long halloos, screams, echoes* and *concourse wild of jocund din.*

These techniques suggest a theory of experience. Wordsworth adds, modifies and repeats, because there is always something more to say. Being is a continuous process. To be true to himself he must be true to his perceptions. This is the deeper motive of his compulsion to be accurate. His concern to mark nuances is his recognition of the ever-changing data of consciousness. Any one statement is never quite right. Saying what he wants to say is a cumulative process, a process of accumulating phrases, clauses, qualifications. Wordsworth does not like to stop. The *and. . .and. . .and. . .* is like the semi-colon and the dash in that they all serve to prolong the sentence. Long sentences, moreover, are a way of binding these many disparate things together. To articulate means *to give voice to, to divide into distinct and significant parts,* and *to join things together.* Wordsworth is very concerned to articulate his experiences in each of these senses.

Wordsworth repeats. He has a need to go over and over things, which is what we do in order to get things right, in order to learn or master them, as when we learn a new language, but with every repetition he brings something new to the poem. He names Winander only by reference to its islands and alludes to it even more indirectly as part of 'the watery vale.' It is both 'the glimmering lake' and 'the steady lake.' His distinctive vocabulary and phrasing are, in part, a result of his need to continuously re-experience and see from all sides whatever he has in mind. 'Watery vale,' 'quivering peals,' 'concourse wild of jocund din' are all examples of this desire for circumlocution. Montaigne calls his essays 'walls without stones.'[8] Wordsworth, too, surrounds his experiences with words.

Repetition in Wordsworth's poetry involves a return to the past. He goes back to the events of his childhood, or continually turns over a given experience in a single poem. Usually it is the experiences that disturb us, that trouble us, that we cannot stop thinking about. If you have a small stone in your shoe it is difficult to forget it, and R.P. Blackmur was fond of pointing out that *scruple* means a small stone. The response of the oyster to an irritating particle of grit is to cover it with layer after layer of pearl.

The sentence (V.364 – 388; 1850) appears to be the record of a single moment of experience, but this is not the case: *'many a time /* At evening. . .' he would stand 'beneath the trees *or* by the glimmering lake. . .'; 'Then *sometimes*. . .' he heard 'the voice / Of mountain torrents; *or* the visible scene / Would enter unawares into his mind. . .' Many experiences have been compressed and amalgamated to create this moment. Its unity is a poetic fiction, but Wordsworth is careful to specify the multiplicity of experiences that go to make it up. Both the unity and the multiplicity are important to him.

Each of Wordsworth's long sentences is a series of qualifications. His habit is to retrace the development of an experience, or rather to re-construct its happening, packing as much as he can into a small space and re-arranging the syntax in an effort to make more room. He makes the subtlest discriminations: after the repeated cries of the owls, there is 'a *lengthened pause*.' The adjective draws it out. This delicate calibration is only the beginning of the description of this moment. The boy is lost in the pause, suspended 'in that silence while he hung / listening. . .' *While, hung* and *listening* all insist on the duration, of the suspense, which is intensified by placing *hung* at the end of the line with its own pause. Then, sometimes, comes 'a gentle shock of mild surprise.' This double oxymoron brings together expectation and fulfilment. The repetition makes a shock of a fine perception and yet softens the blow. The new experience does not efface the old, but is incorporated by it. The matching of opposites maintains the equilibrium of this finely balanced state.

The shock is of a voice:

> . . .a gentle shock of mild surprise
> Has carried far into his heart the voice
> Of mountain torrents. . .

but the object of the sentence is removed from the moment of impact. Wordsworth says: *has carried*. The voice is already inside the boy before he notices it. The event is almost over before it happens. The voice is carried 'far into his heart,' deep inside him. *Far* tells us that it has gone a long way in an instant, and reminds us that the sound is dim and far away. The power of the mountain torrents is muffled and contained. The voice implies communication, as if the boy has absorbed a message. What he hears is a torrent of sound, continuous, enchained, another concourse.

Next Wordsworth changes the sense from hearing to sight, and the same process is repeated: another perception goes deep within the boy, the outside is suddenly inside:

> . . .the visible scene
> Would enter unawares into his mind
> With all its solemn imagery, its rocks,
> Its woods, and that uncertain heaven, received
> Into the bosom of the steady lake.

The action is more comprehensive, the phrases are very general: 'visible scene,' 'solemn imagery.' Everything or everything visible enters the boy's mind. What is perceived appears to be divided in the act of perception: 'the visible scene. . .with all its solemn imagery.' It is as if the scene is a container full of objects. *Imagery* suggests that these things possess meaning, that they are more than themselves. The previous experience shocks, this slips in without anything to mark it off from what the boy is or was. The surprise forms in the listening a boundary between the old and the new. The seeing is unconscious absorption. Wordsworth does not say that the boy *sees*. Instead the *visible* scene enters his mind. The boy is passive if perception can be entirely passive.

The final clause juxtaposes two actions: (a) the visible scene entering the mind unawares, and (b) the uncertain heaven received into the lake. Thus, the two entrances, the two receptions, are made to seem analogous, but in fact the heaven-in-the-lake is part of the visible scene. The juxtaposition in one sentence of the listening and the seeing allows them to feel like successive actions when they are, according to Wordsworth, mutually exclusive. After the calls of the owls, *then sometimes* the boy hears the mountain torrents *or* absorbs the visible scene. Wordsworth uses long sentences to merge separate experiences and he interprets experiences by the manner in which he re-constructs them. He does not need to say anything explicitly: his syntax is an implicit commentary.

There is no mention of reflection or mirroring. The heaven 'is received / Into the bosom of the steady lake.' This suggests that it is welcome and again that the reception is into the body. The bosom is where the heart is and there is a further suggestion of welcome and security in its hint of the child at the mother's breast. *Heaven* (not *sky*) with its connotations of fate is here *uncertain* and the water that is always in motion is *steady*. If the adjectives are reversed, the lines lose most of their force. *Uncertain* gives us the shimmer of the reflection along with our dubious, problematical destinies. *Steady* gives us the brief but absolute stillness of a single now, as if time had stopped.

This whole passage has two parts: the experience of the boy making 'mimic hootings' (364 – 388) and a conclusion (389 – 422) that separates us abruptly from what has gone before. The shift is from the boy's experience to the poet's experience. The poet speaks in his own person. Suddenly there is a change in time. The boy is dead and seems to have died long ago, and the poet is looking at his grave. We are removed from the vivid moments by the lake. Those experiences are made to feel remote. This second part is missing from MS JJ, the oldest surviving draft of the episode. There Wordsworth has everything happening to himself. It is perhaps more convincing to describe the unconscious entry of the visible scene as happening to another person, as we cannot describe that of which we are unaware, but it seems that it is primarily Wordsworth's need to get outside of his own experience that causes him to recast the anecdote. The shift that creates the conclusion would have been impossible without the change from the third to the first person. Thus Wordsworth can look back at the experience from the other side of the grave.

There is a change in tone, in syntax, in the second part of the passage. There is nothing complicated about:

> This boy was taken from his mates, and died
> In childhood, ere he was full twelve years old.

This is a direct, factual statement, but it is followed by a poetic moment that is the composite of a number of actual moments. The poet has stood in the churchyard on many 'summer evenings.' There is an uncertainty that contributes to the impression of the poet being lost in his thoughts:

> . . .*I believe* that there
> A long half hour together I have stood
> Mute, looking at the grave in which he lies!

'*Full* twelve years old' and 'A *long* half hour *together*' may be compared with 'a *lengthened* pause.' There is a finickiness about time in Wordsworth's poetry, and an attempt to be precise about the imprecise in which every detail represents a nuance of feeling.

An important proof that Wordsworth is not a philosophical poet is that he does not try to explain these moments in any systematic way. There is no argument, no insistence; no interpretation is offered. We are unaware of what entered into the poet's mind as he stood in the churchyard. The experience stands for itself and is its own meaning. The remarks on the education of children that follow do not refer back to the dialogue of the boy and the owls, but to what comes before it. The village church is 'forgetful of this Boy / Who slumbers at her feet' (V.401 – 402; 1850).

At the end there is not a word of sorrow or regret. The vale is 'fair' and 'beautiful.' The poet is mute about what he feels, although the feeling, the quality of the moment, appears to be what is most important here. The correspondence of the two episodes is suggested by the repetition of the verb *to hang* at the end of a line: 'the boy hung / Listening,' 'the grassy churchyard hangs / Upon a slope,' but the exact nature of the correspondence is left mysterious. The end of the second part functions like the end of the first part. The images are allowed to echo. We feel their resonance. The poem enters our minds in the same way the visible scene is received into the steady lake.

De Quincey relates how Wordsworth once spoke to him about this episode:

One night, as often enough happened, during the Peninsular war, he and I had walked up Dunmail Raise, from Grasmere, about midnight, in order to meet the carrier who brought the London newspapers,. . . The time had arrived, at length, that all hope for that night had left us: no sound came up through the winding valleys that stretched to the north; and the few cottage lights, gleaming, at wide distances, from recesses amidst the rocky hills, had long been extinct. At intervals, Wordsworth had stretched himself at length on the high road, applying his ear to the ground, so as to catch any sound of wheels that might be groaning along at a distance. Once, when he was slowly rising from this effort, his eye caught a bright star that was glittering between the brow of Seat Sandal and of the mighty Helvellyn. He gazed upon it for a minute or so; and then, upon turning away to descend into Grasmere, he made the following explanation: — 'I have remarked, from my earliest days, that, if under any circumstances, the attention is energetically braced up to an act of steady observation, or of steady expectation, then, if this intense condition of vigilance should suddenly relax, at that moment any beautiful, any impressive visual object, or collection of objects, falling upon the eye, is carried to the heart with a power not known under other circumstances. Just now, my ear was placed upon the stretch, in order to catch any sound of wheels that might come down upon the lake of Wythburn from the Keswick road; at the very instant when I raised my head from the ground, in final abandonment of hope for this night, at the very instant when the organs of attention were all at once relaxing from their tension, the bright star hanging in the air above those outlines of massy blackness fell suddenly upon my eye, and penetrated my capacity of apprehension with a pathos and a sense of the infinite, that would not have arrested me under other circumstances.' He then went on to illustrate the same psychological principle from another instance:. . .[9]

This other 'instance' is his poem of the boy making 'mimic hootings,' in which Wordsworth again uses the metaphor of tension and relaxation. De Quincey shows Wordsworth thinking in terms of moments and combining two very specific experiences in order to derive psychological principles. This is an important gloss on the construction of the autobiographical poem, where, as in De Quincey's story, he remains immersed in the unique details of experiences, and in the subtle graduations of feeling over time: 'Just now. . .at the very instant when I raised my head. . .at the very instant when the organs of my attention were at once relaxing. . .fell suddenly. . .' His purpose is never mere abstraction.

Wordsworth is concerned to show us exactly how we perceive the world and ourselves. This is not philosophy in the ordinary sense of the word. If we read Hume, Hegel, Santayana or Wittgenstein, we rarely find the individual moments of their own lives that have helped them to form their theories. They are more abstract than Wordsworth, so much so that we feel that they are engaged in a different activity. This abstraction is an effort to escape from actuality, a desire for anonymity; they feel they must be impersonal. Wordsworth finds it necessary to leave experience in the context of individual lives — that of the boy who dies young or his own. The philosophers try to stay outside of time, Wordsworth knows that our being is in our history.

The exact length of any individual sentence in Wordsworth's 'Poem (Title not yet fixed upon)' is uncertain, because he never published it,

and because none of the five major extant MSS (A, B, C, D and E) is in
his hand. The punctuation of the MSS appears to vary somewhat
according to the copyist and they represent the work of five copyists.
There is a further complication in that E, the copy from which the
1850 text was allegedly printed, has very little compared to the other
MSS and to the printed text, and it is not known how the punctuation
of the printed text was established.

Wordsworth's work habits, moreover, were not such as to provide
very much material for the study of his punctuation. His rough drafts
are on the whole lightly punctuated. He appears to have done most of
his composing in his head and then either to have jotted it down
rapidly at the first opportunity, often without any punctuation, including full stops, or to have dictated it to someone else (and in this case it
is impossible to know to what degree the punctuation is that of his
amanuensis). Added to this was his extreme dislike of writing.
Wordsworth did not like to hold a pen. He writes to De Quincey
(6.3.1804) of 'the unpleasant feelings which I have connected with the
act of holding a Pen.' He tells his friend Wrangham (early spring
1812): 'My writing desk is to me a place of punishment, and as my
penmanship sufficiently testifies, I always bend over it with some
degree of impatience.' As a result he rarely made a fair copy of a poem,
and when he did he was usually in a hurry to put his pen down.

Nevertheless, Wordsworth took great pains over the final texts of
his compositions, even going so far as to write to friends asking them to
correct misprints in their copies of his poems. As he goes over and over
certain experiences in his poetry, he continuously revises his work,
including the punctuation. After Dorothy Wordsworth wrote out MS
V (DC MS 23), a fair copy of the two-part 1799 version of the autobiographical poem, Wordsworth went through the whole MS making
extensive additions and changes to the punctuation as well as other
revisions.[10] A number of letters survive from Wordsworth to the
printers Biggs and Cottle in Bristol that show his concern with the
second edition of *Lyrical Ballads*. One dated mid-July 1800 is characteristic. It is filled with details of revision of Wordsworth's poems, but
in the hands of Coleridge and Dorothy; Wordsworth wrote only one
line himself, on the address sheet is inscribed: 'Begin the Printing
immediately.' He did not sign his name, merely his initials.[11]

On 29 July 1800, Wordsworth's concern for correctness causes him
to write in a peremptory tone to Humphry Davy (who lived in Bristol)
asking him to help:

Dear Sir,

So I venture to address you though I have not the happiness of being personally known to you. You would greatly oblige me by looking over the enclosed poems and correcting any thing you find amiss in the punctuation a business at which I am ashamed to say I am no adept. I was unwilling to print from the Mss which Coleridge left in your hands, because as I had not looked them over I was afraid that some lines might be omitted or mistranscribed.

It is difficult to know how to interpret this statement by Wordsworth that he is 'no adept' at punctuation. It is an attempt, at a distance, to persuade Davy to give his full attention to the task of correcting Wordsworth's MSS, but also, like Wordsworth's ill-health when composing or revising, and the fact that he did revise endlessly, it suggests a basic uncertainty about his work. Without doubt, during his entire career, Wordsworth, as his correspondence shows, was prepared to make changes in his poems at the suggestion of others and to enter into elaborate discussions about the rightness of his text.[12] Even so, however much his amanuenses, copyists, editors, printers and friends may have contributed to the punctuation (or revision) of his work, anything which Wordsworth accepted must be judged as his.

Although the exact length of any individual sentence in Wordsworth's poem on his own life may be problematical, that most of the sentences are long and complex is not. Moreover, Wordsworth's tendency in his revision of the five most complete MSS (A, B, C, D and E), especially in the first four where there was the most revision, was generally to make his sentences longer. He did this most often by adding phrases. To satisfy this desire for accuracy and completeness he usually needed more words. The poem itself grows from two parts in MS JJ to fourteen books in MS E. Wordsworth appears to use a colon more than a semi-colon, and in many cases where he puts a full stop, he also adds a dash, as if he knows that he must pause, but is still concerned to insist on the unity of experience. He does not want his thought to break off. Perhaps his habit in his rough drafts of writing passages without any punctuation and his frequent omission of full stops can be taken as further proof of this feeling that his experience, his thought, is one continuous process.

These long agglutinative sentences can be found in Wordsworth's earliest work. They are the result of Wordsworth's attempts to confront his own feelings. These lines are from *The Vale of Esthwaite*, probably composed when Wordsworth was about seventeen:

But now a thicker blacker veil
Is thrown o'er all the wavering dale
[   ] assume
[   ] against the gloom
[   ] head seems to rear
[   ] the steeple near
[   ] woods and hills with hamlets grac'd
[   ] flat, and seem a level waste.
[   ] last of all the leafy train
[The] black fir mingles with the plain.
While hills o'er hills in gradual pride
That swell'd along the upland's side
From the blunt baffled Vision pass
And melt into the gloomy mass.
And on its bosom all around
No softly sunken vale is found,
Save those seen faintly [that] combine
To form the Horizon's broken line.
Now holy Melancholy throws
Soft o'er the soul a still repose,
Save where we start as from a sleep
Recoiling from a gloom too deep.
Now too, while o'er the heart we feel
A tender twilight softly steal,
Sweet Pity gives her forms array'd
In tenderer tints and softer shade;
The heart, when pass'd the Vision by,
Dissolves, nor knows for whom nor why.

(103 – 130)[13]

When this passage was reworked by Wordsworth for *An Evening Walk*, the bulk of which was composed when he was nineteen, he made the syntax more complex and both the line and the sentences longer. This is the text as it was first published in 1793:

Unheeded Night has overcome the vales,
On the dark earth the baffl'd vision fails,
If peep between the clouds a star on high,
There turns for glad repose the weary eye;
The latest lingerer of the forest train,
The lone black fir, forsakes the faded plain;

Last evening sight, the cottage smoke no more,
Lost in the deepen'd darkness, glimmers hoar;
High towering from the sullen dark-brown mere,
Like a black wall, the mountain steeps appear,
Thence red from different heights with restless gleam
Small cottage lights across the water stream,
Nought else of man or life remains behind
To call from other worlds the wilder'd mind,
Till pours the wakeful bird her solemn strains
Heard by the night-calm of the wat'ry plains.
— No purple prospects now the mind employ
Glowing in golden sunset tints of joy,
But o'er the sooth'd accordant heart we feel
A sympathetic twilight slowly steal,
And ever, as we fondly muse, we find
The soft gloom deep'ning on the tranquil mind.

$$(363-384)^{14}$$

In both passages the sentences are prolonged in order to register change, the process of twilight. The outer world provides an image of the inner world, but the poet also wants to show how the outside is absorbed by the inside. The action, like that of the boy listening for the owls, is a taking in. Wordsworth has integrated the two worlds more completely in the second passage. This integration is expressed in individual phrases: *accordant heart, sympathetic twilight*. There is nothing like this in the first passage. The second passage is both more definite and more analytical. There are more adjectives and Wordsworth names more of the elements of the scene: 'the cottage smoke,' the *red, small* cottage lights, 'the wakeful bird' — and with 'the sullen dark-brown mere,' and 'like a black wall, the mountain steeps,' he also distinguishes two shades of darkness. He eliminates *Vision, Melancholy* and *Pity*, so that the only actors are now *Night* and the perceiving *mind*. Semi-colons are used extensively in *An Evening Walk* instead of full stops. There are three in the sixteen lines of the first sentence and the two sentences are held together by a dash.

Its complex syntax is apparently what attracted Wordsworth to the poetry of Michelangelo, whose difficult and elaborate sentences seem to repeat the tension of the marble bodies of his sculptures. Wordsworth translated six of his poems and attempted many others. He declares to Sir George Beaumont (17 and 24.10.1805) that Michelangelo's poetry is the most difficult to construe I ever met with, but just what you would expect from such a man, shewing abundantly how conversant his soul was with great things. . .so much meaning has been put by Michael Angelo into so little room, and that meaning sometimes so excellent in itself that I found the difficulty of translating him insurmountable.

These are the same terms in which he praises (11.1802) Milton's sonnets:

. . .upon the whole, I think the music exceedingly well suited to its end, that is, it has an energetic and varied flow of sound crowding into narrow room more of the combined effect of rhyme and blank verse than can be done by any other kind of verse I know of.

This is the music that Wordsworth seeks not only in the narrow rooms of his own sonnets, but also in his long poems where he has all the room he wants. There the crowding is accomplished by the ordonnance of the sentence, as if through his syntax he could lay hold of his meaning. He desires the palpable reassurance of the past made ever present, beyond any possibility of loss. Expression is a means of bringing his feelings into the open and of re-establishing the intangible foundation of his being. He wants, he says, to give 'substance and life' to feelings, 'enshrining, / . . .the spirit of the Past / For future restoration' (XII.284 – 287; 1850). The restoration is to be both of the experience and himself, and this is the purpose for which he tries to keep alive the fire in the embers of memory.

Milton, whose syntax is more complicated than that of any other major English poet before Wordsworth, is Wordsworth's favourite model. His example encourages Wordsworth's disposition to complexity. The great difference between them is that Milton, unlike Montaigne (or even to a certain extent Burton and Browne), does not use his syntax to explore the data of consciousness. This is one reason why Milton is so comfortable with the conventions and techniques of the Homeric poems. Wordsworth knew that he was rejecting this aspect of Milton and felt that he was going beyond him. Sometime early in 1800, still in the midst of deciding on the shape of his autobiographical poem, he composed these lines that were published as part of the 'Preface' to *The Excursion*:

> Urania, I shall need
> Thy guidance, or a greater Muse, if such

Descend to earth or dwell in highest heaven!
For I must tread on shadowy ground, must sink
Deep — and, aloft ascending, breathe in worlds
To which the heaven of heavens is but a veil.
All strength — all terror, single or in bands,
That ever was put forth in personal form —
Jehovah — with his thunder, and the choir
Of shouting Angels, and the empyreal thrones —
I pass them unalarmed. Not Chaos, not
The darkest pit of lowest Erebus,
Nor aught of blinder vacancy, scooped out
By help of dreams — can breed such fear and awe
As fall upon us often when we look
Into our Minds, into the Mind of Man —
My haunt, and the main region of my song.

$$(25-41)^{15}$$

Amid numerous echoes of *Paradise Lost*, Wordsworth calls on Milton's muse, Urania, but hopes for a greater Muse, and then he *passes by* Milton's subject to his own: the human mind, which, he declares, is more fearful and more awe-inspiring.

Keats believed (without knowing the autobiographical poem) that Wordsworth had found a new subject for poetry and that in doing this he had surpassed Milton. He sets forth his views when he writes to John Reynolds (3.5.1818) about his own gloomy efforts to understand life and the growth of individual consciousness. Like Wordsworth, he feels that the problem of what life is about can be solved by understanding how consciousness works. Keats compares human life first to a labyrinth and then to a mansion with many rooms, opened and closed. We are born, he says, into 'the infant or thoughtless Chamber' and then enter 'the Chamber of Maiden-Thought' where intoxicating delight has the effect of

> sharpening one's vision into the heart and nature of Man — of convincing one's nerves that the world is full of Misery and Heartbreak, Pain, Sickness and oppression — whereby this Chamber of Maiden Thought becomes gradually darken'd and at the same time on all sides of it many doors are set open — but all dark — all leading to dark passages — We see not the ballance of good and evil. We are in a Mist. *We* are now in that state — We feel the 'burden of the Mystery', To this Point was Wordsworth come, as far as I can

conceive when he wrote 'Tintern Abbey' and it seems to me that his Genius is explorative of those dark Passages. Now if we live, and go on thinking, we too shall explore them — he is a Genius and superior [to] us, in so far as he can, more than we, make discoveries, and shed a light in them — Here I must think Wordsworth is deeper than Milton — . . .

Of Milton, he says in a penetrating phrase: 'He did not think into the human heart, as Wordsworth has done.'[16] Keats's metaphors, the labyrinth, 'a large Mansion of Many Apartments' and 'those dark Passages,' remind us of the syntax of Wordsworth's sentences and suggest that to make the unconscious conscious it is necessary to follow a winding and twisting path.

How Milton and Wordsworth use elaborate syntax for different purposes can be illustrated by comparing *Paradise Lost* (IX. 1099 – 1115) with Wordsworth's *Yew-Trees*, composed with Milton's text in mind. Milton describes, in a passage that Coleridge considered a masterpiece, how, after eating the fruit of the tree of knowledge, Adam and Eve look for leaves to cover their nakedness:

> So counsell'd hee, and both together went
> Into the thickest Wood, there soon they chose
> The Figtree, not that kind for Fruit renown'd,
> But such as at this day to *Indians* known
> In *Malabar* or *Decan* spreads her Arms
> Branching so broad and long, that in the ground
> The bended Twigs take root, and Daughters grow
> About the Mother Tree, a Pillar'd shade
> High overarch't, and echoing Walks between;
> There oft the *Indian* Herdsman shunning heat
> Shelters in cool, and tends his pasturing Herds
> At Loopholes cut through thickest shade: Those Leaves
> They gather'd, broad as *Amazonian* Targe,
> And with what skill they had, together sew'd,
> To gird thir waist, vain Covering if to hide
> Thir guilt and dreaded shame; O how unlike
> To that first naked Glory.[17]

Milton's sentence fills 17 lines and is deliberately prolonged by semi-colons and colons. He expands it irregularly by adding detail: the tree grows 'in *Malabar* or *Decan*,' it is not the kind known for its fruit, its arms spread and branch, the twigs root in the ground, the branches are 'so broad and long,' — balancing it somewhat by the *there soon* and *There oft*. His characters engage in a series of actions: the Herdsman shuns, shelters and tends; Adam and Eve gather, sew and gird.

Milton begins and ends with Adam and Eve doing things (except for the final exclamation), separating these events, and thereby suspending the action, by the simile of the Indian Figtree. The result is a description of the behaviour of the personified tree and of the Indian Herdsman. Milton uses similes, as Dante does in the *Commedia*, as a way of incorporating the real world in his imaginary world. The Figtree with the Indian Herdsman tending his cattle is at once exotic and ordinary. Milton's description is wholly factual, the image of the tree is not presented as a metaphor, despite its personification as a mother with daughters. The fig tree in India is used to describe the fig tree in Eden.

Wordsworth's *Yew-Trees* is made up of three sentences. The final sentence is 21 lines long, prolonged by semi-colons and dashes, and twice by both. That the second begins with *Of* and the final one with *But* causes the three sentences to run together. Like Milton, Wordsworth takes pleasure in strange-sounding names: *Umfraville* and *Azincour*. He makes more obvious and concentrated use of assonance and consonance, as in 'pining umbrage tinged / Perennially' and 'as if for festal purpose, decked,' and employs more long words than Milton and more abstractions. This increases the effect of concentration and intensity. The abstract and latinate words are important in making possible the easy movement of the poem from the outside to the inside world.

> There is a Yew-tree, pride of Lorton Vale,
> Which to this day stands single, in the midst
> Of its own darkness, as it stood of yore:
> Not loth to furnish weapons for the bands
> Of Umfraville or Percy ere they marched
> To Scotland's heaths; or those that crossed the sea
> And drew their sounding bows at Azincour,
> Perhaps at earlier Crecy, or Poictiers.
> Of vast circumference and gloom profound
> This solitary Tree! a living thing
> Produced too slowly ever to decay;
> Of form and aspect too magnificent

To be destroyed. But worthier still of note
Are those fraternal Four of Borrowdale,
Joined in one solemn and capacious grove;
Huge trunks! and each particular trunk a growth
Of intertwisted fibres serpentine
Up-coiling, and inveterately convolved;
Nor uninformed with Phantasy, and looks
That threaten the profane; — a pillared shade,
Upon whose grassless floor of red-brown hue,
By sheddings from the pining umbrage tinged
Perennially — beneath whose sable roof
Of boughs, as if for festal purpose, decked
With unrejoicing berries — ghostly Shapes
May meet at noontide; Fear and trembling Hope,
Silence and Foresight; Death the Skeleton
And Time the Shadow; — there to celebrate,
As in a natural temple scattered o'er
With altars undisturbed of mossy stone,
United worship; or in mute repose
To lie, and listen to the mountain flood
Murmuring from Glaramara's inmost caves.

Wordsworth uses Milton's metaphor of the trees being a family and borrows his phrase 'a pillared shade,' but Wordsworth's images are obvious metaphors. The yew of Lorton Vale 'in the midst / Of its own darkness' seems to live in an atmosphere of self-created melancholy. Its own nature is the centre of this mystery, and it is explicitly 'a living thing.' There is a temptation to see this as a self-image of the melancholy poet, set apart by the singularity of his genius. Wordsworth always remembered his mother's intimate friend, Miss Hamilton, telling him that his mother had 'said to her, that the only one of her five children about whose future life she was anxious, was William; and he, she said, would be remarkable either for good or evil.'[18] The yew trees, in their gloom and power, evoking fear and hope, can be said to embody this double potential.

Somewhat arbitrarily Wordsworth combines the single yew with the four in Borrowdale. The possibility that they might be a family of five — Wordsworth speaks only of the 'fraternal Four' — reminds us that Wordsworth was one of five children and that, counting his father, there were five men in the family. The poem's geography also has personal associations for him: Lorton Vale is the valley of the River

Cocker north of Crummock Water and the Cocker runs into the Derwent at Cockermouth near Wordsworth's birthplace. The source of the'River Derwent is at the end of Borrowdale, not far beyond the group of yew trees, and the streams that fall from Glaramara into Borrowdale are tributaries of the Derwent. The Derwent, which flows at the end of the garden behind Wordsworth's birthplace, appears as a shaping and tutelary spirit of the poet's character in the autobiographical poem (in which the poem itself is frequently compared to a river). The murmurs of Glaramara's waters — the voice of 'mute repose,' an indeterminate sound that might be speech — are, in truth, the murmurs of the Derwent. It is as if by going away from Cockermouth to Lorton Vale and Borrowdale, Wordsworth has used movement in space to represent movement in time, as if the 'inmost caves' are the recesses of the past.

The language of *Yew-Trees* is active, but unlike Milton, Wordsworth is not primarily interested in reporting action or actuality. This poem, along with *There was a Boy*, is one of the 'Poems of the Imagination.' As Wordsworth describes the trees, he looks away from the present. The Lorton yew is associated with ancient history. The Borrowdale yews are not 'uninformed with Phantasy' and, as a consequence of the structure of this very long sentence, seem almost to become the 'ghostly shapes.' These are feelings on the verge of form-lessness. It is not even clear if the shapes are really there: they '*May* meet at noontide.' They are the constant companions of the poet rather than spirits of the dead. They are an unusual collection and come in pairs, as if in some way each pair restated a basic antithesis.

Fear is named first, after joy the strongest emotion in the autobiographical poem. Hope is trembling and uncertain, weaker than Fear and affected by it. The most unusual combination is Silence and Foresight. Does Silence stand for annihilation and oblivion? Wordsworth associates life with murmurous sounds. There is no poet with a keener ear for dim faraway music. Thinking for him is listening — for an inner voice or some lost echo. Foresight resembles Hope in being always about the future. Fear, Hope and Foresight all depend upon imagination, on the capacity for phantasy. The poet in this poem full of shadows makes death the core of what we are and Time a *memento mori*, although without doubt he wishes the yew of Lorton Vale to be immortal.

The ghostly shapes do nothing. Their 'United worship' is obscure, and it is only one of two alternatives. The lying and listening seem something done by the poet rather than by the six abstract entities.

This shift is a success because of the syntax and the length of the sentence. Wordsworth takes things apart and puts them back together in a single affirmation. There is nothing comparable to this in the passage from *Paradise Lost* where there is no suggestion of the inner world; the 'guilt and dreaded shame' of Adam and Eve are stated outright, they are not embedded in the description.

Wordsworth uses his long sentences to bring together reality and phantasy in order to go from the tangible to the unknown. Each informs the other as the poet specifically says. The yew trees appear as incarnations of mystery. Wordsworth stresses the close relation of 'those *fraternal* Four of Borrowdale / *Joined in one*. . .grove.' Most of all he emphasises the structure of their trunks. He does this five times: *intertwisted, serpentine, up-coiling, convolved* and *Nor uninformed* (using long and unusual words that draw attention to themselves) and he maximises the effect by packing them all together in four lines. The trunks of the yews are the centres of the 'pillared shade.' Wordsworth is trying to describe the core of darkness. This seems to be a matter of inner form: they are *inter*twisted, *in*veterately (which means deep-rooted) convolved and *in*formed with phantasy. It is almost as if these words perform the integration of the tangible and the unknown. They suggest, moreover, the function or meaning of the intertwisting of Wordsworth's sentences.

For Wordsworth his own identity seems to depend on discovering and maintaining the original connection between himself and the world. He seeks to explore and repair his primordial feelings. He writes in MS JJ, the earliest draft of the autobiographical poem, of:

> . . .those first born affinities which fit
> Our new existence to existing things
> And in our dawn of being constitute
> The bond of union betwixt life & joy.[19]

The earliest period of our lives is so crucial because 'The bond of union' is created in the 'dawn of being.'

Wordsworth uses the verb *intertwine* in this context in MS V, a somewhat later draft than MS JJ of the two-part version of the poem, when he addresses the 'Beings of the hills,' 'the woods and open heaths':

> . . .thus from my first dawn
> Of childhood did ye love to intertwine

> The passions that build up our human soul
> Not with the mean and vulgar works of man
> But with high objects, with eternal things. . .

(MS JJ has *interweave*.[20]) Here the child's strongest emotions, the shapers of its phantasies, are bound up with the outside world of nature. *Intertwine* makes it clear that this is a process, not a single event, and emphasises the intricate and intimate nature of the bond. The word is used to introduce the same subject in MS JJ: Wordsworth remembers how the River Derwent sent 'a voice / To intertwine my dreams. . .' and again there is a long meandering sentence trying to describe the origin of being — and this passage was for a time literally the start of the poem.[21]

When in the final version he discusses the growth of man's 'immortal spirit,' and how it reconciles the 'discordant elements' of human character, he compares it to 'harmony in music,' passing immediately to his own self:

> Dust as we are, the immortal spirit grows
> Like harmony in music; there is a dark
> Inscrutable workmanship that reconciles
> Discordant elements, makes them cling together
> In one society. How strange that all
> The terrors, pains, and early miseries,
> Regrets, vexations, lassitudes interfused
> Within my mind, should e'er have borne a part,
> And that a needful part, in making up
> The calm existence that is mine when I
> Am worthy of myself!

> (I.340 – 350; 1850)

Wordsworth sees that he is what he is because of the way diverse feelings have come together in his mind and he recognises that his bad feelings are necessary to his happiness. At peace with himself, he finds that his earliest memories are not just *intertwined* but *interfused*.

Wordsworth employs *interfused* three times in his published works (including *The Prelude*, 1850).[22] He uses it in the *Lines Composed a Few Miles above Tintern Abbey* when explaining how he has learned to hear 'The still, sad music of humanity' in nature, which reverses the process described in the texts above: he now projects upon nature what he previously has apprehended in nature and introjected. As he says, this is part of adult consciousness, not of 'thoughtless youth.' He feels 'a sense sublime / Of something far more deeply interfused' that is at once in the world 'and in the mind of man.' This is the bond of identity, the sense of the relation of all things.

Wordsworth in all these passages knows that he is engaged in the analysis of mental states, and that his dim, vague feelings have nothing to do with mysticism. Wordsworth's religion at the end of his life is a substitute for the continuation of this analysis. He does not under-estimate the difficulty of the task that he sets himself:

> Hard task to analyse a soul, in which,
> Not only general habits and desires,
> But each most obvious and particular thought,
> Not in a mystical and idle sense,
> But in the words of reason deeply weigh'd,
> Hath no beginning.
>
> (II.232–237)

Wordsworth persists in trying to imagine his own origins, his repeated use of *being* showing his concern with the time before thought and self-awareness. The sense of being begins for each baby at its mother's breast:

> Blest the infant Babe,
> (For with my best conjecture I would trace
> Our Being's earthly progress,) blest the Babe,
> Nursed in his Mother's arms, who sinks to sleep
> Rocked on his Mother's breast; who with his soul
> Drinks in the feelings of his Mother's eye!
> For him, in one dear Presence, there exists
> A virtue which irradiates and exalts
> Objects through widest intercourse of sense.
> No outcast he, bewildered and depressed:
> Along his infant veins are interfused
> The gravitation and the filial bond
> Of nature that connect him with the world.
>
> (II.232–244; 1850)

The 'one dear Presence' that animates the world is the presence of the mother. This, in the *Lines Composed a Few Miles above Tintern*

Abbey, is a 'presence that disturbs me with the joy / Of elevated thoughts.' Here it *exalts*, there it *elevates*; it prevents the baby from being *bewildered and depressed* instead of providing *joy*. Here it *irradiates*, there it dwells in 'The light of setting suns. . .the living air and the blue sky.' The interfusing is 'Along his infant veins' just as the River Derwent sent 'a voice / To intertwine my dreams' (MS JJ) or 'That flow'd along my dreams' (MSS A and B). The *infant veins* are like miniature rivers. The words and syntax are similar in each case. The *gravitation* is the force of 'those first born affinities,' the inborn propensities of the infant towards its mother. The *bond of nature* is *filial*. The relation of the child to the mother is the basis of its relation to the world.

Wordsworth insists on the unifying nature of this process (*interfused, bond, connect*) and on its all-pervasive power. Feelings are so intertwined that they become interfused and bonded. They are metamorphosed. The presence of the mother *irradiates* through the being of the child. There is an interpenetration of all the desires and phantasies of the inner world and all the data of perception. Wordsworth refers to the 'intercourse of sense' and to the 'intercourse of touch,' and to how the baby is:

> . . .creator and receiver both,
> Working but in alliance with the works
> Which it beholds.
>
> (II.258−260; 1850)

He calls this 'the first / Poetic spirit of our human life' (II. 260−261; 1850). The poet, too, is a 'creator and receiver both.' Imagination enables him to create poetry as the mother and infant create being. Wordsworth returns so often to his earliest moments and is so often overpowered by the presence of nature that it is as if these primordial feelings were not sufficiently interfused, as if his connection to the world keeps dissolving so that he uses poetry to re-create this essential unity.

This discussion by Wordsworth is a triumph of self-analysis, of autobiography. He makes it clear that he is attempting a reconstruction of his own experiences:

> From early days,
> Beginning not long after that first time
> In which, a Babe, by intercourse of touch
> I held mute dialogues with my Mother's heart,

I have endeavoured to display the means
Whereby this infant sensibility,
Great birthright of our being, was in me
Augmented and sustained.

(II.265 – 272, 1850)

He is looking for himself in the mirror of memory and in describing the
mother and baby as he would a landscape, he endeavours to give voice
to the 'mute dialogues' of the 'intercourse of touch' in order to free
himself from the painful emptiness of silence in the unconscious. He is
comforted when he is in touch with the presence of another being,
when he hears:

the mountain flood
Murmuring from Glaramara's inmost caves.

He bridges the silence with the sound of his own voice.

The most significant moments in the autobiographical poem, and
in most of Wordsworth's poetry, are when something from the depths
comes to the surface. This, moreover, is the metaphor Wordsworth
chooses to sum up the activity of composing his long poem:

As one who hangs down-bending from the side
Of a slow-moving boat, upon the breast
Of a still water, solacing himself
With such discoveries as his eye can make
Beneath him in the bottom of the deep,
Sees many beauteous sights — weeds, fishes, flowers,
Grots, pebbles, roots of trees, and fancies more,
Yet often is perplexed and cannot part
The shadow from the substance, rocks and sky,
Mountains and clouds, reflected in the depth
Of the clear flood, from things which there abide
In their true dwelling; now is crossed by gleam
Of his own image, by a sun-beam now,
And wavering motions sent he knows not whence,
Impediments that make his task more sweet;
Such pleasant office have we long pursued
Incumbent o'er the surface of past time
With like success, nor often have appeared
Shapes fairer or less doubtfully discerned

Than these to which the Tale, indulgent Friend!
Would now direct thy notice.

(IV.256 – 276; 1850)

Here is one of the best examples of Wordsworth's use of long sentences to bring the life of the mind to consciousness. The sentence extends over twenty-one lines. Virtually every phrase is qualified. The poet keeps changing direction and breaking in on himself. He proceeds without urgency, without any clearly defined purpose, and accepts whatever he happens to find. He muses and drifts. This is the reflective mood that produces the poem. Wordsworth is not conducting a philosophical investigation; he does not seek another order for his experiences beyond the order in which they happen. He is 'solacing himself' with his discoveries. For him a metaphor is truer than any system and allows him to enjoy the uncertainty of his conclusions. He is not interested in presenting a realistic or vivid picture of the lake floor because he is looking into himself. He offers not a description of things seen, but the sensation of the process of seeing.

The verb to *hang* has a special virtue to Wordsworth. It is the crucial verb in the examples from Virgil, Shakespeare and Milton that he employs in the 'Preface' of 1815 to show how 'the full strength of the imagination' can be involved in a single word.[23] The boy who 'blew mimic hootings' to the owls 'hung / Listening' for their response, and Wordsworth tells how, going to steal eggs, he has:

hung

Above the raven's nest, by knots of grass
And half-inch fissures in the slippery rock
But ill-sustained, and almost (so it seemed)
Suspended by the blast that blew amain,

(I.330 – 334; 1850)

listening to the 'strange utterance' of the wind. He compares himself in this passage to 'one who hangs down-bending' from the side of a boat seeking out the secrets of the deep. He is suspended over 'the surface of past time.' (Wordsworth revises MS A to read: 'floating upon' and retains this reading in MSS B and C.)

The suspense is also a matter of syntax. The simple sentence is complex enough: *As one who hangs from the side of a boat upon the water, such office have we pursued o'er the surface of past time,* but thirteen lines separate the first part of the simile from the second; the conclusion is withheld and the syntax illustrates how difficult it is to distinguish one perception or memory from another. The 'rocks and sky, / Mountains and clouds' are all reflected in 'the clear flood,' but at first glance it appears that they are to be differentiated, *rock* from *sky*, *mountains* from *clouds*, as examples of substances and shadows. The ambiguity is created by the syntax. The objects are paired, like *shadow* and *substance*, and in each case a solid object is paired with a nebulous one. The true substances, nevertheless, are the things which abide in the deep. The things of the world are shadows, and yet they are *reflected in the depth* rather than on the surface. The sense demands that *now is* modifies either *still water* or *clear flood*, yet grammatically it modifies *one*. The gleam is in the mind. *Sent he knows not whence* is a very roundabout way of describing the origin of the *wavering motions* and seems to say the opposite of what it means. Wordsworth no sooner completes the simile than he extends it: *with like success*, and immediately begins another: *nor often have appeared / Shapes fairer. . .than these. . .*, which serves to muffle the original comparison and makes the sentence still longer. Thus the boundaries of the simile are obscured and it is absorbed stylistically into the poet's discourse.

Wordsworth still has in his mind the image of the mother and the baby. As the visible scene before the boy listening on the shore of Winander 'is received / Into the bosom of the steady lake,' the poet in the boat moves 'upon the breast / Of a still water' — and looks into the breast. Near the end of the verse paragraph he regrets that the world has lured his mind from the 'firm habitual quest / Of feeding pleasures.' This may be compared with how in his description of the nursing couple the baby 'with his soul / Drinks in the feelings of his Mother's eye' (II.236 – 237; 1850). 'Feeding pleasures' are those that build up identity. So often in Wordsworth's poetry the poet drinks in the landscape and his style is shaped by his desire to absorb what he sees.

Wordsworth in this passage seeks to record the action of remembering, moments in which reality and phantasy mingle without interfusing. Perception is at the pitch of day-dreaming. Objects are indefinite and indistinct, like murmurous sounds. He tries to confront the whole contents of the mind, and, as in the episode on Snowden, feels that he is looking into an abyss. Revising MS A he changes 'nor have we often look'd / On more alluring shows' (IV.265) to read: 'nor often in the abyss / Have we discovered more alluring shows.' This is retained in MSS B and C, but changed again in MS D. In this description of memory, time is all but eliminated, past and present, shadow and substance, are there on equal terms, interrupted now and again by glimpses of the self: the 'gleam / Of his own image.' The changes of the mind's focus are the 'wavering motions.'

After Wordsworth perhaps the two most notable builders of long, complex sentences are Henry James and Marcel Proust, and they construct them for much the same reasons. Joyce, Faulkner and Beckett often abandon the sentence in favour of a more or less unordered series of words and phrases, as if to resolve consciousness into mere sensation and by this fragmentation to affirm a more elemental continuity. The work as a whole becomes the statement and in a sense takes the place of the sentence. No author after Proust, so far, has equalled or attempted to equal his syntactic control of his material. Browning, Hopkins and Hardy continue with the developments initiated by Wordsworth, but it is Mallarmé who pushes the poetic sentence to its limits. The poets who follow him work with syntactic fragments as often as the prose writers, and poets such as Cummings and Williams, in many poems, have dispensed with punctuation altogether.

James believes that characters are interesting in proportion to their consciousness of their respective situations.

> But there are degrees of feeling — the muffled, the faint, the just sufficient, the barely intelligent, as we may say; and the acute, the intense, the complete, in a word — the power to be finely aware and richly responsible. . . Their being finely aware. . .*makes* absolutely the intensity of their adventure, gives the maximum of sense to what befalls them.[24]

James multiplies his words in order to marshal all the degrees of feeling and mark every conceivable nuance. For him, as for Wordsworth, feeling is never simple and all his naming is only suggestion, only approximation. He celebrates the power of 'the stray suggestion, the wandering word, the vague echo. . .to penetrate as finely as possible. This fineness it is that communicates the virus of suggestion, anything more than the minimum of which spoils the operation.' James believes 'that life has no direct sense whatever,' while Wordsworth believes that its sense is more accessible, but both believe in the precision of circumlocution and repeated re-statement.[25] James tries to create characters who appear to us as Wordsworth appears to himself.

James is aware that his style implies a particular view of experience

(a characteristically European view that dates from the new meaning
that the word acquires in the lifetime of Montaigne) — and it is one
that is shared by Wordsworth and Proust:

> Experience is never limited, and it is never complete; it is an
> immense sensibility, a kind of huge spider-web of the finest silken
> threads suspended in the chamber of consciousness, and catching
> every air-borne particle in its tissue. It is the very atmosphere of the
> mind; and when the mind is imaginative — much more when it
> happens to be that of a man of genius — it takes to itself the
> faintest hints of life, it converts the very pulses of the air into
> revelations.[26]

The emphasis of all three authors is on the fineness of consciousness.
They register the shadows of each sensation as well as the light, that
which is barely perceptible seems to them to be most important. They
seek to communicate 'the very atmosphere of the mind.' Wordsworth
who hears 'Low breathings coming after me' (I.323; 1850) and 'a
breath-like sound' from the hazel leaves stirred 'by the straggling wind'
(IV.183 – 185; 1850), who is alert to 'the bleak music' of a dry stone
wall (XIII.320; 1850) and is wooed to poetry by the blessing of the
'gentle breeze' seems one of those geniuses who literally 'converts the
very pulses of the air into revelations.'

James, like Wordsworth and Proust, uses long sentences to analyse
consciousness. This is how in *The Wings of the Dove* (Chapter XXIV)
he begins his description of Milly Theale's growing appreciation of the
Palazzo Laporelli in Venice where she has come to stay:

> Not yet so much as this morning had she felt herself sink into posses-
> sion; gratefully glad that the warmth of the Southern summer
> was still in the high florid rooms, palatial chambers where hard
> cool pavements took reflexions in their lifelong polish, and where
> the sun on the stirred sea-water, flickering up through open
> windows, played over the painted 'subjects' in the splendid
> ceilings — medallions of purple and brown, of brave old melan-
> choly colour, medals as of old reddened gold, embossed and berib-
> boned, all toned with time and all flourished and scolloped and
> gilded about, set in their great moulded and figured concavity (a
> nest of white cherubs, friendly creatures of the air) and appreciated
> by the aid of that second tier of smaller lights, straight openings to
> the front, which did everything, even with the Baedekers and

photographs of Milly's party dreadfully meeting the eye, to make of
the place an apartment of state.[27]

The location of this event in the chronology of Milly's morning is not
made clear. It is her awareness of herself sinking into possession that is
important. She absorbs her surroundings. A series of moments is
combined almost but not quite into one. The syntax is used to convey
the elaborateness of the palace and the complexity of her perception.
The sentence seems to follow Milly's gaze, but whether she is walking
from room to room or only remembering is unstated and blurred. Her
movement is only implicit in the plurals: *rooms, chambers, pave-
ments, ceilings*. Outside and inside are merged. The present and the
past are as one — all perception is of the present and belongs to the
inner world. As in Wordsworth's description of hanging over the boat,
a process is represented by a moving scene, nothing is described in any
detail, the adjectives are deliberately unspecific. Milly's impression is
everything. The rooms are *high* and *florid*, the ceilings are *splendid*
and their '*subjects*' are only alluded to. The colours of the sky and sea
are omitted. There is no reference to any furniture. Wordsworth in the
same way merely mentions 'weeds, fishes, flowers, / Grots, pebbles,
roots of trees,' 'rocks and sky / Mountains and clouds.' The abstractness of both descriptions derives from their being pictures of mental
events. The flickering light denotes the play of attention.

The sentences of Proust are, on the whole, even longer than those of
James. He is more self-interested and concerned with his own perceptions than James and more interested in the things of the
world — they are what he perceives — and a more accurate observer
of objects, but he is equally ready to expatiate on a sensation or pursue
a vague emotion, equally attuned to the vibrations of the spider web of
experience. As in Wordsworth description of the countryside is a way
of gaining access to the world of phantasty and the workings of the
imagination. Proust's description of water-lilies in the Vivonne shades
off into the infinite:

Ailleurs, un coin semblait réservé aux espèces communes qui
montraient le blanc et le rose proprets de la julienne, lavés
comme de la porcelaine avec un soin domestique, tandis qu'un
peu plus loin, pressées les unes contre les autres en une véritable
plate-bande flottante, on eût dit des pensées des jardins qui
étaient venues poser comme des papillons leurs ailes bleuâtres et

glacées sur l'obliquité transparente de ce parterre d'eau; de ce parterre céleste aussi: car il donnait aux fleurs un sol d'une couleur plus précieuse, plus émouvante que la couleur des fleurs elles-mêmes; et, soit que pendant l'après-midi il fit étinceler sous les nymphéas le kaléidoscope d'un bonheur attentif, silencieux et mobile, ou qu'il s'emplît vers le soir, comme quelque port lointain, du rose et de la rêverie du couchant, changeant sans cesse pour rester toujours en accord, autour des corolles de teintes plus fixes, avec ce qu'il y a de plus profond, de plus fugitif, de plus mystérieux — avec ce qu'il y a d'infini — dans l'heure, il semblait les avoir fait fleurir en plein ciel.[28]

(Elsewhere a corner seemed reserved for the ordinary species, that showed the neat white and rose of the rocket-flowers, like porcelain washed with housewifely care, while a little further on, pressed against each other in a veritable floating border, one would have said that pansies from gardens had come and alighted like butter-flies with bluish and glazed wings on the transparent obliquity of this watery flower-bed; of this celestial flower-bed also: for it provided the flowers with a soil whose colour was more precious, more moving, than the colour of the flowers themselves, and whether during the afternoon it made the kaleidoscope of an atten-tive, silent and mobile happiness sparkle beneath the water-lilies, or whether it filled, towards the evening, like some far off port, with the rose and the reverie of the sunset, changing continuously in order to remain always in harmony, around the corollas of the more stable tints, with that which was most profound most fugitive, most mysterious — with what there was of infinity — in the hour, it seemed to have caused them to flower in the midst of the sky.)

Proust moves in the space of a single sentence from the ordinary: *espèces communes, soin domestique*, to *ce qu'il y a de plus profond, de plus fugitif, de plus mystérieux*. As so often in Wordsworth, reality is assimilated to thought. This is a movement into twilight. (The point of departure of Proust's great work is the moment before sleep. Signifi-cantly there is nothing in the context of this sentence that requires any reference to twilight.) The water-lilies seem *des pensées des jardins*, only temporarily there, like butterflies. The water fills up *du rose et de la rêverie* and suggests *quelque port lointain*, some remote destination across strange seas of thought.

This description of Proust's is not especially realistic, except as it describes thought. There is not a single colour in Wordsworth's account of hanging over the side of the boat. The force of James's description resides in the *brave, old melancholy colour* not in the *purple and brown*. Similarly, Proust does not try to name the colour of the river. He states that it is *plus précieuse, plus émouvante* than the colour of the flowers, that it forms the *kaléidoscope d'un bonheur attentif, silencieux et mobile*. Like Wordsworth, like James, he makes use of generalities, abstractions, in an effort to come to terms with change.

Proust is closer to Wordsworth than to James in that his work is more deliberately autobiographical. *À la Recherche du temps perdu* resembles the autobiographical poem in that it is based on a number of 'spots of time.' They are 'scattered everywhere' (XII.224; 1850), and occur and recur without warning. For Proust, exactly as for Wordsworth, they provide new courage and demand long sentences:

Alors on eût dit que les signes qui devaient, ce jour-là,
me tirer de mon découragement et me rendre la foi dans
les lettres, avaient à cœur de se multiplier, car, un maître
d'hôtel depuis longtemps au service du prince de Guer
mantes m'ayant reconnu et m'ayant apporté dans la
bibliothèque où j'étais, pour m'éviter d'aller au buffet,
un choix de petits fours, un verre d'orangeade, je m'es
suyai la bouche avec la serviette qu'il m'avait donnée;
mais aussitôt, comme le personnage des *Mille et une Nuits*
qui sans le savoir accomplissait précisément le rite qui
faisait apparaître, visible pour lui seul, un docile génie
prêt à le transporter au loin, une nouvelle vision d'azur
passa devant mes yeux; mais il était pur et salin, il se
gonfla en mamelles bleuâtres; l'impression fut si forte que
le moment que je vivais me sembla être le moment actuel;
plus hébété que le jour où je me demandais si j'allais
vraiment être accueilli par la princesse de Guermantes ou
si tout n'allait pas s'effondrer, je croyais que le domestique
venait d'ouvrir la fenêtre sur la plage et que tout m'in
vitait à descendre me promener le long de la digue à
marée haute; la serviette que j'avais prise pour m'essuyer
la bouche avait précisément le genre de raideur et d'em
pesé de celle avec laquelle j'avais eu tant de peine à me
sécher devant la fenêtre, le premier jour de mon arrivée à

Balbec, et, maintenant, devant cette bibliothèque de
l'hôtel de Guermantes, elle déployait, réparti dans ses
pans et dans ses cassures, le plumage d'un océan vert et
bleu comme la queue d'un paon.[29]

(Then one would have said that the signs which, that very day, were
to lift me out of my discouragement and restore my faith in literature had determined to multiply, for when a butler, who had been
for a long time in the service of the Prince de Guermantes, having
recognised me and brought to me in the library where I was, in
order to save my going to the buffet, a selection of *petits fours*, a
glass of orangeade, I wiped my mouth with the napkin he had given
me; but immediately, like the character in *The Thousand and One
Nights* who without knowing it performed precisely the rite that
caused the appearance, visible to his eyes alone, of a docile genie
ready to transport him far away, a new vision of azure passed before
my eyes, but it was pure and saline, it swelled as bluish breasts; the
impression was so strong that the moment that I was living seemed
to me to be the actual moment; more dazed than the day when I
asked myself whether it was true that I was going to be received by
the Princess de Guermantes or whether everything was not going to
collapse, I believed that the servant had just opened the window on
the beach and that everything invited me to go down and walk the
length of the sea-wall at high tide; the napkin that I had taken to
wipe my mouth had precisely the kind of stiffness and starchiness of
the one with which I had had so much difficulty in drying myself in
front of the window, the first day of my arrival at Balbec, and, now,
in front of the bookcases of the hotel de Guermantes it unfolded,
distributed among its surfaces and fractures, the plumage of an
ocean green and blue like the tail of a peacock.)

Here phrase is added to phrase so as to assemble as a unity every essential element of the experience. The wholeness of these experiences is
vital to both authors. Mundane details are insisted upon: the plate of
petit fours, the glass of orangeade, the texture of the napkin, as if they
guarantee the truth of memory. Their definiteness is in marked
contrast to the indefiniteness that seems to be the core of the moment.
The rite that makes the genie appear is performed unknowingly.
These moments are gifts, not acts of the will. They happen without
warning — suddenly the world merges with phantasy. This merger is

made explicit by the reference to the *Thousand and One Nights*. (Wordsworth cherished his copy of the Arabian Nights as 'a precious treasure' (V.960; 1850) and it is an 'Arab of the Bedouin tribes' (V.77; 1850) who leads him into the dream world.) Here the old servant of the prince de Guermantes acts as a genie and the narrator is transported into himself, he passes through reality as through a gate: he imagines the windows being opened upon the beach and the sea, the shore of a bygone time.

Wordsworth thinks of phantasy as a bridge to the world:

> Of the same isthmus, which our spirits cross
> In progress from their native continent
> To earth and human life. . .
>
> (V.536 – 538; 1850)

and states that his song might dwell:

> On that delightful time of growing youth,
> When craving for the marvellous gives way
> To strengthening love for things that we have seen;
> When sober truth and steady sympathies,
> Offered to notice by less daring pens,
> Take firmer hold of us, and words themselves
> Move us with conscious pleasure.
>
> (V.539 – 545; 1850)

By means of their respective 'spots of time,' Wordsworth and Proust cross back over this bridge to an earlier time, before consciousness of language. Wordsworth, discussing (V.496 – 507; 1850) the value of 'The tales that charm away the wakeful night / In Araby,' declares:

> Dumb yearnings, hidden appetites, are ours,
> And *they must* have their food.

The vision of Balbec happens when the narrator is eating and begins with a saline taste and the swelling of *mamelles bleuâtres*. He redis-covers all of Combray and his childhood in the taste of the tea-soaked crumbs of the madeleine. (These cakes also suggest the sea shore as they 'semblent avoir été moulés dans la valve rainurée d'une coquille de Saint Jacques' ('seemed to have been moulded in the grooved valve of a scallop shell').)[30]

The *vision d'azur* after the narrator wipes his mouth with the napkin is a glimpse of infinite space, as in the other example from Proust. The experience is over when the connection with the earlier memory has been made. Proust differs from Wordsworth in that what is remembered is usually another specific and well defined moment; he uses fewer abstractions and more objects to cope with formlessness while Wordsworth's special memories are usually of barely adumbrated feelings and disembodied presences, set out with a certain indeterminacy — although in this sentence of Proust's the re-experiencing of the narrator's first day at Balbec ends in a vivid sensation of pure colour, the shimmering green and blue of the ocean and the peacock's tail. Both authors feel that their 'minds / Are nourished and invisibly repaired' by these 'spots of time.' Wordsworth speaks of renovation after depression and trivial occupations; Proust, of fatigue, sadness and recovering lost faith.

Wordsworth's long sentences are the result of his desire for wholeness. They are expressions of longing. They show him plainly at work in his poems, how he continuously elaborates and refines and how he repeatedly returns to his subject. They enable him to connect past and present, and to go back and forth between his phantasies and the world. The subordination is sometimes tenuous, illustrating Valéry's aphorism: 'Think?. . .To think is to lose the thread.'[31] He employs them, as do James and Proust, to represent the stream of consciousness. Wordsworth, however, is concerned to trace consciousness to its origins.

Wordsworth, after the simile of hanging over the side of a slow-moving boat, mentions the vanity of worldly pleasures and how they stop 'the quiet stream / Of self-forgetfulness' (IV.296 – 297; 1850). He recovers the sensation of his identity from the 'spots of time' by seeking there the time before self-consciousness, and when its history is fully re-experienced, the self can be forgotten without anxiety, and allowed to change. Nietzsche observes:

> . . .we are not *subtle* enough to perceive the probably absolute *flow* of *becoming*; the *permanent* only exists thanks to our coarse organs that sum up and reduce things to general designs, although nothing ever exists *in that form*. The tree is a new thing every instant; we affirm the form because we do not seize the subtlety of an absolute movement.[32]

Wordsworth's style is the result of his effort to represent 'the probably absolute *flow* of *becoming*.'

His long sentences are born of his way of apprehending the world and perfected in the writing of the autobiographical poem. Choosing to write about himself is probably the most important step in his development as a poet: his best poems come after this decision, made sometime in 1798, possibly between January and March, certainly by October.

The long, complex sentences are not simply a characteristic of the autobiographical poem or of Wordsworth's blank verse — the same syntactical habits inform even his short poems. *I wandered lonely as a cloud* is one of his most famous lyrics. It is composed of four six-line stanzas. The first two describe the host of golden daffodils dancing in the wind and each stanza is a complete sentence. When the poet starts to meditate on what he sees and on the nature of meditation, his thought is allowed to continue as one sentence until the conclusion:

> The waves beside them danced; but they
> Out-did the sparkling waves in glee:
> A poet could not but be gay,
> In such a jocund company:
> I gazed — and gazed — but little thought
> What wealth the show to me had brought:
>
> For oft, when on my couch I lie
> In vacant or in pensive mood,
> They flash upon that inward eye
> Which is the bliss of solitude;
> And then my heart with pleasure fills,
> And dances with the daffodils.

The sentence is lengthened in order to analyse the vision of 'that inward eye.'

4

The Meaning of Feeling

The Recluse, which casts its shadow over the greater part of Wordsworth's career, is probably the most obscure of all his poetic ventures, not simply because it was never finished, but because Wordsworth's idea of the poem kept changing — and because, or so it seems, he wanted it at a certain point to remain nebulous. It is as if by not completing *The Recluse* he could continue to enjoy the hope of doing great work and continue to possess the ideal, as though a poet who had committed himself to such a task need never feel guilty about his vocation or how he lived his life. *The Recluse*, it appears, was simultaneously a free pardon and a self-punishment.

Coleridge is the person who appears to have persuaded Wordsworth that he ought to write a philosophical poem. During February and March 1798 they saw each other regularly and it is in March 1798 that Wordsworth mentions starting *The Recluse*. Coleridge, after seeing the rough drafts, writes to Cottle (7.3.1798) of 'The Giant Wordsworth,' and declares that what he has read is 'superior, I hesitate not to aver, to anything in our language which in any way resembles it.' From that point on he never forgets about *The Recluse* or allows Wordsworth to forget about it. He writes to Wordsworth:

> I am anxiously eager to have you steadily employed on 'The Recluse'. . . My dear friend, I do entreat you go on with 'The Recluse' (*c*.10.9.1799).
> I long to see what you have been doing. O let it be the tail-piece of 'The Recluse!' for of nothing but 'The Recluse' can I hear patiently' (12.10.1799).
> I grieve that 'The Recluse' sleeps (2.1800).

His letter to Thomas Poole (14.10.1803) reveals his relentless interest:

> I rejoice therefore with a deep & true Joy, that he has at length yielded to my urgent & repeated — almost unremitting — requests & remonstrances — & will go on with the Recluse exclusively. — A

Great Work. . . — the having been out of it has been his Disease — to return into it is the specific Remedy, both Remedy & Health.

and he several times opposes the writing of short poems.

Over the years Coleridge's clamour for *The Recluse* was taken up by Wordsworth's family and other friends:

[Dorothy Wordsworth to Catherine Clarkson:] William is quite well, and very busy, though he has not looked at *The Recluse* or the poem on his own life; and this disturbs us (27.3.1821).
[Lamb to Wordsworth:] For your head (I do not flatter) is not a nob or the end of a ninepin — unless a Vulcanian hammer could fairly batter a Recluse out of it, then would I bid the smirch'd God knock and knock lustily, the two-handed skinker (22.1.1830).
[Mary Wordsworth to Henry Crabb Robinson:] We hope. . .that the Poet may leave home with a perfect holiday before him — and, but I dare not say so — return to *The Recluse*; and let me charge you, not to encourage the Muse to *vagrant* subjects (28.9.1836).
[Barron Field to Wordsworth:] Oh! continue *The Recluse*. I wish I was Moxon. I would make you such an offer for it as could ruin me and enrich my children (17.12.1836).[1]

This is proof of Wordsworth's commitment to the notion of *The Recluse*: if he had rejected it for any reason, I do not believe that Dorothy and Mary would have joined in the chorus.

De Selincourt comments that Wordsworth 'used *The Recluse* as a covering title for all the blank verse which he was writing in the early years with a view to the great philosophical poem.'[2] The first part of this statement may be true, but it is not the case that Wordsworth had one, unchanging idea of 'the great philosophical poem.' Since there is, moreover, no evidence to show that Wordsworth ever took a serious interest in philosophy, when he speaks, as he does in the 'Preface' to *The Excursion*, of his 'determination to compose a philosophical poem,' what does he have in mind?

To begin, *The Recluse* can be seen as the matrix from which Wordsworth produced two long poems and the completion of each poem altered the matrix. Coleridge does not appear to have taken any notice of this. He endorses Wordsworth's changing idea of *The Recluse* as if it was a constant, because his own idea did not change, and his reactions to the two finished poems show him preferring the abstract ideal to what he saw as an imperfect reality.

For all Coleridge's admiration of what he calls Wordsworth's 'divine Self-biography,' he could only think of it as an adjunct to, and a preparation for, *The Recluse*, and it was obvious to him that it was not truly a philosophical poem; there was too much about Wordsworth's life in it for that. He describes it to Lady Beaumont (26.3.1804) as 'the biographical or philosophico-biographical Poem to be prefixed or annexed to the Recluse.' *The Excursion* published in July 1814 also disappointed Coleridge. Again this was not the hoped-for philosophical poem, and as he wrote to Lady Beaumont (3.4.1815), he preferred 'the Work on the Growth of his own spirit,' but this did not keep him from seeing clearly the nature of *The Excursion*. Wordsworth, he thinks:

> having by the conjoint operation of his own experiences, feelings, and reason *himself* convinced *himself* of Truths, which the generality of persons have either taken for granted from their Infancy, or at least adopted in early life, he has attached all their own depth and weight to doctrines and words, which come almost as Truisms or Common-place to others.

Coleridge objects to *The Excursion* because it is about common experience, because Wordsworth has attached the whole depth and weight of his own individual feelings to the truths of human development.

Coleridge recognises Wordsworth's preoccupation with his own thoughts and with the earliest years of childhood, but for him introspection is not an end in itself. He believes, as he states in the *Biographia Literaria*, that:

> There is a *philosophic. . .consciousness*, which lies beneath or (as it were) *behind* the spontaneous consciousness natural to all reflecting beings.

This must be discriminated from the 'mere reflection and *re*-presentation' that he criticises in *The Excursion*, and demands a systematic approach; it must be treated as other than experience.[3] Thus Coleridge's character prevented him from fully understanding that of Wordsworth. To Wordsworth his own development was a momentous process, a succession of eerie and potent moods that were connected because they had all happened to him and that were manageable, because they were all grounded in the world — because they had happened at particular times in particular places. To him the under-powers were apprehended through these events. That these feelings were, to a degree, shared by everyone was reassuring and seemed somehow to make them more intelligible.

Lady Beaumont showed Coleridge's letter criticising *The Excursion* to Wordsworth. There followed an exchange of letters that reveals how completely at odds were their two conceptions of *The Recluse*. Wordsworth, whose feelings were still hurt, wrote to Coleridge (22.5.1815):

> I have rather been perplexed than enlightened by your *compara-tive* censure. One of my principal aims in the Ex^n: has been to put the commonplace truths, of human affections especially, in an interesting point of view; and rather to remind men of their knowledge, as it lurks inoperative and unvalued in their own minds, than to attempt to convey recondite or refined truths. Pray point out to me the most striking instances where I have failed, in producing poetic effect by an overfondness for this practice, or through inability to realize my wishes.

Wordsworth affirms that 'one of his principal aims' was to describe feeling, and in this endeavour the ordinary is his touchstone for truth. He does not think of first principles — a phrase that recurs like a refrain in Coleridge's prose — or of any system. He rejects Coleridge's notion of philosophy as 'recondite or refined truths' that were no part of his purpose.

Coleridge replied immediately (30.5.1815) and at length, addres-sing Wordsworth as 'My honored Friend.' Wordsworth had begun his letter by asking Coleridge not to publish the poem, *Lines to William Wordsworth: composed for the greater part on the same night after the finishing of his recitation of the Poem in 13 Books, on the growth of his own Mind* (January 1807), of which Coleridge had given Lady Beaumont a copy. Coleridge said that he would not publish it because of 'it's *personality* respecting myself.' Then he reveals how far he is from appreciating the greatness of Wordsworth's autobiographical poem and of understanding Wordsworth's approach to experience:

> It is for the Biographer, not the Poet, to give the *accidents* of *individual* Life. Whatever is not representative, generic, may be indeed most poetically exprest, but is not Poetry.

Such accidents — the 'knots of grass / And half-inch fissures in the slippery rock' and the constellation of the sheep, the 'whistling hawthorn' and the dry stone wall — are vital to Wordsworth's poetry. They are the language of memory. Wordsworth resists the representative when it swallows up his individuality and embraces the everyday when it stands for the world. He seems troubled by the uniqueness of his experiences, the separateness of each moment makes it difficult to maintain the continuity of his self.

After attempting to reassure Wordsworth that he has no plans to publish the poem dedicated to him, Coleridge undertakes an elaborate and clumsy justification of his remarks to Lady Beaumont, but insisting on, rather than retracting, his criticisms. He is disappointed in *The Excursion* because it is not what he expected. He considered 'the Poem on the growth of your own mind' as 'the EXCURSION' and had anticipated that, having completed it, Wordsworth would 'begin a *Philosophical Poem*.' As for Wordsworth's declared intention 'to place commonplace Truths in an interesting point of View,' he feels that this, too, has already been done in Wordsworth's two volumes, *Poems* (1815), which had just appeared, and in any case it could be a beginning, but not an end in itself:

> Now this I supposed to have been in your two Volumes of Poems, as far as was desirable, or p[ossible,] without an insight into the whole Truth — . How can common [trut]hs be made permanently interesting but by being *bottomed* in our common nature — it is only by the profoundest Insight into Numbers and Quantity that a sublimity & even religious Wonder become attached to the simplest operations of Arithmetic, the most evident properties of the Circle or Triangle — .

Wordsworth's examinations of the everyday perceptions of ordinary people are compared to the 'simplest operations of Arithmetic.' Wordsworth immerses himself in the nuances of his moods, Coleridge wishes for an algebra of feeling. His very metaphor declares his need of abstraction. Wordsworth realises that his extreme feelings can only be understood by referring them to the experiences of others. This is for him a way out of loneliness. He is reassured by the commonplace which has the security of a daily routine. Coleridge is reassured when he escapes from particulars to a phantasy world in which he can do everything by thought.

Coleridge thinks in terms of system: the mind arranging all its objects together in an order of its own making:

I looked forward to the Recluse, as the *first* and *only* true Phil. Poem in existence. Of course, I expected the Colors, Music, imaginative Life, and Passion of *Poetry*; but the matter and arrangement of *Philosophy* — not doubting from the advantages of the Subject that the Totality of a System was not only capable of being harmonized with, but even calculated to aid, the unity (Beginning, Middle, and End) of a *Poem*.

This is a hard blow to Wordsworth. Coleridge finds both of his long poems wanting. He dismisses the fabric of both poems as so much raw material, as mere 'Colors, Music, imaginative Life, and Passion,' and demands a greater remove from reality, both 'the matter and arrangement of *Philosophy*.' This criticism constitutes a further objection to Wordsworth's use of biographical forms. Philosophy has its own plots that are other than the plot of a man's life. (Coleridge discovered the difficulty of combining the two in his own autobiography.) Next follows Coleridge's amazing synopsis of what he envisaged as the contents of *The Recluse*, the most detailed account that survives of how he imagined it, and, significantly perhaps, the last extant letter in which he mentions *The Recluse* to Wordsworth. There is no better document to show the depths to which the two friends misunderstood each other:

I supposed you first to have meditated the faculties of Man in the abstract, in their correspondence with his Sphere of action, and first, in the Feeling, Touch, and Taste, then in the Eye, & last in the Ear, to have laid a solid and immoveable foundation for the Edifice by removing the sandy Sophisms of Locke, and the Mechanic Dogmatists, and demonstrating that the Senses were living growths and developements of the Mind & Spirit in a much juster as well as higher sense, than the mind can be said to be formed by the Senses — . Next, I understood that you would take the Human Race in the concrete, have exploded the absurd notion of Pope's Essay on Man, Darwin, and all the countless Believers — even (strange to say) among Xtians of Man's having progressed from an Ouran Outang state — so contrary to all History, to all Religion, nay, to all Possibility — to have affirmed a Fall in some sense, as a fact, the possibility of which cannot be understood from the nature of the Will, but the reality of which is attested by Experience & Conscience — Fallen men contemplated in the different ages of the World, and in the different states — Savage — Barbarous — Civilized — the lonely Cot, or Borderer's Wigwam — the Village — the Manufacturing Town — Sea-port — City — Universities — and not disguising the sore evils, under which the whole Creation groans, to point out however a manifest Scheme of Redemption from this Slavery, of Reconciliation from this Enmity with Nature — what are the Obstacles, the *Antichrist* that must be & already is — and to conclude by a grand didactic swell on the necessary identity of a true Philosophy with true Religion, agreeing in the results and differing only as the analytic and synthetic process, as discursive from intuitive, the former chiefly useful as perfecting the latter — in short, the necessity of a general revolution in the modes of developing & disciplining the human mind by the substitution of Life, and Intelligence (considered in it's different powers from the Plant up to that state in which the difference of Degree becomes a new kind (man, self-consciousness) but yet not by essential opposition) for the philosophy of mechanism which in every thing that is most worthy of the human Intellect strikes *Death*, and cheats itself by mistaking clear Images for distinct conceptions, and which idly demands Conceptions where Intuitions alone are possible or adequate to the majesty of the Truth. — In short, Facts elevated into Theory — Theory into Laws — & Laws into living & intelligent Powers — true Idealism necessarily perfecting itself in Realism, & Realism refining itself into Idealism. —

Such or something like this was the Plan, I had supposed that you were engaged on — .

It is difficult to say which is more remarkable: that Wordsworth ever entertained such a scheme (if we can believe that he did) or that Coleridge urged it on him. Their separate approaches illustrate the definition by their contemporary, Ranke, of the difference between poetry and philosophy. Poetry, he says, tries 'to represent the infinite by the finite,' philosophy tries 'to explain the finite by the infinite.'[4] The generality and impersonality of Coleridge's plan seems compounded of Pope's *An Essay on Man*, Akenside's *The Pleasures of the Imagination*, Erasmus Darwin's *The Botanic Garden* and his own day-dream of a supreme set of abstractions — that ultimate statement of the origin of life that he yearns for so often in his work and that finds expression in his project for the *Logosophia* (the systematic work 'on the PRODUCTIVE LOGOS human and divine, with, and as the introduction to, a full commentary on the Gospel of St. John' that Coleridge announces in the *Biographia Literaria*).[5] That neither *The Recluse* nor the *Logosophia* were ever completed shows the phantastic and unworkable nature of both plans, and after all it is not surprising that Wordsworth came to feel that Coleridge's day-dream was an inadequate form for the expression of his fears and hopes.

Coleridge's plan for *The Recluse* also resembles the philosophical sections of the *Biographia Literaria* (Chapters 5 – 9 and 12 – 13) that were to be written that summer and autumn, so that what Coleridge was recommending to Wordsworth he was meditating for his own purposes as well.[6] In the *Biographia Literaria* he starts with a consideration of the nature of human perception and a refutation of mechanical and materialistic theories of the mind, concentrating on Hartley rather than Locke (Chapters 5 – 9). He omits 'the Human Race in the concrete,' the 'Ouran Outang state' and the Fall, but he concludes his argument with a 'grand didactic swell' and ten theses to demonstrate 'the necessary identity of a true Philosophy with true Religion' (Chapters 12 – 13). It is essentially the same design, although, characteristically, both discussions break off before the arguments are fully developed, both with references to the *Logosophia* where it is promised that these matters will be settled systematically. Coleridge projects the programme upon the future as he projected it upon Wordsworth — in order to postpone doing it himself. Both men seem to have tried to steady themselves by setting themselves impossible tasks.

Coleridge reaffirms in the *Biographia Literaria* (1817) his faith in his notion of *The Recluse*:

What Mr Wordsworth *will* produce, it is not for me to prophecy: but I could pronounce with the liveliest convictions what he is capable of producing. It is the FIRST GENUINE PHILOSOPHIC POEM.[7]

He maintained this conviction to the end of his life. Talking to his son-in-law, Henry Nelson Coleridge, on 21 July 1832, he sketched his idea of the poem in virtually the same terms as he had to Wordsworth in the letter of 30 May 1815:

Then the plan laid out, and, I believe, partly suggested by me, was that Wordsworth should assume the station of a man in mental repose, one whose principles were made up, and so prepared to deliver upon authority a system of philosophy. He was to treat man as man, — a subject of eye, ear, touch, and taste, in contact with external nature, and informing the senses from the mind, and not compounding a mind out of the senses; then he was to describe the pastoral and other states of society, assuming something of the Juvenalian spirit as he approached the high civilization of cities and towns, and opening a melancholy picture of the present state of degeneracy and vice; thence he was to infer and reveal the proof of, and necessity for, the whole state of man and society being subject to, and illustrative of, a redemptive process in operation, showing how this idea reconciled all the anomalies, and promised future glory and restoration. Something of this sort was, I think, agreed on. It is, in substance, what I have been all my life doing in my system of philosophy.[8]

Coleridge's deep personal involvement in the idea that Wordsworth should write a philosophical poem is apparent throughout his remarks. As he writes to Wordsworth (12.10.1799):

That it is to be addressed to me makes me more desirous that it should not be a poem of itself. To be addressed, as a beloved man, by a thinker, at the close of such a poem as 'The Recluse,' a poem *non unius populi*, is the only event, I believe, capable of inciting in me an hour's vanity — vanity, nay, it is too good a feeling to be so called; it would be self-elevation produced *ab extra*.

By assuming responsibility for *The Recluse*, Coleridge lives vicariously in Wordsworth's work. He needs Wordsworth to share his guilt for the poetry he does not write — in particular for his projected long poem, *The Brook*, which he describes in 1817 in words that are very close to those of Wordsworth's early descriptions of *The Recluse*:

I sought for a subject, that should give equal room and freedom for description, incident, and impassioned reflections on men, nature, and society, yet supply in itself a natural connection to the parts, and unity to the whole. Such a subject I conceived myself to have found in a stream, traced from its source in the hills. . .to the lonely cottage and its bleak garden won from the heath. . .to. . .the market-town, the manufactories, and the seaport.[9]

Coleridge seeks to bind Wordsworth to him as if thereby to strengthen himself with Wordsworth's toughness, and with his plan for a philosophical poem, he, in a sense, takes over Wordsworth.[10] This is what he does, to a limited extent, in the *Biographia Literaria*. How else can we explain why half of Coleridge's autobiography is devoted to Wordsworth's poetry? The psychology is similar to that of Coleridge's plagiarisms. Plagiarism means to kidnap or steal a man.

Coleridge, by urging Wordsworth to write a philosophical poem, is willing him to do something that he cannot do himself. The subject was 'in substance, what I have been all my life doing in my system of philosophy.' It would indeed be a 'self-elevation produced *ab extra*.' There is, in addition, an element of aggression in Coleridge's repeated recommendations. There had always been some rivalry in their friendship and the wounds that resulted from their misunderstanding in 1810 never entirely healed.[11] Coleridge was not above setting Wordsworth a task that he could not complete or whose completion might depend on his help. Certainly he knew that Wordsworth would not like what he was saying about his poetry in the *Biographia Literaria*. He tells R.H. Brabant (28.7.1815): 'I have no doubt that Wordsworth will be displeased.'[12] These interconnected motives moved Coleridge to put the full force of his spellbinding personality behind his notion of *The Recluse*, and it is perhaps impossible to overestimate the effect of his 'urgent & repeated — almost unremitting — requests & remonstrances.'

Wordsworth's response was anything but simple. He brooded intermittently upon *The Recluse* without ever writing anything that remotely resembled Coleridge's plan and in the end could not go on with it even on his own terms. He was the first of the two to put the other in his autobiography. He made the story of his life 'the poem to Coleridge,' but this was probably more in answer to his inner promptings than to Coleridge's urgings, although perhaps he felt the intensity of Coleridge's interest as a unifying force.

The feeling that someone else is there, that there is another person in the world, is an essential element in Wordsworth's poetry and a deep craving in the man himself. Upon the existence of this presence depends the unity of his perceptions, the wholeness of his self and the possibility of communication, including self-communication. Thus, he personifies the surrounding landscape in order not to be alone. This is why every sound in nature is apprehended as language, as the world speaking to the poet, and why he so often demands the actual presence of another real person in poems where he seems to be preoccupied with talking to himself. Many of Wordsworth's most successful poems are of this form: *Lines Composed a Few Miles Above Tintern Abbey*, *Nutting* and *Ode: Intimations of Immortality from Recollections of Early Childhood*. Why did he address the poem on his own life to a man rather than a woman, to Coleridge rather than Dorothy? I would hazard that it is because it is the story of his coming of age, of his choice of a vocation and entry into the world as a man. This, which is felt as occurring in competition with other men, needs the support of a man, just as in most tribes the rites of passage from boyhood to manhood are administered by men only. Wordsworth turns to Coleridge as he turns to Milton and Spenser.

There is, in any event, no doubt that Coleridge was successful, at least temporarily, in using *The Recluse* to cause Wordsworth to depend upon him. When in 1804 Wordsworth thought that Coleridge was going to be absent, either for a long convalescence in Malta or permanently, if he did not recover, he wrote to him (6.3.1804):

> I am very anxious to have your notes for the Recluse. I cannot say how much importance I attach to this, if it should please God that I survive you, I should reproach myself for ever in writing the work if I had neglected to procure this help

and a subsequent report that Coleridge had taken a turn for the worse increased his anxiety about the future of the poem (29.3.1804):

> Your last letter but one informing us of your late attack was the severest shock to me, I think, I have ever received,. . .I cannot help saying that I would gladly have given 3 fourths of my possessions for your letter on The Recluse at that time. I cannot say what a load it would be to me, should I survive you and you die without this memorial left behind. Do for heaven's sake, put this out of the reach of accident immediately.

The intimate nature of Wordsworth's dependence upon Coleridge can be illustrated from Wordsworth's manuscripts. A small pocket notebook used in Germany in 1798 (DC MS 16) shows him at mid-point of what was then to be a two-part autobiography. After the conclusion of the First Part, and a sum of the lines completed so far, Wordsworth writes:

> Here we pause
> Doubtful; or lingering with a truant heart

> slow & of stationary character
> Rarely adventurous studious more of peace
> And soothing quiet which we here have found. — [13]

His resistance to continuing his self-analysis combines with the peace that he achieves in working through his past to produce a mood of doubt, weakness and inertia. This mood, repeatedly described in Book I (1805), is part of the creative process in Wordsworth, and it is in this state of mind that he turns to Coleridge. On the *verso* page he starts the final half of the poem:

> 2nd Part
> Friend of my heart & Genius we had reach'd
> A small green island which I was well pleased
> To pass not lightly by for though I felt
> Strength unabated yet I seem'd to need
> Thy cheering voice or ere I could pursue
> My voyage, resting else for ever there

This passage was later cancelled. That many such apostrophes are included demonstrates Wordsworth's appreciation of the psychological value of Coleridge's presence (as well as his gratitude) — and his commitment to the representation of mental process. The function of Coleridge is to cheer Wordsworth on. When he is moving again, Coleridge is no longer necessary and then, often, the lines in which he was invoked can be dispensed with.

There is an example of this dependence in MS A where Wordsworth's struggle to get right the crucial description of the 'spots of time' (XI.258 – 397) can be seen. To resolve the difficulty that he felt in moving from the summary statement (258 – 279) to the first example, Wordsworth invokes Coleridge:

> Philosopher and Friend a willing ear
> While I record a casual incident
> With grateful recollection

(f.301b)

These lines are revised *and* cancelled. The passage, calling on Coleridge as 'Philosopher and Friend,' in a slightly different form each time, is reintroduced on two more occasions (f.304a and 304b) and then at the top of the next page (f.305a) Wordsworth seemingly starts

again, but writes only: 'Philosopher and Friend.'[14] This invocation
vanishes in the final version; moreover, neither in the 1805 nor 1850
text, nor in any published poem does Wordsworth address Coleridge
as 'Philosopher.' The epithet is reserved for more private discourse.
The rough drafts indicate that Coleridge is especially valued for his
knowledge, as a 'Genius' and 'Philosopher.' Wordsworth draws from
Coleridge the courage that he needs to make an extra effort, the cancelled passages showing the degree to which he had absorbed the sus-
taining presence of Coleridge, speaking ('Thy cheering voice') and listening ('a willing ear'), into himself. They suggest, furthermore, that
in Wordsworth's mind, Coleridge, not himself, is the philosopher.

The example of Coleridge, in fact, caused Wordsworth to shy away
from philosophy. 'Urgent' & repeated. . .requests' went both ways.
This emerges from Coleridge's letter to Thomas Poole, 16 March
1801, where he writes that although he has overthrown Hartley's
'doctrine of Association. . .and with it all the irreligious metaphysics
of the modern Infidels,' he has decided to pause in his pursuit of the
solution 'to the process of Life & Consciousness' because of
'Wordsworth's advice or rather fervent intreaty.' However much
Wordsworth may have enjoyed listening to Coleridge talk about
philosophy — and this cannot be documented in any satisfactory
way — from at least this point onwards he must have heard him with a
certain wariness, and to the end of his life he believed that the study of
philosophy, especially German philosophy, had been a major cause of
what he saw as Coleridge's failure to get his work done. His turning
away from the subject was not only the result of the bias of his mind,
but also because he feared that what had happened to Coleridge could
happen to him — together with a lurking sense that philosophy and
poetry were antithetical. The Sunday after Coleridge's death the
Reverend R.P. Graves walked over to Rydal Mount and spoke with
Wordsworth about Coleridge:

> Wordsworth, as a poet, regretted that German metaphysics had so
> much captivated the taste of Coleridge, for he was frequently not
> intelligible on this subject; whereas if his energy and his originality
> had been more exerted in the channel of poetry, an instrument of
> which he had so perfect a mastery, Wordsworth thought he might
> have done more permanently to enrich the literature and to
> influence the thought of the nation, than any other man of the
> age.[15]

Thus each man contributed to the myth of the other: Coleridge started the notion that Wordsworth was a philosophical poet, and Wordsworth fostered the belief that the study of philosophy had prevented Coleridge from writing poetry.

Several years later, in 1840, Wordsworth writes to Henry Crabb Robinson of the 'serious charge of Plagiarism brought against Coleridge in the last number of Blackwood:'

> With the part concerning the imputation of thefts from Schelling, having never read a word of German metaphysics, thank Heaven! though I doubt not that they are a good diet for some tastes I feel no disposition to meddle.[16]

The emotion of 'thank Heaven!' recalls his 'fervent intreaty' to Coleridge, yet again suggesting that Wordsworth's ignorance of philosophy was a deliberate choice; it is as if he felt that this ignorance was a guarantee of his originality.

*

Everything that we know about Wordsworth's reading and books supports the view that he never concerned himself very much with philosophy. Three subjects in particular engaged his interest: poetry, history and travel. Poetry was his overriding passion and, in Mr Justice Coleridge's phrase, his 'principal scholarship,' and the other two subjects were on many occasions pressed into the service of poetry.[17] Replying to an offer from De Quincey to buy some second-hand books for Wordsworth, Dorothy gave this account of his library and interests (7.7.1808):

> His library is in fact little more than a chance collection of odd books (setting aside the poets, and a few other Books that are to be found everywhere). Therefore in general I may say that he wants all that is valuable and can be procured *very cheap*. . . Clarendon — Burnet — any of the elder Histories — translations from the Classics chiefly — historical — Plutarch's Lives, — Thucydides, *Tacitus* (I think he said) — (by the bye, he *has* a translation of Herodotus), Lord Bacon's Works — Milton's prose Works — in short, any of the good elder writers. . .

and she adds a postscript: 'My brother wishes very much to have Josephus's writings.' Her description is confirmed by De Quincey's own succinct judgement in 1839 of Wordsworth's reading:

In fact, there were only two provinces of literature in which Wordsworth could be looked upon as well read — Poetry and Ancient History. Nor do I believe that he would much have lamented, on his own account, if all books had perished, excepting the entire body of English poetry, and, perhaps, 'Plutarch's Lives.'[18]

To William Mathews, who had asked him to write at length his observations on modern literature, Wordsworth answers (3.8.1791):

> You might as well have solicited me to send you an account of the tribes inhabiting the central regions of the African Continent. God knows my incursions into fields of modern literature. . .are absolutely nothing.

and he says much the same thing to Francis Wrangham (4.11.1807): 'I might as well live at St. Kilda for any commerce I have with passing Literature. . .' These replies are especially interesting as they show Wordsworth playing the part of the recluse — and the terms of his comparisons point to his taste for travel books. Writing to Wrangham in early spring 1812(?), Wordsworth declares:

> I see no new books except by the merest accident;. . .The only *modern* Books that I read are those of travels, or such as relate to Matters of fact; and the only modern books that I care for; but as to old ones,. . .scarcely any thing comes amiss to me.

Wordsworth has no desire to keep up with any subject; he looks backward rather than forward. His preference, as in his own life, is for ancient history. Outside of poetry, he has little taste for fiction, speculation or abstraction. He is a pedestrian who keeps his feet firmly on the ground of 'Matters of fact.'

A fortnight after Wordsworth died, on 7 May 1850, a Kendall bookseller, John Hudson, made an inventory of the books in Rydal Mount. The two notebooks that he used are now in the Wordsworth Library.[19] Copies of the sale catalogue for the auction on 19, 20 and 21 July 1859 at Rydal Mount of nearly three thousand books from Wordsworth's library also survive.[20] They do not constitute a complete record, and the greater part of the works that they list were acquired after Wordsworth's move to Rydal Mount in May 1813; nevertheless, on their testimony Wordsworth did not possess the major works of any major philosopher.[21] There are very few philosophical books and those that are noted appear to be a totally random collection.[22]

The references to philosophers and philosophy in Wordsworth's prose are extremely sparse and perfunctory. Those that he makes to Aristotle are typical. There are some problematic echoes of the *Poetics* in the 'Preface' to *Lyrical Ballads* (added in 1802).[23] They do not appear to derive from any study of the text — although 'Aristotle on Poetry 2v' was in the library at Rydal Mount — because when Wordsworth does mention Aristotle by name, he misquotes him and tells us that his knowledge is second-hand: 'Aristotle, I have been told, has said, that Poetry is the most philosophic of all writing. . .' What Aristotle in fact says is that poetry is more philosophical than history.[24] The only other mention of Aristotle occurs in a letter to Sir George Beaumont (12.3.1805) after John Wordsworth's death where Wordsworth copies out a passage from the *Nicomachean Ethics* that he believes portrays his brother's character. Here, too, his knowledge is second-hand, and it is something that he has merely happened across: 'I will transcribe a passage that I met with the other day in a review. . .'

The whole passage in which Wordsworth misquotes Aristotle is worth considering, because it shows how Wordsworth imbues old terms, including *philosophic*, with his own meaning:

> Aristotle, I have been told, has said, that Poetry is the most philosophic of all writing: it is so: its object is truth, not individual and local, but general, and operative; not standing upon external testimony, but carried alive into the heart by passion; truth which is its own testimony, which gives competence and confidence to the tribunal to which it appeals, and receives them from the same tribunal. Poetry is the image of man and nature.[25]

The emphasis on general truth demonstrates the extent to which Wordsworth participates in the tradition represented by Coleridge's criticisms of the autobiographical poem and *The Excursion*. Here, however, we witness that tradition being transformed: with *operative*, a word that Wordsworth apparently borrows from Davenant that in this context presents truth as dynamic, changing; and with the idea that truth is a matter of feeling, that our appeal is not to anything outside ourselves, but to the tribunal of our own heart.[26] To put his theory into practice, he resorts — as Coleridge saw — to the 'individual and local.' Operative truth, truth in action, cannot be represented in any other way, and the 'individual and local' is, of course, the domain of feeling, where we find ourselves if we must appeal only to our own experience.

Owen and Smyser in their commentary on the 'Preface' point out that there *philosophic* probably means 'precise, authentic, adequate to the subject,' and that, generally, for Wordsworth, 'to speak more philosophically' means 'to speak more precisely.'[27] When Wordsworth in the *Essay, Supplementary to the Preface* (1815) states: TASTE,. . .like IMAGINATION, is a word which has been forced to extend its services far beyond the point to which philosophy would have confined them,' they construe *philosophy* as 'accurate verbal usage' and as 'the mode of thought which insists and depends upon accuracy of verbal usage.'[28] This puts Wordsworth's 'determination to compose a philosophical poem' in a new light. Poetry as 'the most philosophic of all writing' becomes the most rigorously precise of all writing — and is concerned with the detailed representation of the inner truth of human feelings, truth carried into the heart by passion. The matter, however, is neither simple nor clear-cut because Wordsworth's usage (as when he speaks of 'operative' truth) is inhabited by old theories as well as by new practice, a lexical range that embodies his ambivalence about the project.

This ambivalence is present in his description of himself thinking about composing a philosophical poem:

> Then, last wish,
> My last and favourite aspiration! then
> I yearn towards some philosophic Song
> Of Truth that cherishes our daily life;
> With meditations passionate from deep
> Recesses in man's heart, immortal verse
> Thoughtfully fitted to the Orphean lyre;
> But from this awful burthen I full soon
> Take refuge, and beguile myself with trust
> That mellower years will bring a riper mind
> And clearer insight.

(I.228–238)

There is every reason to take literally Wordsworth's statement that the idea was an 'awful burthen.' To satisfy both Coleridge and himself was impossible. If he could not write about himself, about his experience, that which Coleridge rejected as 'Truism or Commonplace,' he had nothing to say. Perhaps he cherished the plan in the hope of self-transformation and self-transcendence, but the work could only go forward if he in some sense repeated himself, if he returned again to his childhood and everyday life, rewriting in another form the poem on his own life or *The Excursion*. Perhaps he was stopped in part by a desire for an impossible originality. Certainly in conceiving of *The Recluse* as 'his great work' he thereby made it the focus of his ambition and aggressive phantasies, so that by not writing it he sought to prevent the fulfilment of his aggression.[29] That in this passage, probably composed early in 1804, he sees the rejection of the project as running away and self-deception suggests that this account of yearning followed by dread accurately represents his procrastinations and postponements over the next forty-odd years.

*

The history of *The Recluse* is complicated, and there are long periods of time in which it is difficult to catch any glimpse of the project in the surviving documents. Because of Wordsworth's habit of keeping several poems or subjects going at once and moving from one to the other, sometimes without finishing any of them, the whole history of *The Recluse* will probably not be clear until all of Wordsworth's manuscripts are properly edited. However, if we look closely at exactly what Wordsworth said about it and at the sections of it that he did write, we see that when the work took a real rather than an imaginary shape, it was of a piece with his other work. From beginning to end, Wordsworth thought of it as a poem giving 'pictures' (1798) or 'views' (1814) of 'Nature, Man, and Society,' that is, as a means of unifying diverse and diffuse experiences. Moreover, he always appears to have envisaged the work as a set of life histories, although he quickly concluded that it could only be made coherent by being presented as the thoughts or narrative of a single individual: the recluse — with other characters telling their stories to him.

The first mention that Wordsworth makes of his new idea for a long poem is in a letter to James Tobin dated 6 March 1798. He tells him:

> I have written 1300 lines of a poem in which I contrive to convey most of the knowledge of which I am possessed. My object is to give pictures of Nature, Man, and Society. Indeed I know not any thing which will not come within the scope of my plan. . . If you could collect for me any books of travels you would render me an essential service, as without much of such reading my present labours cannot be brought to a conclusion.

A few days later his poem has a title. To James Losh he says (11.3.1798): 'I have written 1300 lines of a poem which I hope to make of considerable utility; its title will be *The Recluse; or views of Nature, Man, and Society.'* These 1300 lines cannot be identified with any certainty and there is no one surviving MS of the time that corresponds to this description. Wordsworth appears to have in mind a group of drafts in different stages of completion: what he had so far composed of *The Ruined Cottage*, possibly *The Old Cumberland Beggar* and possibly the encounter with the discharged soldier (later incorporated into Book IV of the autobiographical poem).[30] Wordsworth's words seem to promise some abstract and comprehensive statement about the nature of things, but behind them loom the figures of three peripatetic, older men: the pedlar, the beggar and the soldier.

Pope writes of *An Essay on Man* (his poem on 'Nature, Man, and Society'): 'I thought it more satisfactory to begin with considering *Man* in the abstract. . .'[31] Despite some attempts in this direction, Wordsworth was never satisfied by 'considering Man in the abstract.' A man's identity cannot be found in what he shares with other men. Within five days of writing to Tobin, he had found it necessary to create an individual, the recluse, around whom to collect his thoughts. His poems required a definite human centre, usually a version of himself, of 'the Author retired to his native mountains.' To an extent, this idea of himself as a recluse was an accurate description of his life at Grasmere, but it was also a myth, the part that he invented for himself to play for over fifty years. He is the man for whom modern literature, as he tells Mathews, is as remote as 'the tribes inhabiting the central regions of the African continent' and who, as he says to Wrangham, is so isolated in Grasmere that he might as well be in St Kilda.

Wordsworth's poems are concerned with particular human lives. For him, the knowledge of the 'deep / Recesses in man's heart' is a knowledge of the world. This is why he asks Tobin to collect '*any* books of travels' he can and why they are '*essential*' to the completion of the poem. His request can be understood as a demand for more reality. It is as if he hoped to extend by his reading the contact with the earth provided by his innumerable walks, where each step reaffirmed that he was not alone with his thoughts. There was in Wordsworth a basic restlessness that caused him to identify with all wanderers and vagabonds; he felt their experience as a continuation of his own. Travel books, perhaps the most unphilosophical of all works, furnished experience in an easily assimilable form and offered support in his struggle to prevent himself from falling into what he calls the 'abyss of idealism.'[32]

Wordsworth repeats the same abstract title as he had written it to Losh, *The Recluse or views of Nature, Man and Society*, in a letter to De Quincey (6.3.1804) in which he sketches his future plans. He tells De Quincey that he is in the midst of 'writing a Poem on my own earlier life:'

> This Poem will not be published these many years, and never during my lifetime, till I have finished a larger and more important work to which it is tributary. Of this larger work I have written one Book and several scattered fragments: it is a moral and Philosophical Poem; the subject whatever I find most interesting, in Nature Man Society, most adapted to Poetic illustration. To this work I mean to devote the Prime of my life and the chief force of my mind. I have also arranged the plan of a narrative Poem. And if I live to finish these three principal works I shall be content.

At this point *The Recluse* appears to be still *The Ruined Cottage*. What evidence there is suggests that the 'one book and several scattered fragments' belong to the stories of Margaret and the pedlar, however, they are now conceived as following on from the 'Poem on my own earlier life.' The 'narrative poem' is a mystery and there is nothing to suggest that it has any relation to the other two poems. The subject of *The Recluse* is to be 'whatever I find most interesting in Nature Man Society, most adapted to Poetic illustration.' This is not the language of a systematic thinker, Wordsworth trusts to the bias of his mind and poetic values are his standard.

When he writes to Sir George Beaumont (3.6.1805) to announce that he has completed the poem on his own life, Wordsworth states:

> This work may be considered as a sort of portico of the Recluse, part of the same building, which I hope to be able erelong to begin with, in earnest; and if I am permitted to bring it to a conclusion, and to write, further, a narrative Poem of the Epic kind, I shall consider the *task* of my life as over.

He continues to view the narrative poem as separate from the other two works, that he thinks of as connected, and he uses (for the first time?) the metaphor of a building to express this unity. He retains this metaphor when, nine years later, he writes the 'Preface' to *The Excursion*.

The 'Preface' (1814) is the *locus classicus* for *The Recluse*. It seems to define more or less the final form the idea took in his imagination. *The Excursion* is published as 'BEING A PORTION OF THE RECLUSE, *A Poem*' and Wordsworth undertakes to explain this title as follows:

> Several years ago, when the Author retired to his native mountains, with the hope of being enabled to construct a literary Work that might live, it was a reasonable thing that he should take a review of his own mind, and examine how far Nature and Education had qualified him for such employment. As subsidiary to this preparation, he undertook to record, in verse, the origin and progress of his own powers, as far as he was acquainted with them. That Work, addressed to a dear Friend, most distinguished for his knowledge and genius, and to whom the Author's Intellect is deeply indebted, has been long finished; and the result of the investigation which gave rise to it was a determination to compose a philosophical poem, containing views of Man, Nature, and Society; and to be entitled, the Recluse; as having for its principal subject the sensations and opinions of a poet living in retirement. — The preparatory poem is biographical, and conducts the history of the Author's mind to the point when he was emboldened to hope that his faculties were sufficiently mature for entering upon the arduous labour which he had proposed to himself; and the two Works have the same kind of relation to each other, if he may so express himself, as the ante-chapel has to the body of a gothic church.[33]

He views *The Excursion* somewhat as a narrative digression in which other voices intervene in the monologue of the poet:

> the first and third parts of The Recluse will consist chiefly of meditations in the Author's own person; and that in the intermediate part (The Excursion) the intervention of characters speaking is employed, and something of a dramatic form adopted.[34]

The Recluse is now conceived as a three-part *magnum opus* in which he has incorporated the narrative poem — which has become *The Excursion*. That it is published as the second part of his 'philosophic Song' amply demonstrates (as the letters cited at the beginning of this chapter confirm) how far apart were Wordsworth's and Coleridge's notions of what constitutes a philosophical poem. The characters in

The Excursion talk about a wide range of subjects, but their talk is of their personal feelings and of the histories of others, and they do not speak until their own histories are established. Wordsworth, as he says to Coleridge (22.5.1815), wants 'rather to remind men of their knowledge, as it lurks inoperative and unvalued in their own minds, than to attempt to convey recondite or refined truths.'

Wordsworth apologises for 'saying. . .so much of performances either unfinished or unpublished,' as if he dislikes committing himself to a plan. The only thing upon which he is clear and insistent is the autobiographical form of *The Recluse*, which will have 'for its principal subject the sensations and opinions of a poet living in retirement' and 'will consist chiefly of meditations in the Author's own person.' *Sensations*, *opinions*, *meditations* are words that stress the informal and personal nature of the feelings involved. Wordsworth specifically repudiates any purpose of offering formal or systematic philosophy: 'It is not the Author's intention formally to announce a system: it was more animating to him to proceed in a different course. . .' He does add that if he is successful in conveying 'clear thoughts, lively images, and strong feelings' — these being the units in which he works — 'the Reader will have no difficulty in extracting the system for himself.' This last seems like a sop to Coleridge, as well as an affirmation that his experience does have a unity. Finally, Wordsworth appends a passage of 107 lines from the conclusion of the first book of *The Recluse* 'as a kind of *Prospectus* of the design and scope of the whole Poem.'[35]

These lines state in a forthright manner not simply the autobiographical nature of *The Recluse*, but the commitment that this requires to the representation of mental events. Its subject will be:

> the Mind of Man —
> My haunt, and the main region of my song.
>
> (40–41)

and neither mind nor man in the abstract:

>   . . .and if with this
> I mix more lowly matter; with the thing
> Contemplated, describe the Mind and Man
> Contemplating; and who, and what he was —
> The transitory Being that beheld
> This Vision, when and where, and how he lived; —
> Be not this labour useless.
>
> (93–99)

There is no justification or explanation of why it might not be useless. Wordsworth simply trusts his feelings. Coleridge and the literary tradition to which they both belonged may have caused him to feel that this was 'lowly matter,' but he did not give it up. His belief was that 'such theme / May sort with highest objects' (99–100), and, acting on this almost instinctive conviction, he proposes a new realism in poetry. Every 'thing / Contemplated' needs to be related to the life history of 'the Mind and Man / Contemplating.' The interpretation of the actions of the mind involves the reconstruction of a specific human 'life, because a man's feelings cannot be understood without knowing 'when and where, and how he lived.'

After declaring that the human mind is his subject, Wordsworth immediately finds it necessary to emphasise the value of the ordinary. There is no need for the poet to go beyond the physical, beyond the tactile realm of everyday reality, because beauty is:

> a living Presence of the earth,
> Surpassing the most fair ideal Forms
> Which craft of delicate Spirits hath composed
> From earth's materials. . .

$$(42–45)$$

Paradise is not 'a mere fiction of what never was' but 'A simple produce of the common day' (51, 55). It is as if he seeks to free himself from all phantasy. The words that he will use in his poem will 'speak of nothing more than what we are' (59).

Of the first and third parts of *The Recluse*, Wordsworth produced only one complete book, *Home at Grasmere* (which in MS D DC MS 76 is clearly marked: '*The Recluse — Part first Book first*') and three fragments.[36] He made a start on *Home at Grasmere* in 1800, finished drafting it (MS B DC MS 59) in 1806, worked on it again between 1809 and 1812 (when he moved some of the material to *The Excursion*), and in 1812–1814 began a thorough revision that he never finished.[37] The three fragments were composed probably in 1808.[38] As all of this was done before the 'Preface' to *The Excursion* was written, it is clear that when Wordsworth says there that 'the Recluse will consist chiefly of meditations in the Author's own person,' he has something definite in mind. The texts confirm that he was thinking of more autobiography.

Home at Grasmere takes up his story at the point at which he leaves off in the earlier poem. The most recent event that Wordsworth mentions in the 1805 version of his autobiographical poem (aside from the *now* which is the time of the final passage) is his grief after his brother John's death on 6 February 1805. He describes the summer of 1797 when he and Coleridge walked 'on Quantock's grassy Hills' (XIII.386), but only alludes to the 'permanent abode' that received him along with the 'Sister of my heart' (XIII.331 – 332). William and Dorothy moved into Dove Cottage in December 1799. *Home at Grasmere* is a celebration of their life in their new home.

There are many similarities between Book I of the autobiographical poem and *Home at Grasmere*. To begin again Wordsworth needed to perform the same inaugural rituals. Both poems open with the account of a particular moment where much is made indeterminate and where the poet is a wanderer with no definite course who is seeking a home. In the earlier poem he is suddenly free of the bondage of the city; in *Home at Grasmere*, he is 'A roving School-boy,' an 'Adventurer' (2) vividly aware of his 'unfettered liberty' (37), and much later there is a description of being 'immured' in 'the vast Metropolis' (592 – 624).[39] The description of the poet's journey to his new dwelling place (I.1 – 115; HG 152 – 188) is followed by a consideration of possible subjects for a long poem (I.157 – 238; HG 664 – 860). The invocations of the poet's sister (HG 75 – 109, 246 – 255, 428) take the place of the addresses to Coleridge (I.55, 116, 144, 645 – 663). The composition of both poems is for Wordsworth the fulfilment of a duty. He does not want, in the autobiographical poem, to be 'a false steward who hath much received / And renders nothing back' (I.270 – 271) and, therefore, he rejects the voluptuousness of rural walks of which no record is kept, 'given up / To vacant musing, unreprov'd neglect / Of all things' (I.252 – 256). The same thought (with *unreproved* and the idea of walking) is repeated in *Home at Grasmere*:

> Yet 'tis not to enjoy that we exist,
> For that end only; something must be done.
> I must not walk in unreproved delight
> These narrow bounds and think of nothing more. . .
>
> (664 – 667)

This suggests that those moments of unfocused meditation that are so prominent in Wordsworth's poetry are especially dear to him because he is uneasy about simply enjoying his existence. Poetry, as a form of action that places the highest value on day-dreaming, offers the perfect compromise.

Although in *Home at Grasmere*, Wordsworth is not so specific about the subjects that he has considered and rejected, he does cover much the same ground as in the autobiographical poem. He speaks of his great love of battle stories and of the excitement with which he heard:

> of danger met
> Or sought with courage, enterprize forlorn,
> By one, sole keeper of his own intent,
> Or by a resolute few, who for the sake
> Of glory fronted multitudes in arms.
>
> (715 – 720)

These lines are a perfect summary of the stories of the race of Odin, Sertorius and followers, the unknown man, the 'one Frenchman,' Gustavus I and William Wallace; and he is still thinking of 'the groves of Chivalry,' the knights reposing by the fountain-side and 'the Fortunate Isles' of Sertorius when he asks:

> Paradise and groves
> Elysian, Fortunate Fields — like those of old
> Sought in the Atlantic Main — why should they be
> A history only of departed things,
> Or a mere fiction of what never was?
>
> (800 – 804)

At the end of this new inventory, Wordsworth again rejects stories of heroic combat as matter for a long poem. As before, the activity of composing the poem is described in the poem, and the subject is treated momentarily almost as an adjunct:

> A Voice shall speak, and what will be the Theme?
>
> (753)

but the old question receives the old answer. He looks forward to another journey into himself. He believes that the poem is there in the unending stream of his phantasies, aware that his own consciousness is his subject whatever he may speak about:

> On Man, on Nature, and on Human Life,
> Musing in Solitude, I oft perceive

Fair trains of imagery before me rise,
Accompanied by feelings of delight
Pure, or with no unpleasing sadness mixed;
And I am conscious of affecting thoughts
And dear remembrances, whose presence soothes
Or elevates the Mind, intent to weigh
The good and evil of our mortal state.
To these emotions, whencesoe'er they come,
Whether from breath of outward circumstance,
Or from the Soul, an impulse to herself,
I would give utterance in numerous Verse.

(754 – 766)

Here it is the process of imagining that is described and the uncertainty that is valued. The content of these 'trains of imagery' is not discussed. The emphasis is on feeling: 'feelings of delight,' 'affecting thoughts,' 'these emotions.'

Home at Grasmere is not the start of a philosophical poem in any ordinary sense of the word, but the continuation of the story of Wordsworth's own life and exploration of his inner feelings. The three other surviving pieces that seem to have been intended for *The Recluse* and that are, as far as we know, as close as Wordsworth ever came to the second book: 'Pressed with conflicting thoughts of love and fear,' *The Tuft of Primroses* and *To The Clouds*, are also autobiographical.

'Pressed with conflicting thoughts of love and fear' is the description of a restorative moment — and the 'Friend' whom the poet addresses is Coleridge. He tells how on a winter morning he was walking through 'the great City,' completely lost in his thoughts and not knowing where he was going, when suddenly he looked up and beheld the hushed street stretching before him:

Deep, hollow, unobstructed, vacant, smooth,
And white with winter's purest white,

and at the end of the street:

The huge majestic Temple of St. Paul
In awful sequestration, through a veil,
Through its own sacred veil of falling snow.

The moment did not end his uneasiness, but provided 'An anchor of

stability,' and reassuring evidence of the 'Imagination's holy power.'
The experience of a relaxation of concentration producing an intense
perception is that of the boy waiting for the owls to reply on the shore
of Winander (V.389–413). There is no doubt that this vision of St
Paul's in the snow represents an actual experience of Wordsworth's,
one that can be dated as occurring on his visit to London in the spring
of 1808, because he describes it in the same vivid terms in a letter to Sir
George Beaumont (8.4.1808).

The point of departure for a *Tuft of Primroses* may have been an
episode like that recorded in Dorothy's journal for 30 December 1802:

> We stopped our horse close to the ledge opposite a tuft of primroses
> three flowers in full blossom and a Bud, they reared themselves up
> among the green moss. We debated long whether we should pluck
> [them] and at last left them to live out their day, which I was right
> glad of at my return the Sunday following for there they remained
> uninjured either by cold or wet.[40]

After addressing the primroses in the poem, Wordsworth alludes to a
series of very specific, local events whose significance is wholly
personal: Sara Hutchinson's illness in the spring of 1808 (37–62), the
death of old Mr Sympson of High Broadrain on 27 June 1807 and of
other friends that summer and before (71–77, 132–218), the felling
of 'the giant sycamore near the parsonage house' and of 'all the finest
firtrees that overtopped the steeple tower' in the summer of 1807
(78–131).[41] The poem is like a diary of Wordsworth's feelings. He
includes next, as if in search of even greater authenticity, a historical
document: a version of St Basil's letter to Gregory Nazianzen inviting
him to become a recluse (346–420); prefaced by an analysis of Basil's
own withdrawal from the world (264–346) in which Basil's sister's
exhortations play an important part (305–317). This is followed by
praise of solitary communities and concludes with a celebration of
ruined monasteries, mentioning by name: Tintern Abbey (477),
Fountains Abbey (481) and the Grande Chartreuse (513) — providing yet another version of the visit first described in *Descriptive
Sketches*.

To The Clouds is another report of a specific moment in the poet's
life. 'These verses were suggested,' Wordsworth tells Isabella Fenwick,
'while I was walking on the foot-road between Rydal Mount and
Grasmere. The clouds were driving over the top of Nab Scar across
the vale; they set my thoughts agoing, and the rest followed almost

immediately.'[42] Trying to explain his sense of vocation and his possession of a great gift, Wordsworth states in *Home at Grasmere*:

> but yet to me I feel
> That an internal brightness is vouchsafed
> That must not die, that must not pass away.

> (674 – 676)

The gift, as stated there, is not poetry, but the 'internal brightness,'
not the vision of anything particular, but a feeling of intensity that
must be preserved. Poetry is the means of maintaining this internal
state. At the close of *To the Clouds*, Wordsworth describes how the sun
showers the clouds with 'all but beatific light.' He insists on the
richness and transience of the image:

> . . .too transient. . .did not. . .credulous desire
> Nourish the hope that memory lacks not power
> To keep the treasure unimpaired. Vain thought!

> (87 – 91)

The metaphor is the same: the poem is an act of memory and the poet
is anxious to keep hold of a vague, cloudy vision of disappearing,
changing light.

The clouds coming over Nab Scar in *To the Clouds* are:

> Ascending from behind the motionless brow
> Of that tall rock, as from a hidden world. . .

> (2 – 3)

After they have passed, the poet sees:

> a calm descent of sky conducting
> Down to the unapproachable abyss,
> Down to that hidden gulf from which they rose
> To vanish. . .

> (34 – 37)

The clouds are the poet's thoughts suddenly visible 'behind the
motionless brow' of the thinker, just as, in the autobiographical poem,
the imagination is 'an unfathered vapour' rising from the mind's abyss

(VI.592–596; 1850). Wordsworth when he looks at the sky full of clouds feels that he is looking into the depths of his mind. His 'soul' finds in this scene:

> A type of her capacious self and all
> Her restless progeny.
>
> (52–53)

The reasons why Wordsworth never completed *The Recluse* are complex. Perhaps it was never finished because it was to be a continuation of the poem on his own life, and Wordsworth understood, at least unconsciously, that the crucial events in his development were in his early, not his later, years, knew that the 'deep / Recesses in man's heart' are full of the shadows — and the inner brightness — of childhood, and that it is in this cave that the imagination has its source. For him the answer to the question 'What do I feel?' always seems to involve a journey back to his beginnings. If we trust to the evidence of his poems, Wordsworth was aware that he was continuing to change such that it was increasingly difficult for him to find his way back to that fading brightness. His withdrawal to Grasmere was, as he says in *Home at Grasmere*, 'a last retreat' (147). Perhaps that he retreated rather than advanced brought an eventual surrender. To continue the story of his life in *The Recluse* meant an increasing concentration on the most recent past. As a poet he was 'not used to make / A present joy the matter of my Song' (I.55–56), and perhaps as a man he found in his adult self things that he was unwilling to face. To work so close to the present, moreover, involved coming to terms with the thought of his approaching death. Wordsworth, as a child, would not accept that he could die and believed that he would be translated to heaven like Enoch and Elijah, and it is not unlikely that vestiges of this resistance remained.[43] In any case, he was unable to go on and *The Recluse* became a ruined cathedral.

At the end of his autobiography, *Memories, Dreams, Reflections*, Jung states:

> There is nothing I am quite sure about. . .I know only that I was born and exist, and it seems to me that I have been carried along. I exist on the foundation of something I do not know. In spite of all uncertainties, I feel a solidity underlying all existence and a continuity in my mode of being.[44]

Wordsworth shares this sense of something deeply interfused that connects him with the world. His poetry is a record of his effort to commune with this something and thereby to strengthen the bond. His uncertainties and his acute awareness of its existence suggests that for him the connection may have been fragile — just enough. Sometimes he distrusts the power that carries him along, at other times it is as if he feels that he himself is responsible for the near obliteration of this underlying presence and then he is overwhelmed by fears of disintegration. This can be a desperate state, because what is at risk is — in Jung's phrase — the continuity of his mode of being.

Jung, like Wordsworth, ends by interpreting this solidity in religious terms, thus incorporating it in a fixed and fully developed system of meaning. Shakespeare speaks of the endless jar of right and wrong in which justice resides, Jung thinks of the endless jar of meaning and meaninglessness in which our being resides. 'Meaninglessness,' he says, 'inhibits fullness of life and is therefore equivalent to illness. Meaning makes a great many things endurable — perhaps everything.'[45] The energy with which Wordsworth works to understand what has happened to him, his everlasting rethinking of his perceptions and revising of his poems, is part of the body's persistent desire for health. Again: it is his being that is at stake. Communication is not only a sensation, an attempt to touch the intangible, it is also the creation of meaning. Wordsworth's struggle to get in touch with his feelings and the elusive but definite presence that underlies his experience is a process of interpretation. Moment by moment he established the significance of his life.

5

The Poetry of Consciousness

Wordsworth was a man who continually struggled not to be over-whelmed by his feelings. The difficulty of the struggle in his early years determined in part the deliberate order, self-isolation and conserva-tism of his later years. Evidence of the intensity and turbulence of Wordsworth's inner life can be found throughout his work, but there is no better example than the remarks that he made to Isabella Fenwick in 1843 on the subject of his great *Ode: Intimations of Immortality from Recollections of Early Childhood.* He tells her:

> . . .I was often unable to think of external things as having external existence, and I communed with all that I saw as something not apart from, but inherent in, my own immaterial nature. Many times while going to school I have grasped at a wall or tree to recall myself from this abyss of idealism to the reality. At that time I was afraid of such processes.[1]

This is an extraordinary confession: that often the world existed for him only when he made an effort and that without this effort he could not escape from his phantasies. Johnson was joking when he said that he kicked a stone in order to refute Berkeley. Wordsworth reaches out to the wall and the tree like a drowning man, in a gesture of desperate need. He was, he says, afraid. The fear of being engulfed and the fear of falling seem to be united in this experience, and as Wordsworth relates it we have the illusion that he is still walking to the school: 'Many times while going to school have I grasped at a wall or tree. . .' He says 'this abyss' as if it is yawning in front of him.

These experiences were very important to Wordsworth and he spoke of them to others beside Isabella Fenwick. R.P. Graves told the poet's nephew:

> I remember Mr. Wordsworth saying that, at a particular stage of his mental progress, he used to be frequently so rapt into an unreal transcendental world of ideas that the external world seemed no

longer to exist in relation to him, and he had to reconvince himself
of its existence *by clasping a tree*[2]

and Bonamy Price, after Wordsworth's death, recalled a walk they
had taken together:

> The venerable old man raised his aged form erect; he was walking
> in the middle, and passed across me to a five-barred gate in the wall
> which bounded the road on the side of the lake. He clenched the top
> bar firmly with his right hand, pushed strongly against it, and then
> uttered these ever-memorable words: 'There was a time in my life
> when I had to push against something that resisted, to be sure that
> there was anything outside me. I was sure of my own mind; every-
> thing else fell away, and vanished into thought.'[3]

For Wordsworth writing poetry was like reaching out a hand to steady
himself. His poems were a way of pushing against these primitive
moods that sometimes threatened to overpower him and that he
thought of as forming 'the starting-place of being.' Because the imagination has its source in this abyss of the mind, and because composing
meant facing up to the totality of the inner situation (including the
imagination), Wordsworth cultivated as well as feared these moods.
Self-absorption was a means of holding on to the self, a defence against
vanishing into thought — and a way of wooing the muse.

These accounts reveal how great was Wordsworth's sense of the
separateness of the inner and outer worlds, and how conscious he was
of moving back and forth between two realms, the one dream-like and
cloudy, the other substantial and definite. His realisation of the degree
to which perception is creation might have been impossible without
the memory of the world intermittently emerging from the mists of
phantasy. This is a recurring image in his poetry and one that he constantly uses to describe the mind. Nowhere is this clearer than in his
description of climbing to the top of Snowdon to watch the sunrise.
This passage is the great conclusion to his greatest poem, and, as soon
as he had drafted it, he recognised its value. When he enlarged the
poem from five books to thirteen, and then from thirteen to fourteen,
he kept the description of the ascent of Snowdon for the final book.[4]
The mind is perhaps the implicit subject of all art; it is Wordsworth's
explicit subject.

In one of these excursions, travelling then

Through Wales on foot, and with a youthful Friend,
I left Bethkelet's huts at couching-time,
And westward took my way to see the sun
Rise from the top of Snowdon. Having reach'd
The Cottage at the Mountain's foot, we there
Rouz'd up the Shepherd, who by ancient right
Of office is the Stranger's usual Guide;
And after short refreshment sallied forth.

It was a Summer's night, a close warm night,
Wan, dull and glaring, with a dripping mist
Low-hung and thick that cover'd all the sky,
Half threatening storm and rain; but on we went
Uncheck'd, being full of heart and having faith
In our tried Pilot. Little could we see
Hemm'd round on every side with fog and damp,
And, after ordinary travellers' chat
With our Conductor, silently we sank
Each into commerce with his private thoughts:
Thus did we breast the ascent, and by myself
Was nothing either seen or heard the while
Which took me from my musings, save that once
The Shepherd's Cur did to his own great joy
Unearth a hedgehog in the mountain crags
25   Round which he made a barking turbulent.
This small adventure, for even such it seemed
In that wild place and at the dead of night,
Being over and forgotten, on we wound
In silence as before. With forehead bent
Earthward, as if in opposition set
Against an enemy, I panted up
With eager pace, and no less eager thoughts.
Thus might we wear perhaps an hour away,
Ascending at loose distance each from each,
And I, as chanced, the foremost of the Band;
When at my feet the ground appear'd to brighten,
And with a step or two seem'd brighter still;
Nor had I time to ask the cause of this,
For instantly a Light upon the turf
Fell like a flash: I look'd about, and lo!
The Moon stood naked in the Heavens, at height

Immense above my head, and on the shore
I found myself of a huge sea of mist,
Which, meek and silent, rested at my feet:
A hundred hills their dusky backs upheaved
All over this still Ocean, and beyond,
Far, far beyond, the vapours shot themselves,
In headlands, tongues, and promontory shapes,
Into the Sea, the real Sea, that seem'd
50 To dwindle, and give up its majesty,
Usurp'd upon as far as sight could reach.
Meanwhile, the Moon look'd down upon this shew
In single glory, and we stood, the mist
Touching our very feet; and from the shore
At distance not the third part of a mile
Was a blue chasm; a fracture in the vapour,
A deep and gloomy breathing-place thro' which
Mounted the roar of waters, torrents, streams
Innumerable, roaring with one voice.
The universal spectacle throughout
Was shaped for admiration and delight,
Grand in itself alone, but in that breach
Through which the homeless voice of waters rose,
That dark deep thoroughfare had Nature lodg'd
The Soul, the Imagination of the whole.

A meditation rose in me that night
Upon the lonely Mountain when the scene
Had pass'd away, and it appear'd to me
The perfect image of a mighty Mind,
Of one that feeds upon infinity,
That is exalted by an underpresence,
The sense of God, or whatsoe'er is dim
Or vast in its own being, above all
One function of such mind had Nature there
75 Exhibited by putting forth, and that
With circumstance most awful and sublime,
That domination which she oftentimes
Exerts upon the outward face of things,
So moulds them, and endues, abstracts, combines,
Or by abrupt and unhabitual influence
Doth make one object so impress itself

Upon all others, and pervade them so
That even the grossest minds must see and hear
And cannot chuse but feel. The Power which these
Acknowledge when thus moved, which Nature thus
Thrusts forth upon the senses, is the express
Resemblance, in the fulness of its strength
Made visible, a genuine Counterpart
And Brother of the glorious faculty
Which higher minds bear with them as their own.
This is the very spirit in which they deal
With all the objects of the universe;
They from their native selves can send abroad
Like transformations, for themselves create
A like existence, and, whene'er it is
Created for them, catch it by an instinct;
Them the enduring and the transient both
Serve to exalt; they build up greatest things
From least suggestions, ever on the watch,
100   Willing to work and to be wrought upon,
They need not extraordinary calls
To rouze them, in a world of life they live,
By sensible impressions not enthrall'd,
But quicken'd, rouz'd, and made thereby more fit
To hold communion with the invisible world.
Such minds are truly from the Deity,
For they are Powers; and hence the highest bliss
That can be known is theirs, the consciousness
Of whom they are habitually infused
Through every image, and through every thought,
And all impressions; hence religion, faith,
And endless occupation for the soul
Whether discursive or intuitive
Hence chearfulness in every act of life
Hence truth in moral judgements and delight
That fails not in the external universe.

(XIII.1 – 116)

Wordsworth starts by carefully locating the episode in his own life.
The narration is elaborately circumstantial and full of the almost
euphemistic expressions that are so characteristic of him. They
abound at the beginning: 'youthful Friend,' 'couching-time,' 'Rouz'd

up the Shepherd,' 'by ancient right / Of office' 'the Stranger's usual Guide,' 'short refreshment,' 'sallied forth,' and show us Wordsworth's need to transform his experience. The opening is like a diary entry, but in the grand style. The place name, 'Bethkelet,' that the shepherd living at the foot of the mountain had the right by custom to be the guide, the encounter of the dog and the hedgehog, none of these things seems crucial to the description of the 'sea of mist,' but they are necessary to establish the reality of the experience. They balance it as our waking life balances our dreams. This is Wordsworth grasping at a tree or pushing against a five-bar gate. These particulars emphasise the uniqueness of the experience. They make it a moment distinguishable from all other moments and ward off the chaos of undifferentiated sensation.

The progress up the mountain is a movement from the outer to the inner world. The climbers are soon isolated, 'Hemm'd round on every side with fog and damp.' After some polite conversation, each of the three men sinks 'into commerce with his private thoughts.' The poet becomes completely self-absorbed:

> and by myself
> Was nothing either seen or heard the while
> Which took me from my musings. . .

These are interrupted only by the dog barking at the hedgehog. The smallness of this incident serves as a measurement of the larger silence. The mountain is 'lonely.' The moon and clouds seem to emerge from the poet's thoughts just as the 'sea of mist' merges with 'the real sea.' Here the inner world is made continuous with the outer world and the whole scene becomes 'The perfect image of a mighty Mind.' This is the end to which this poem on the growth of the poet's mind builds.

The progress up the mountain is also a movement from darkness to enlightenment. At the foot of Snowdon they were under the mist, 'Low-hung and thick that cover'd all the sky,' and were soon engulfed by it. 'Little could we see,' the poet says. The time is 'the dead of night.' Then a sudden flash of light intrudes upon his day-dreams like an idea and he, who has been looking down at nothing, looks about. The moon reveals a vast panorama of earth and sky of which it is a part. The poet gazes 'as far as sight could reach.' The darkness is illuminated by the moon, instead of fog there is a landscape, the fog forms tongues, the roar of waters becomes a voice, then the scene passes and is replaced by understanding. The description is followed by a long interpretation of the event.

Knowledge has to be paid for. The idea is as old as the myth of Eden that tells us that its price is innocence and shows us that in the world of experience what we are is always at risk. The cost of venturing into the mind, which is only hinted at in the Snowdon narrative, is clearly stated in *Home at Grasmere*:

> For I must tread on shadowy ground, must sink
> Deep, and aloft ascending, breathe in worlds
> To which the heaven of heavens is but a veil.
> All strength, all terror, single or in bands,
> That ever was put forth in personal form —
> Jehovah, with his thunder, and the choir
> Of shouting Angels and the empyreal thrones —
> I pass them unalarmed.

> (HG.781 – 788)

The 'shadowy ground' resembles the 'huge sea of mist.' The poet must 'sink / Deep' (as into the 'blue chasm') and ascend 'aloft' (as to the mountain top) to breathe in the new worlds. This means confronting: 'All strength, all terror. . . / That ever was put forth in personal form.' Although Wordsworth declares himself 'unalarmed' by Jehovah's thunder and the angels' shouting, there is nothing that he finds more fearful or awful than looking into the human mind:

> Not Chaos, not
> The darkest pit of lowest Erebus,
> Nor aught of blinder vacancy scooped out
> By help of dreams can breed such fear and awe
> As fall upon us often when we look
> Into our Minds, into the Mind of Man,
> My haunt and the main region of my Song.

> (HG.788 – 794)

Haunt summons up an underworld of ghosts, '*My* haunt' shows us that Wordsworth felt himself irresistibly drawn to the twilight of his subject. The 'blue chasm' is 'deep and gloomy,' and a 'dark deep thoroughfare,' — a road into the night of the mind. *Homeless* to describe the 'voice of waters' is like *haunt* in that it conjures up rootless, restless, ever-changing spirits, who press to speak to us in an uncanny language.

That poets are explorers and likewise exposed to dangers is implied by the passage of over a hundred lines that Wordsworth later thought of including in his analysis of what he saw from the peak of Snowdon. He relates two mundane experiences of his own of how nature imposes herself on man, and then episodes from the lives of Columbus, Gilbert, Park and Dampier, all stories of great fear or suffering. Wordsworth's feelings when watching a storm blow over Coniston and when seeing a horse standing motionless against 'a clear silver moonlight sky' near Grasmere are set equal to Mungo Park's despair in the jungle of the Niger and to James Dampier's narrow escape from death in a canoe off Nicobas in the worst storm that he had ever known.[5]

The mind for Wordsworth is an abyss. He associates it with chaos (when 'the earth was without form, and void; and darkness *was* upon the face of the deep'), the bottom of the underworld and threatening dreams, — with something blind, vacant and 'scooped out' that we can 'look into.' That 'fear and awe' then *fall* upon us suggests the vertigo of looking over the edge of a precipice. He refers in his great *Ode* to the child's ability to read:

> the eternal deep,
> Haunted for ever by the eternal mind. . .

This is the 'mighty mind' 'exalted by an underpresence' (XIII.71, a phrase that in both MSS A and B is altered to 'underconsciousness').[6] The sources of the poet's power are conceived of as coming from below, and this is perhaps why Wordsworth's two greatest descriptions of the imagination are set high in the mountains: near the top of the Simplon Pass and on the summit of Snowdon. Thus, the whole world is revealed as subject to the imagination and made a metaphor for the mind itself. Heidegger, commenting on a poem by Rilke, states:

> What Rilke calls Nature is not contrasted with history. Above all, it is not intended as the subject matter of natural science. Nor is Nature opposed to art. It is the ground for history and art and nature in the narrower sense.[7]

Wordsworth's poetry about nature is not any more specific than it is, because he is constantly trying to look through nature to his own mind and being.

The 'blue chasm' of Snowdon is a 'breathing-place,' a place literally of inspiration, and thereby related to the metaphor of the 'half-conscious' external breeze and the 'corresponding . . .creative. . .vital breeze' (I.1 – 4; 41 – 44) with which Wordsworth starts the poem. Also at the start is Wordsworth's recollection of the Derwent's murmurs blending with his nurse's song. On Snowdon, there is a similar sense of varied melody and of many indistinct mutterings becoming one voice. For Wordsworth the imagination is a disembodied voice that speaks to us without interruption like the sound of running water heard at a distance.

Coleridge covers the same ground in *Kubla Khan*, which is explicitly the report of a dream produced 'without any sensation or consciousness of effort,' and which echoes with songs, cries and the sound of subterranean waters. There, the sacred river, Alph, whose name indicates the poem's concern with origins, sinks 'in tumult' 'through caverns measureless to man' to the ocean. Before disappearing underground, it runs through a 'deep romantic chasm' 'A savage place!' 'enchanted' and 'haunted,' that is also a 'breathing-place':

> And from this chasm, with ceaseless turmoil seething,
> As if this earth in fast thick pants were breathing,
> A mighty fountain momently was forced. . .[8]

The garden of Xanadu is related to a vision of a woman playing a dulcimer and singing. The poet's desire is to revive her music within himself so that he is able to-recreate at will this lost and awesome paradise.

Wordsworth calls 'the homeless voice of waters' the 'Soul, the Imagination of the whole,' and throughout the passage he insists on the unity of the experience. The mist merges with the sea, the moon looks down 'In single glory,' and the innumerable streams are 'roaring with one voice.' The scene is 'The universal spectacle.' 'The whole' exists as a whole because of the soul or imagination. Wordsworth shares Coleridge's belief that the imagination is esemplastic (shaping into one), and the source of its power, as Wordsworth presents it here, is that it connects consciousness with the unconscious. The imagination is the 'thoroughfare' which enables the cloudy thoughts and shapeless voices of the unconscious to enter consciousness. Without it the mind is divided.

The passage is a good example of how Wordsworth employs the vocabulary of religion for the purposes of psychological analysis. Only the religious words express the strength, the awfulness (in the full sense of the word) and the sacredness of what he felt. Even so, neither *soul* nor *imagination* is adequate to express his meaning; he needs them both. Similarly, although the scene offers 'the perfect image of a mighty Mind,' he needs four more phrases to complete his thought. The 'mighty Mind': (a) 'feeds upon infinity,' and (b) is 'exalted by an underpresence' — two ways of describing the abyss of the unconscious — and, as this still is not enough to communicate his emotion, Wordsworth compares this 'underpresence' to: (c) 'the sense of God,' and (d) 'whatso'er is dim or vast in its own being,' phrases which adumbrate his uncertainty before his perceptions and the tentativeness of his explorations. That it is 'dim *or* vast' is a further indication that the many vague panoramas and dissolving views in Wordsworth's poetry stand for what is obscure within the poet's self. The mind, he says, is exalted by its sense of the unfathomable darkness 'in its own being.'

There is no mysticism here (or anywhere in Wordsworth's work). Wordsworth never makes any such claims for his experience. On the contrary, he specifies in his comments to Isabella Fenwick on the *Ode: Intimations of Immortality from Recollections of Early Childhood* that he has extrapolated the notion of 'a pre-existent state' from his memories of childhood:

> To that dream-like vividness and splendour which invests objects of sight in childhood, every one, I believe, if he would look back, could bear testimony, and I need not to dwell upon it here: but having in the Poem regarded it as presumptive evidence of a prior state of existence, I think it right to protest against a conclusion, which has given pain to some good and pious persons, that I meant to inculcate such a belief. It is far too shadowy a notion to be recommended to faith, as more than an element in our instincts of immortality.

He makes it clear that he does not ask the reader to believe in the poem as a report of any religious vision. The poem has its source in 'particular feelings or *experiences* of my own mind' that he believes to be part of common experience: '. . .I took hold of the notion of pre-existence as having sufficient foundation in humanity for authorizing me to make for my purpose the best use of it I could *as a Poet*' (my italics).[9] God in the account of the climb up Snowdon is associated with dimness and vastness, and is one of a series of metaphors. *Soul* recurs in

Wordsworth's descriptions of the imagination. The 'first great gift' in his inventory of his poetic powers is 'the vital soul' (I.161). Discussing the confirmation at Cambridge of his vocation, he declares: 'The Poet's soul was with me at that time' (VI.55), and in his apostrophe to the imagination upon crossing the Alps, he says: 'to my Soul I say / I recognise thy glory' (VI.531 – 532).

Although Wordsworth continues by declaring — in remote and awkward phrases — that great minds are 'truly from the Deity':

> . . .the consciousness
> Of whom they are habitually infused
> Through every image,

and by asserting the existence of divine love (XIII.157 – 158), the burden of his meditation is to explain the workings of the imagination. The emphasis throughout is on the power of the mind. When the scene disappears, it is retained in the poet's memory as a metaphor that reveals, 'above all' / 'One function' of ' a mighty Mind': how the mind imposes its thoughts upon the world, how thinking virtually changes the nature of the world. The syntax is so convoluted because 'Nature' is treated both as an agent that operates upon minds and as a mind itself. This entanglement shows Wordsworth's uncertainty about the sources of the mind's power. His experience tells him that it comes from within, and this is how he pictures it in the image he makes of the events on Snowdon: it is like the voice of the waters continuously rising up from the 'blue chasm.' The unconscious is the infinity that feeds the imagination. And yet its force is so overwhelming, so alien, so 'awful and sublime' that, when he comes to interpret this image, part of him maintains that it comes from without. What Wordsworth means by 'Nature' 'putting forth. . .That Domination' — his phrase is strange — '. . .upon the outward face of things' is not entirely clear. It seems to refer to 'Nature' bringing together mountains, streams, clouds and moon in the Snowdon episode. That is 'the outward face of things.' Making 'one object so impress itself / Upon all others,' however, refers to the way in which the scene is apprehended. This is the inward face of perception. 'Nature,' moreover, moulds, endues, abstracts and combines like the imagination.

Repeatedly Wordsworth calls attention to the tremendous energies at play in the mind. His language suggests that consciousness is a war between sensation and the will. 'Nature' *exerts* a *domination*, *makes* one object *impress* itself upon another and *thrusts forth upon the senses*. The grossest minds *cannot chuse but feel*. As for higher minds, *they are Powers*. The syllogistic form of the meditation (note the 'thus. . .thus' (85) and the 'hence. . .Hence. . .Hence. . .' (107, 114−115)) represents part of Wordsworth's attempt to encompass the totality of these energies. He includes 'all the objects in the universe,' and, refers to 'every image' and 'every thought, / And all impressions,' that pass through a 'higher' mind. The many superlatives and commodious abstractions are part of the struggle to comprehend the whole by connecting everything to something else.

Earlier in the poem, Wordsworth in fact uses the word *war* to describe the relation between the world and the poetic power that he felt within him almost like another self:

> A plastic power
> Abode with me, a forming hand, at times
> Rebellious, acting in a devious mood,
> A local spirit of its own, at war
> With general tendency, but for the most
> Subservient strictly to the external things
> With which it commun'd.
>
> (II.381−387)

For him the imagination lives its own ever-changing life, but the change and violence end abruptly in *commun'd*, in a hush of concentration that suggests the baby's rapt study of its mother's face, a study that Wordsworth recognises as 'the first / Poetic spirit of our human life' (II.237−280). Hostile to 'general tendency,' the imagination is subdued only by 'external things.' Only definite, particular objects produce peace and communion. The projection of the poet's phantasies upon the world is seen as controlling the world, as establishing obedience and *dominion* (compare *domination*, XIII.77). Wordsworth closes this paragraph, as he does all his longer poetic descriptions of the imagination in a mood of reverence, and, like the Snowdon episode, with *hence* repeated three times:

> An auxiliar light
> Came from my mind which on the setting sun
> Bestow'd new splendor, the melodious birds,
> The gentle breezes, fountains that ran on,
> Murmuring so sweetly in themselves, obey'd
> A like dominion; and the midnight storm

Grew darker in the presence of my eye.
Hence my obeisance, my devotion hence,
And hence my transport.

(II.387–395)

Wordsworth believes that the poetic power is connective rather than analytic:

. . .more poetic as resembling more
Creative agency. I mean to speak
Of that interminable building rear'd
By observation of affinities
In objects where no brotherhood exists
To common minds.

(II.400–405)

Valéry comes to the same conclusion in his 'Introduction à la méthode de Léonard de Vinci' (1894):

The secret, that of Leonardo, like that of Bonaparte, like that of anyone who possesses even once the highest intelligence, — is, and can only be, in the relations they find, — that they are forced to find, — *between things of which the law of continuity escapes us.*[10]

The poet's mind, therefore, is a vast structure of connections, an 'interminable building,' and Wordsworth's religion may be described as an attempt to find a mirror image of this structure in the world. He obtained from religion the same satisfactions that he obtained from geometry:

Mighty is the charm
Of those abstractions to a mind beset
With images, and haunted by itself;
And specially delightful unto me
Was that clear Synthesis built up aloft
So gracefully, even then when it appear'd
No more than as a plaything, or a toy
Embodied to the sense, not what it is
In verity, an independent world
Created out of pure Intelligence.

(VI.178–187)

His thoughts on the 'plastic power' of the imagination in Book II lead him on, again as in the Snowdon episode, to a description of the bliss of consciousness:

> Thus did my days pass on, and now at length
> From Nature and her overflowing soul
> I had receiv'd so much that all my thoughts
> Were steep'd in feeling; I was only then
> Contented when with bliss ineffable
> I felt the sentiment of Being spread
> O'er all that moves, and all that seemeth still,
> O'er all, that, lost beyond the reach of thought
> And human knowledge, to the human eye
> Invisible, yet liveth to the heart,
> O'er all that leaps, and runs, and shouts, and sings,
> Or beats the gladsome air, o'er all that glides
> Beneath the wave, yea, in the wave itself
> And mighty depth of waters.

> (II.415–428)

The feeling of wholeness that is projected in the *Lines Composed a Few Miles above Tintern Abbey* and at the end of the Snowdon meditation exists here as an inner state, as 'the sentiment of Being,' the joy of just existing. This feeling is beyond words, virtually beyond consciousness, and yet heart-felt:

> beyond the reach of thought
> And human knowledge, to the human eye
> Invisible, yet liveth to the heart. . .

Here there is another 'invisible world' and a 'mighty depth of waters,' another 'blue chasm.'

When in the Snowdon meditation Wordsworth actually describes how 'higher minds' work, his language becomes sharper and more confident, and he has no need of religious language:

> This is the very spirit in which they deal
> With all the objects of the universe;
> They from their native selves can send abroad
> Like transformations, for themselves create
> A like existence, and, whene'er it is

Created for them, catch it by an instinct;
Them the enduring and the transient both
Serve to exalt; they build up greatest things
From least suggestions, ever on the watch,
Willing to work and to be wrought upon,
They need not extraordinary calls
To rouze them, in a world of life they live,
By sensible impressions not enthrall'd,
But quicken'd, rouz'd, and made thereby more fit
To hold communion with the invisible world.

(XIII.91 – 105)

Although he uses the third person plural and makes no mention of poetry, this is introspection. What the poet sends abroad — the world here is a foreign country — is a transformation of his native self, and *native* seems to be an attempt in this context to distinguish a primitive version of the self, the self of infancy as opposed to the self of maturity. The passage is completely abstract, an abstractness that is a measurement of Wordsworth's self-consciousness. Wordsworth stands outside the mental processes and observes them; he is concerned to define the mind in terms of its operations. To find a greater degree of abstraction it is necessary to go to Freud's *Project for a Scientific Psychology* (1895) and to Valéry's notebooks (1894 – 1945) which show his lifelong effort to devise an algebra of thought.

Wordsworth's poetry contains many passages like this one where he first describes his feelings and then derives theoretical conclusions from them, developing what might be called an *ad hoc* theory of the mind. This, such as it is, is never fully articulated, but is present as a set of unspoken (or half-spoken) assumptions, that he has not worked out systematically, and that find their way into his poetry when he needs to follow his feelings to something that he can believe in as a conclusion. Often these conclusions are rather perfunctory religious statements or, as in this case, shade off into such statements. His religious beliefs mark the limits of his knowledge of the mind. The very abstract passages are never far away from the description of a definite moment or a particular feeling; they are the result of Wordsworth's capacity to enter into reality in very specific terms. Although many of his successors have been freer, few, perhaps only Valéry and Stevens, have been as successful in making great poetry about the data of consciousness.

Why did Wordsworth in his theory-making stop where he did and why is he less thoroughgoing than Valéry or Stevens? The answer is hidden in the details of his life (which perhaps we could not interpret even if we could recover them) and leads to the question of why he wrote poetry. Some suggestions can be made instead of answers. R.D. Laing says that:

> Orphans and adopted children sometimes develop a tremendously strong desire to find out 'who they are' by tracing the father and mother who conceived them. They feel incomplete for want of a father or mother, whose absence leaves their concept of self incomplete.

This desire may be satisfied by seeing something tangible, such as a tombstone which 'seems to allow "closure".'[11] The poem is to the poet as the tombstone is to the child and provides him with an analogous sense of completion. Poem and tombstone both are objects, concrete, palpable, that supply unchanging form to the dimmest feelings. Wordsworth wrote to reaffirm his sentiment of being. His invention of the autobiographical poem was the invention of a self. This involved not only making an order of his feelings and coping with his guilt, but also coming to terms with his genius, as so many of his most theoretical and greatest passages are on the subject of the creative power of the mind. Autobiography to Wordsworth meant an examination of the sources of poetry, and more theory would have taken him too far away from his subject: himself.

Valéry and Stevens, who are more theoretic than Wordsworth, are less personal and use the idea of the self to detach themselves from their own lives. Stevens sees this abstraction as a prerequisite for poetry. The example of Stevens illustrates how Wordsworth's way of thinking about the imagination has continued to the present. Wordsworth (and Coleridge) are Stevens's point of departure. Their terms echo in his work. Thinking about the origins of poetry, he distinguishes between sensibility and imagination — rather than between fancy and imagination — and emphasises the power of the mind to make things:

> the operative force within us does not, in fact, seem to be sensibility, that is to say, the feelings. It seems to be a constructive faculty, that derives its energy more from the imagination than from the sensibility.[12]

Wordsworth's description of 'higher minds' is like a sketch for Stevens's 'figure of a poet,' although Stevens is more conscious than Wordsworth of the nature of abstraction. The poet, Stevens insists, must abstract both his self and the world:

> He will consider that although he has himself witnessed, during the long period of his life, a general transition to reality, his own measure as a poet, in spite of all the passions of the lovers of truth, is the measure of his power to abstract himself, and to withdraw with him into his abstraction the reality on which the lovers of truth insist. He must be able to abstract himself and also to abstract reality, which he does by placing it in his imagination.[13]

Stevens makes abstraction appear more an act of will than Wordsworth for whom it is an almost uncontrollable impulse of 'higher minds' that 'need not extraordinary calls / To rouze them.' The two poets share the sense of a profound division between the self and the world that is created and, in a way, repaired by the imagination, and the belief that, as Stevens puts it:

> if for the poet, the imagination is paramount, and if he dwells apart in his imagination, as the philosopher dwells in his reason, and as the priest dwells in his belief. . . He is thinking of those facts of experience of which all of us have thought and which all of us have felt with such intensity. . .[14]

The separation, isolation and loneliness of the individual, especially the artist, is the theme or counterpoint of most of the poetry, if not of all art, composed from Wordsworth to the present. The greater the stress on the uniqueness of our individuality, the more we have become separated from every other thing, including each other. This increasing self-awareness and self-definition has turned poets upon their own feelings as if they were the most *real* things available, as, paradoxically, the most knowable and the most mysterious.

Wordsworth in his poetry uses the landscape in a new way in order to define his states of mind. He maps in space what he feels in time, forming what is amorphous into a unified scene with its own metaphoric structure. He is aware of what he is doing *and* makes this awareness part of the poem:

> A meditation rose in me that night

Upon the lonely Mountain when the scene
Had pass'd away, and it appear'd to me
The perfect image of a mighty Mind. . .

(XIII.66 – 69)

For Wordsworth and the poets who follow him only the landscape is commensurate with the moods of the mind, nothing else is at once as various and definite. The thorn's 'mass of knotted joints,' the sky's 'peculiar tint of yellow green,' 'the rainbow of the salt sand-wave' and 'the virteous pour of the full moon just tinged with blue' are like the calibrations of an infinitely subtle instrument of measurement.[15] Every particular of a landscape can be made to correspond to a nuance of mood, thereby generating a complete language in which to discuss feeling. As a result, poets have a compelling motive for looking at the minutiae of a landscape, and poetry is increasingly filled with objects and precise observation.

Hopkins invented *inscape* to denote a thing's uniqueness.[16] The word is in keeping with his almost microscopic scrutiny of the world. He sees every object as a landscape and feels that its essential form is somehow inward. As landscape became a habitual metaphor, poets began to play with both terms of the metaphor, and to devise their own countries. (This is how the landscapes of Stevens, Neruda, Quasimodo and Montale, for example, differ from those of Wordsworth.) Imaginary landscapes are, of course, as old as storytelling, but they had not been produced before by authors capable of making real ones.

The descriptions of landscape in Wordsworth and subsequent poets are usually associated with intense and elusive feelings, and the description is a way of fully experiencing the feeling. The idea that perception of the world involves a projection of ourselves is clearly stated by Stevens:

> when we look at the blue sky for the first time, that is to say: not merely see it, but look at it and experience it. . .few people realize that they are looking at the world of their own thoughts and the world of their own feelings.[17]

His choice of the sky as his example here and his repeated use of it in his poetry reveals his preoccupation with evanescent sensations, a metaphor and preoccupation shared by Wordsworth, as all his twilights and sunsets demonstrate.

Stokes writes:

There is a long history of indistinctness in Turner's art, connected throughout with what I have called an embracing or enveloping quality,. . . The power grew in Turner of isolating the visionary effectiveness that belongs to a passing event of light: it entailed some loss of definition in the interest of emphasis upon an overall quality. To one who complained, Turner is said to have replied: 'Indistinctness is my forte.'[18]

Turner (1775–1851) is almost an exact contemporary of Wordsworth. 'The passing event of light' can be equated in the work of both artists with the passing event of feeling. The enveloping power, as it grew in Wordsworth, was analytic and consequently entailed a gain in definition and in complexity. He writes to Landor (21.1.1824) that:

in poetry it is the imaginative only, viz., that which is conversant [with], or turns upon infinity, that powerfully affects me, — perhaps I ought to explain: I mean to say that, unless in those passages where things are lost in each other, and limits vanish, and aspirations are raised, I read with something too much like indifference. . .

The history of the indistinctness in Wordsworth's poetry is the history of his struggle to describe the workings of his mind, and is related to the images of clouds and mist that are his chief metaphor in representing thought. This indistinctness is of a piece with his concern with growth, development, process — 'where things are lost in each other, and limits vanish.' The clouds are one of the places where we can observe process most clearly, and their continuous self-translation occurs in the larger setting necessary for a complex model of the mind.

This is as evident in the famous passage on walking over the Alps as it is in the description of climbing Snowdon:

> Imagination — here the Power so called
> Through sad incompetence of human speech,
> That awful Power rose from the mind's abyss
> Like an unfathered vapour that enwraps,
> At once, some lonely traveller. I was lost;
> Halted without an effort to break through;
> But to my conscious soul I now can say —
> 'I recognise thy glory:' in such strength
> Of usurpation, when the light of sense
> Goes out, but with a flash that has revealed

The invisible world, doth greatness make abode,
There harbours; whether we be young or old,
Our destiny, our being's heart and home,
Is with infinitude, and only there;
With hope it is, hope that can never die,
Effort, and expectation, and desire,
And something evermore about to be.
Under such banners militant, the soul
Seeks for no trophies, struggles for no spoils
That may attest her prowess, blest in thoughts
That are their own perfection and reward,
Strong in herself and in beatitude
That hides her, like the mighty flood of Nile
Poured from his fount of Abyssinian clouds
To fertilise the whole Egyptian plain.

　　The melancholy slackening that ensued
Upon those tidings by the peasant given
Was soon dislodged. Downwards we hurried fast,
And, with the half-shaped road which we had missed,
Entered a narrow chasm. The brook and road
Were fellow-travellers in this gloomy strait,
And with them did we journey several hours
At a slow pace. The immeasurable height
Of woods decaying, never to be decayed,
The stationary blasts of waterfalls,
And in the narrow rent at every turn
Winds thwarting winds, bewildered and forlorn,
The torrents shooting from the clear blue sky,
The rocks that muttered close upon our ears,
Black drizzling crags that spake by the way-side
As if a voice were in them, the sick sight
And giddy prospect of the raving stream,
The unfettered clouds and region of the Heavens,
Tumult and peace, the darkness and the light —
Were all like workings of one mind, the features
Of the same face, blossoms upon one tree;
Characters of the great Apocalypse,
The types and symbols of Eternity,
Of first, and last, and midst, and without end.

(VI.592 – 640; 1850)

The imagination is, in a curious phrase that at once personifies and depersonalises, 'Like an unfathered vapour,' an expression that reveals Wordsworth's concern for origins. The 1805 text reads: 'I was lost as in a cloud.' As on the Snowdon climb, the poet is enveloped in a mist: His isolation is stressed. He is not simply surrounded, he is enwrapped, and even before this happens, the traveller is *lonely* (not *alone*). The poet is 'lost' and 'without an effort to break through.' He is content to allow the inner world to impose itself. Wordsworth expresses it so that his passiveness seems a choice, a surrender of self-control for greater self-knowledge, but although the experience puts him in touch with the 'heart and home' of being, which he locates in 'the invisible world,' he rarely speaks of the *self* and to this degree he is not self-conscious. He refers here, as he does so often, to his *soul*. The idea of the soul is our wish for immortality, one of Wordsworth's most powerful wishes.[19] Infinitude stands for immortality. The vague, dissolving panoramas in his poetry assert not only the potential of the self, but also express his desire not to die, a desire for world without end.

The passage is a description of mental action in terms very similar to those used to describe the climb up Snowdon. The whole landscape, whose components are itemised one after another, resembles the 'workings of one mind' and forms a single identity, 'the features / Of the same face.' This mind is divided into two parts, 'the darkness and the light', the unconscious and the conscious. The imagination rises 'from the mind's abyss,' formless and obscure like the voice of the waters through the 'blue chasm.' The 1805 version reads: 'to my Soul I say' where the 1850 reads: 'to my conscious soul I now can say,' showing Wordsworth's need to mark the difference in self-awareness which has been brought about by the experience: only *now* does he understand what happened to him. The revision implies perhaps that there is an unconscious soul, which would correspond to 'The Soul, the Imagination of the whole' lodged in the 'dark deep thoroughfare' of the mind in the Snowdon passage. The uncertainty in Wordsworth's use of the word *soul* is illustrated by his changing 'The mind beneath such banners militant' to 'Under such banners militant, the soul.'

Greatness comes from the capacity of the imagination to take over perception. The unconscious mind usurps the world. From Snowdon's summit the poet sees 'the real Sea. . . Usurp'd upon as far as sight could reach' (XIII.49,51). This appropriation by the imagination depends none the less upon perception: it is 'the light of sense' which 'Goes out' and the change is from outer to inner:

> the light of sense
> Goes out, but with a flash that has revealed
> The invisible world. . .

It is as if one landscape has been replaced by another. The extraordinary economy of words conveys the speed of mental events. The poet suddenly sees into his mind where the darkness is an illumination and the invisible, visible. This play of opposites is consequent upon the mind's division into light and darkness. There is in the mind, as in the Alps, a frontier to be crossed.

After this momentary flash of glory, Wordsworth returns abruptly from the Egyptian plain to the Swiss mountains, and the process begins again, only now he moves slowly *through* the visible scene to 'the unfettered clouds' and the cloudlike image of a tree covered in blossom. The alpine landscape, its details added up like a column of figures, is read as a message of the end of time and of time without end. The present becomes the future. Here, unlike Snowdon, the poet descends into the chasm and goes all the way to the bottom. The imagination is 'That awful Power' which seems to engage the soul 'Under such banners militant' in some unspecified war. The menace and wonder of its incomprehensible strength are communicated in the words with which Wordsworth colours the description of the Simplon Pass: *melancholy, gloomy, thwarting, bewildered, forlorn, tumult, darkness, Apocalypse.* As in the 'blue chasm' of Snowdon there are voices in the abyss:

> The rocks that muttered close upon our ears,
> Black drizzling crags that spake by the way-side
> As if a voice were in them, the sick sight
> And giddy prospect of the raving stream. . .

The adjectives used for the stream: *sick, giddy, raving,* portray madness and 'the *unfettered* clouds' not only add to this image of terrible freedom, but may be said to suggest the chains used to secure madmen.

On Snowdon the poet watches 'the real Sea. . .dwindle' into the 'sea of mist.' The merging of the real and the imaginary in the Alps is treated somewhat differently in that each section of the passage has its climax in a cloudy abstraction: infinitude and eternity. There is, however, a similar double landscape in the image of the soul overcome by beatitude:

That hides her, like the mighty flood of Nile
Poured from his front of Abyssinian clouds
To fertilise the whole Egyptian plain.

The mobile, liquid plain of the Nile in flood (another sea virtually) usurps the solid reality of the Egyptian earth. This is an image of the imagination at work. In the previous book, Wordsworth has shown that he associates knowledge of the nature of poetry with a flood in an Arab country. The shell carried by the Arab in the dream of the two books holds 'the voice of waters' (XIII.63), a message:

in an unknown tongue,
Which yet I understood, articulate sounds,
A loud prophetic blast of harmony;
An Ode, in passion uttered, which foretold
Destruction to the children of the earth
By deluge, now at hand.

(V.93 – 98; 1850)

Near the end of the dream, this flood of 'the waters of the deep' (VI.130; 1850) appears like a mirage on the horizon, as 'over half the wilderness diffused, / A bed of glittering light' (VI.128 – 129; 1850). Wordsworth states that in his wakening moments he *often* (V.141; 1850) imagined this dream Arab as a 'maniac' (V.160; 1850):

crazed
By love and feeling, and internal thought
Protracted among endless solitudes. . .

(V.145 – 147; 1850)

Here he is afraid that imagination may destroy the stability of his 'internal thought,' afraid that his reason, being over-powered, should be lost. The metaphor of the Nile shows the good side of the flooding imagination, the 'raving stream' the other side. The Nile, of course, issues from a vaporous 'fount' high in the mountains, hidden by the 'Abyssinian clouds.' (These clouds seem also to enwrap the Abyssinian maid in Coleridge's *Kubla Khan* who sings of Mount Abora. Abora, which is not on any map, is a proper noun formed by Coleridge from the names of two rivers in Bruce's *Travels to Discover the Source of the Nile* and the name of a mountain that Milton locates 'By Nilus head' in

Paradise Lost.[20] Thus both Coleridge and Wordsworth locate the head waters of the imagination in the dark continent.)

Wordsworth in *To the Clouds* (discussed in Chapter 4) specifically equates clouds with thoughts. They come, he says, 'as from a hidden world.' With their intangibility and constantly changing shapes, they represent the imaginative powers, appearing the very substance of phantasy. They form the poet's day-dreams (as in *The Excursion*, II.827 – 881) as well as his private hell. Wordsworth, in an early prose fragment (1787?), describes the 'mist which descends slowly into the valley' with its 'burthen of ghosts,' and in another of similar date (1787 or 1788?), he imagines the bottom of the soul in terms that remind us of his looking into the mind in *Home at Grasmere*; here are both the tumult and the peace:

> In anger you may sometimes see the bottom of the soul. Sea Storm. Calm. —
> The spectres are busy shrouding the vale [?s]
> with wan white mist, shrieking and wailing. . .[21]

The unreal in Wordsworth half creates the real: this is the imagination's power. Perception, however, is only half creation. The mind may create 'a world of life' where the 'greatest things' are built up 'From least suggestions,' but they are, nevertheless, 'suggestions,' intimations, of reality. The world with its trees, dry stone walls and five-bar gates constantly imposes itself upon the imagination: this is nature's 'domination.' Wordsworth's images of the mind usually communicate a sense of the coming and going of reality in order to show perception and imagination in action. This is why he prefers half-hidden landscapes. The country emerging from the mist is both the world apprehended through the continuous day-dream of consciousness, and the unconscious becoming conscious.

The success of any metaphor depends upon its truth. Wordsworth can envisage the mind's unity because he recognises its major complexities, above all, that the interaction of the inner world and the outer world provides a model of the mind's *inner* workings: that the unconscious is to the conscious as the whole mind is to the world; and that the two integrating powers, perception and imagination, which perform the interaction, work in analogous ways, each combining the unreal and the real. Perception participates in the world as imagination participates in perception. Wordsworth's stories of clasping trees and walls in order to reassure himself that there was a reality that existed independently of his own thoughts suggest that he felt all this as a split within himself — which he was constantly trying to heal. By becoming a poet, he devoted his total energies to this task, perceiving and imagining became his life's work. He made a career of integration.

Wordsworth comprehends the mind as a whole, because he sees it as a single landscape and he chooses panoramic views, or a long perspective, so as to delimit consciousness and to include at least some note of uncertainty or phantasy. Also, the long perspective stands for time, the vague blue distances are the past and the future. The landscapes that Wordsworth employs are almost invariably composed of the same elements: shadow and light, cloudy and definite shapes, details of particular moments and abstract generalities. He especially enjoys looking down on a valley full of mist. This is a fundamental image in his poetry — one of the most characteristic movements of his mind — and its elements (or their equivalents) are repeated in descriptions that are not landscapes.

This use of landscape is made possible by his understanding that inner tensions and conflicts are an integral part of the mind's make-up and by his capacity to accept his own ambivalent feelings:

> The mind of Man is fram'd even like the breath
> And harmony of music. There is a dark
> Invisible workmanship that reconciles
> Discordant elements, and makes them move
> In one society. Ah me! that all
> The terrors, all the early miseries
> Regrets, vexations, lassitudes, that all
> The thoughts and feelings which have been infus'd
> Into my mind, should ever have made up
> The calm existence that is mine when I
> Am worthy of myself! Praise to the end!
> Thanks likewise for the means!

(I.351 – 362)

Wordsworth goes on to state that he has been favoured in knowing extremes of pleasure and pain, and to suggest that he is a great poet in part because he has been afraid:

> But I believe
> That Nature, oftentimes, when she would frame

A favor'd Being, from his earliest dawn
Of infancy doth open out the clouds,
As at the touch of lightning, seeking him
With gentlest visitation; not the less,
Though haply aiming at the self-same end,
Does it delight her sometimes to employ
Severer interventions, ministry
More palpable, and so she dealt with me.

(I.362–371)

The real is marked by the shadow of the unreal, as is the present by the past and joy by fear. Despite the terrors of the deeps of the mind and the discords of being, he is disposed to optimism. He finds, at the end of his poem, that the possibilities of human development make the mind more beautiful than any landscape and hopes that Coleridge will join him in composing poetry that will demonstrate:

how the mind of man becomes
A thousand times more beautiful than the earth
On which he dwells. . .

(XIII.439–441)

Wordsworth's favourite image of the countryside shrouded in mist is the one with which he opens his first long poem, *The Vale of Esthwaite* (1787):

[?] avaunt! with tenfold pleasure
I [?] the landskip's various treasure.
Lark! O Lark, thy Song awake
Suspended o'er the glassy lake
And see, the mist, as warms the day,
From the green vale steals away;
And ah! yon lingering fleecy streak,
As breaks the rainbow, soon shall break;
Now like a [   ] silver zone
On the lake's lovely bosom thrown
Yet round the mountain tops it sails
Slow born[e] upon the dewy gales.
And on yon summit brown and bare,
That seems an island in the air,

> The shepherd's restless dog I mark,
> Who, bounding round with frequent bark,
> Now leaps around the uncovered plain,
> Now dives into the mist again;
> And while the guiding sound he hears
> The [   ] shepherd lad appears
> Who knows his transport while he sees
> His cottage smoking from the trees,
> [?   ] knows the shepherd boy
> And clasps his clinging dog for joy.[22]

The poet appears to be urging himself to take possession of the land-scape's 'various treasure,' and the older word, *landskip*, that Wordsworth may have found in Milton, sounds an archaic note. Poem and landscape emerge from the mist together, and the poet seems almost to adopt the point of view of the lark high over the lake as he describes the scene.

This image recurs in Wordsworth's work like an obsession. There is a shorter and earlier version of it in *Anacreon* (1786):

> . . .As silvered by the morning beam
> The white mist curls on Grasmere's stream,
> Which, like a veil of flowing light,
> Hides half the landskip from the sight.
> Here I see the wandering rill,
> The white flocks sleeping on the hill,
> While Fancy paints, beneath the veil,
> The pathway winding through the dale,
> The cot, the seat of Peace and Love,
> Peeping through the tufted grove.

> (37 – 46)

Another shorter version is in *Septimi Gades* (1794?):

> When shouts and sheepfold bells and sound
> Of flocks and herds and streams rebound
> Along the ringing dale,
> How beauteous, round that gleaming tide,
> The silvery morning vapours glide
> And half the landscape veil.

Methinks that morning scene displays
A lovely emblem of our days,
Unobvious and serene;
So shall our still lives, half betrayed,
Show charms more touching from their shade,
Though veiled, yet not unseen.

$$(55-66)^{23}$$

Both texts reveal the poet's concern that what is veiled need not be unknown, and in the second, by using the image as an 'emblem' of all our days, he begins to develop its metaphoric power.

Wordsworth describes the shepherd's dog moving freely in and out of the mist at length in the autobiographical poem:

> I remember, far from home
> Once having stray'd, while yet a very Child,
> I saw a sight, and with what joy and love!
> It was a day of exhalations, spread
> Upon the mountains, mists and steam-like fogs
> Redounding everywhere, not vehement,
> But calm and mild, gentle and beautiful,
> With gleams of sunshine on the eyelet spots
> And loop-holes of the hills, wherever seen,
> Hidden by quiet process, and as soon
> Unfolded, to be huddled up again:
> Along a narrow Valley and profound
> I journey'd, when, aloft above my head,
> Emerging from the silvery vapours, lo!
> A Shepherd and his Dog! in open day:
> Girt round with mists they stood and look'd about
> From that enclosure small, inhabitants
> Of an aerial Island floating on,
> As seem'd, with that Abode in which they were,
> A little pendant area of grey rocks,
> By the soft wind breath'd forward. With delight
> As bland almost, one Evening I beheld,
> And at as early age (the spectacle
> Is common, but by me was then first seen)
> A Shepherd in the bottom of a Vale
> Towards the centre standing, who with voice,
> And hand waved to and fro as need required

Gave signal to his Dog, thus teaching him
To chace along the mazes of steep crags
The Flock he could not see: and so the Brute
Dear Creature! with a Man's intelligence
Advancing, or retreating on his steps,
Through every pervious strait, to right or left,
Thridded a way unbaffled; while the Flock
Fled upwards from the terror of his Bark
Through rocks and seams of turf with liquid gold
Irradiate, that deep farewell light by which
The setting sun proclaims the love he bears
To mountain regions.

(VIII.81 – 119)

The description is playful with its 'eyelet spots / And loop-holes,'
floating islands and pendant rocks. Wordsworth enjoys grappling with
the complex indistinctness and 'quiet process' of this double landscape. His pleasure is in moving in and out of the mist like the dog.
After the metamorphoses of the mist, he concentrates on the shepherd
herding sheep he cannot see and on the possibility of communication
through the ever-changing, obscure and 'silvery vapours.' Again we
are made aware that beneath the mist there is a complete and definite
landscape waiting to be explored, and it is with the latent sense of this
undiscovered country that Wordsworth studies the horizons of his
poetry.

This incident (VIII.81 – 119) is the first of a series of anecdotes
about shepherds, including one on how the mist can magnify objects:

. . .on rainy days
When I have angled up the lonely brooks
Mine eyes have glanced upon him, few steps off,
In size a Giant, stalking through the fog,
His Sheep like Greenland Bears. . .

(VIII.398 – 402)

Different shepherds become one shepherd who is suddenly made, in
quick succession, very large and very small. This is the way the mind
moulds, endues, abstracts, combines. The shepherd is changed into
'the human form' which is like 'an index' to a collection of very abstract
feelings:

> like an index of delight,
> Of grace and honour, power and worthiness.
>
> > (VIII.415–416)

He has become 'an imaginative form' (VIII.419). The scene is pervaded by a necessary cloudiness: the 'rainy days,' 'the fog,' 'shady promontory,' 'the deep radiance of the setting sun' — a glow, not a light — and the vagueness of the 'distant sky.' Wordsworth using these images of shepherds wants to depict how he 'was introduced / To an unconscious love and reverence / Of human nature' (VIII.412–414), as if he wants to show us how our dreams validate the world, that all knowledge, and love, takes shape first in the mists of the mind.

To conclude the autobiographical poem, Wordsworth returns to the image of the lark in *The Vale of Esthwaite*. The work is seen as a whole in terms of this metaphor:

> > Anon I rose
> As if on wings, and saw beneath me stretch'd
> Vast prospect of the world which I had been
> And was; and hence this Song, which like a lark
> I have protracted, in the unwearied Heavens
> Singing, and often with more plaintive voice
> Attemper'd to the sorrows of the earth. . .
>
> > (XIII.370–376)

The poet now identifies unambiguously with the lark, but he is both the bird and the earth. The landscape open before him is his entire past and self, a world in itself: 'the world which I had been / And was.' There is no mist because the exploration has been completed. Similarly, at the end of the first book, after he has succeeded in recalling so much of his early life, he remarks that memory can:

> . . .almost make Infancy itself
> A visible scene, on which the sun is shining. . .
>
> > (I.662–663)

Discussing the 'spots of time' (XI.258) — the very phrase suggests something sharply focused in a field of indistinctness — Wordsworth appears to remember the mind's abyss when he declares 'Oh! / Mystery

of Man, from what a depth / Proceed thy honours!' (XI.329 – 330). He
states that he is lost (XI.330), as he was when enwrapped by imagination on the downward slopes of the Simplon Pass. Then:

> The days gone by
> Come back upon me from the dawn almost
> Of life: the hiding-places of my power
> Seem open; I approach, and then they close;
> I see by glimpses. . .

> (XI.334 – 338)

This is the form of all Wordsworth's looking into the mind, a seeing by
glimpses, with *dawn* reminding us of all those mornings when the
valleys are full of mist. The 'spots of time' are:

> Among those passages of life in which
> We have had deepest feeling that the mind
> Is lord and master, and that outward sense
> Is but the obedient servant of her will.

> (XI.270 – 273)

and, near the end of his analysis, Wordsworth portrays himself waiting
on 'the highest summit' of a crag:

> I watch'd,
> Straining my eyes intensely, as the mist
> Gave intermitting prospect of the wood
> And plain beneath.

> (XI.361 – 364)

These images of the mind can be found in the last poems as in the first.
On the Banks of a Rocky Stream is his final attempt to represent the
whole of the mind in action. This is the penultimate poem in Hayden's
edition:

> Behold an emblem of our human mind
> Crowded with thoughts that need a settled home,
> Yet, like to eddying balls of foam
> Within this whirlpool, they each other chase
> Round and round, and neither find

An outlet nor a resting-place!
Stranger, if such disquietude be thine,
Fall on thy knees and sue for help divine.

Thoughts are the cloudy 'balls of foam.' The whirlpool is a watery abyss. By making it the central image, Wordsworth emphasises his fear of being engulfed, the threatening downward tug of the imagination. The poem is an unambiguous statement of why Wordsworth became religious in the middle of his life: to seek refuge from the chaos of his mind. He went to church for the same reason that he lived most of his life in the neighbourhood of Grasmere: to find 'a settled home.' The poem reveals the despair that he never mastered.

Wordsworth tells Isabella Fenwick that his difficulty in admitting 'the notion of death as a state applicable to my own being. . .was not so much from [feelings] of animal vivacity. . .as from a sense of the indomitableness of the spirit within me.' He connects the child's feeling of omnipotence with the poet's capacity for creation:

With a feeling congenial to this, I was often unable to think of external things as having external existence, and I communed with all that I saw as something not apart from, but inherent in, my own immaterial nature.[24]

Vision for Wordsworth is, as his remarks prove, a self-communion, infinitude is his indomitable potential. The unrealised is as yet immaterial. He finds in the 'kindling edge' of consciousness and the vaporous dark of the unconscious 'the spirit within me,' 'my own immaterial nature.'[25]

6
Ideas of Order

Wordsworth came to think of all his poetry as contributing to his description of mind and there is evidence to show that the idea was in his thoughts from almost the beginning of his poetic career. The purpose of the poems in *Lyrical Ballads* is, he declares, 'to follow the fluxes and refluxes of the mind when agitated by the great and simple affections' and to trace 'the primary laws of our nature.'[1] Dictating a note to Isabella Fenwick in 1843, he suddenly breaks out: 'Archimedes said that he could move the world if he had a point whereon to rest his machine. Who has not felt the same aspirations as regards the world of his own mind?'[2] This is a simple statement of the complex motive that caused Wordsworth to regard all his poetry as a single work, the external point that enabled him to know himself, the fulcrum that he hoped would allow him to command his mental world.

Every poem — every work of art — implies a theory of reality, usually unstated, and of which, especially before Wordsworth, the poet or artist is most often unaware. The section 'Moods of My Own Mind' in *Poems, in Two Volumes*, for example, is promised on essentially the same theory as the autobiographical poem. The assumption of the title and of the poems is that being is a succession of moods: states of often very diffuse feelings without distinct beginnings or ends. Existence is feeling — subtle, immediate, irreducible, mutable. The idea that everything is feeling, including our perception of our own history, is the idea that sets the tone for all subsequent European poetry down to the present, and this feeling, however abstract, is always personal, and understood as being the autochthonous and vital substance of the self. Wordsworth, moreover, speaks of poetry not as the philosophy, but as 'the history or science of feelings.'[3] The ground of poetry is particular events. The procedures of poetry are empirical. He declares in the 'Advertisement' to *Lyrical Ballads* (1798): 'The majority of the following poems are to be considered as experiments,' and repeats in the 'Preface' (1800) that the poems were 'published as an experiment.'[4]

To understand being as a succession of moods is to accept that every mood is worth recording. This idea, as Wordsworth acted upon it, had many poetic consequences. The scope of poetry is enlarged so as to include, at least in principle, all human experience, notably the experience we call *ordinary*. Any mood becomes a proper subject for poetry and any person, a baby, child, shepherd, leech-gatherer or poor mad woman, can be the protagonist or subject of a poem.

This emphasis on moods is a movement away from action. When a story is told, it is usually told for the sake of its moods. What happens in Wordsworth's poetry is the poet's perceptions. Knowledge in his poetry is always of experience, and the mood is the unit into which the perceiver divides or gathers his most indefinite perceptions. Wordsworth is the first European poet to make a thoroughgoing attempt to represent feeling from the inside, to be vividly aware of feeling as having an outside and an inside.

Feelings have cloudy boundaries, moods are more or less amorphous. Any poet who seeks to mark their boundaries has to solve special problems of form. Each poem in 'Moods of My Own Mind', for example, is of a different form. Wordsworth's short poems mark, perhaps, the first stirrings of the notion that the form of the poem should be the form of the experience and that each experience has its own form (so that for some poets after Wordsworth, any rhyme scheme or any metre is felt to be forced). This is the distinction that Coleridge makes, criticising Pope (in 1817), between form as superimposed and form as proceeding. The sense that every experience is unique and has in poetry its own unique form also gives rise to the thought that form must have a meaning. Whitman and Baudelaire decisively broke the old moulds of form not long after Wordsworth's death. (The first edition of *Leaves of Grass* was published in 1855, as were Baudelaire's first two prose poems; *Le Spleen de Paris* appeared in 1869.) Their work may be said to take Wordsworth's idea that there is 'no essential difference between the language of prose and metrical composition' to its logical conclusion.[5] This new freedom, however, is not complete freedom. Stevens speaks for the poets who come after Wordsworth when he says: 'The essential thing in form is to be free in whatever form is used. A free form does not ensure freedom. As a form, it is just one more form.'[6]

Experience is a function of time. To think of the past as our experience (rather than our wisdom or as something impersonal) evidently demands a recognition that we change. Men have always been surrounded by examples of change. They have watched the seasons change and each other grow old, but the conviction that life is a process and that the self is part of this process seems to come with the development of autobiography, and does not appear in poetry until Wordsworth. To think of perception as an event is to conceive of perception as occurring in time. This means that feeling is understood not as a fixed quantity but as a continuous operation, and memory as the history of the self. 'Moods of My Own Mind' constitutes a historical approach to feeling. The poet's moods are discreet and unique events, and yet form a series. Wordsworth was not content to let the poems stand as separate compositions. His title indicates the radical character of his working assumptions.

The poems are pervaded by a keen sense of time passing. To the butterfly, in the first poem of the section, the poet says:

> Stay near me — do not take thy flight!
> A little longer stay in sight![7]

The mood lasts as long as the butterfly stays in one place, and his feelings are as finely nuanced as the dust on the butterfly's wings. Addressing the gypsies, Wordsworth begins: 'Yet are they here?' He condemns them for not having done anything while he has been away. They have no tasks, he declares. This is not a simple contrast of idleness and work, as all the poet has done is gone for a walk. His has been the labour of perception:

> — Twelve hours, twelve bounteous hours, are gone while I
> Have been a Traveller under open sky,
>   Much witnessing of change and chear,
>   Yet as I left I find them here!

He is compelled not only to specify the exact period he has been gone, but also to repeat it, such is his sense of how much can happen in any finite period of time. Similarly, in the second poem to a butterfly, he states: 'I've watch'd you now a full half hour' and concludes:

> And summer days when we were young,
> Sweet childish days, that were as long
>   As twenty days are now!

Eleven of the thirteen poems concentrate on a particular object and in the other two moods are described by itemising a collection of objects, as in the poem written in March at Brother's Water:

The cock is crowing,
The stream is flowing,
The small birds twitter,
The lake doth glitter,. . .

Feeling is precipitated by the perception of an object and the moment of its apprehension provides the boundary of the mood, as, to a certain extent, does the description of the thing itself. The 'five blue eggs' in the sparrow's nest, like Proust's tea-soaked madeleine and uneven paving stone, summon up the past. 'Dead times revive in thee', Wordsworth says to the butterfly, and calls it the 'Historian of my Infancy.' He listens to the cuckoo:

. . .till I do beget
That golden time again.

A single moment seems to him virtually infinite because it contains the whole of his past.

Moods become objects in Wordsworth's poetry and so does language. The tools of composition invade his thought. His words are objects like the paper upon which he writes them. He imagines them as having mass:

Words, a Poet's words more particularly, ought to be weighed in the balance of feeling and not measured by the space which they occupy upon paper.

His sense of their individuality, their independence, leads to a certain dissatisfaction with their expressiveness:

now every man must know that an attempt is rarely made to com-municate impassioned feelings without something of an accom-panying consciousness of the inadequateness of our powers, or the deficiencies of language.[8]

This is the view that causes Wordsworth constantly to modify his state-ments and to engage in endless revision. He understands that our words are part of what we feel, that their functions in the poet's mind are analogous, if not identical, to that of the five blue eggs in the sparrow's nest. As present sensations participate in every memory, so the experience of language participates in every representation of feeling. 'The interest which the mind attaches to words is,' he writes, 'not only as symbols of the passion, but as *things*, active and efficient, which are of themselves part of the passion.'[9] Thus, every work of literature is in some sense *about* language. After Wordsworth writers become increasingly aware of this and develop the new consciousness illustrated by Hazlitt's comment that Turner's pictures are 'representations not properly of the objects of nature as of the medium through which they were seen.'[10]

The poems of 'Moods of My Own Mind' may appear unremarkable to us because our poetry is founded upon the same assumptions. Their radical originality is demonstrated by the outraged cries of the reviewers of *Poems, in Two Volumes*.[11] Byron in *Monthly Literary Recreations* (July 1807) refers to their 'deformity,' while the *Critical Review* (August 1807) condemns Wordsworth for 'drivelling to the redbreast. . .and to a common pilewort. . .'

> Is it possible for Mr. Wordsworth not to feel that while he is pouring out his nauseous and nauseating sensibilities to weeds and insects, he debases himself to a level with his idiot boy, infinitely below his pretty Celandine and little butterfly?

Jeffrey in *The Edinburgh Review* (October 1807), writing of 'the new poets', says:

> Their peculiarities of diction alone, are enough, perhaps, to render them ridiculous; but the author before us really seems anxious to court this literary martyrdom by a device still more infallible, — we mean, that of connecting his most lofty, tender, or impassioned conceptions, with objects and incidents, which the greater part of his readers will probably persist in thinking low, silly, or uninteresting. . . It is possible enough, we allow, that the sight of a friend's garden-spade, or a sparrow's nest, or a man gathering leeches might really have suggested to such a mind ['of extraordinary sensibility habituated to solitary meditation'] a train of powerful impressions and interesting reflections; but it is certain, that, to most minds, such associations will always appear forced, strained, and unnatural; and that the composition in which it is attempted to exhibit them, will always have the air of parody, or ludicrous and affected singularity.

This opinion was shared by at least one of Wordsworth's friends.

Southey writes to Miss Seward in December 1807:

> It is the vice of Wordsworth's intellect to be always upon the stretch
> and strain — to look at pile-worts and daffodowndillies through
> the same telescope which he applies to the moon and the stars, and
> to find subject for philosophising and fine feeling in every peasant
> and vagabond he meets. Had I been his adviser, a greater part of his
> last volume should have been suppressed. . .

('Moods of My Own Mind' is in the last volume.)

Consciousness changes everything that it touches, including itself.
We are afraid of change because it transports us from the known into
the unknown, and afraid of consciousness because it means having to
confront again all that we are, good and bad. Wordsworth recognises
this when he states that neither chaos nor the bottom of hell breeds
'such fear and awe' as looking into our minds. This is the source of the
apprehension in these reviews of *Poems, in Two Volumes*. Their
premise is expressed, a few years after the poet's death, by the hero of
Notes from Underground (1864):

> I swear, gentlemen, that to be too conscious is an illness — a real
> thorough-going illness. For man's everyday needs, it would have
> been quite enough to have the ordinary human unconsciousness,
> that is, half or a quarter of the amount which falls to the lot of a
> cultivated man of our unhappy nineteenth century. . . I am firmly
> persuaded that a great deal of consciousness, every sort of con-
> sciousness, in fact, is a disease.[12]

To the artist new consciousness is a call for new orders.

*

De Selincourt comments in his 'Preface' (1940) to *The Poetical Works
of William Wordsworth* that 'the classification and order in which
Wordsworth arranged his poems. . .will not stand logical examination,' and Owen, who has discussed the scheme in more detail than
anyone else (1969), states that 'no meaningful interpretation can be
given it as a whole.'[13] This is, I believe, not the case. In spite of his own
opinion of Wordsworth's plan, de Selincourt adopts it for his edition
because 'it has for the student this supreme value, that it was the poet's
own arrangement, and, since he gave it much thought and set some
store by it, it is, in a measure, illuminative of his mind.'[14] The problem
is to show what it illuminates.

Wordsworth's first attempt to order his poems is in *Poems, in Two*

Volumes (1807), the first collection of short poems that he published under his own name. The table of contents divides them into groups, with first an untitled group, and then:

> Poems Composed During a Tour, Chiefly on Foot
> Sonnets
> > Part the First. — Miscellaneous Sonnets
> > Part the Second — Sonnets Dedicated to Liberty
> Poems Written During a Tour in Scotland
> Moods of My Own Mind
> The Blind Highland Boy

The last group, a large one, carries the title of the first poem in the group. Here are the rudiments of all Wordsworth's arrangements of his poems. Altogether, from 1815 to 1850, he supervised seven collected editions of his poetry and in every one he attempted a similar classification. He sustained the desire to order his work for forty-three years. After *Lyrical Ballads*, he never published a collection of short poems without indicating that they were part of some larger whole. Perhaps his fondness for writing sonnets had something to do with his finding them a handy unit for building sequences: the sonnet is to other lyric forms as the brick is to field stone.

Wordsworth turned the idea of an order for his poems over in his mind even when there was no opportunity of putting it into effect. He explains to Coleridge, in a letter of 5 May 1809, how he means to arrange them 'if they are ever republished during my lifetime.' He sets forth eight categories:

(1) 'Poems relating to childhood, and such feelings as rise in the mind in after life in direct contemplation of that state' (a remark which shows how he felt himself to be divided by his memory)

(2) poems that 'relate to the fraternal affections, to friendship and to love and to all those emotions which follow after childhood, in youth and early manhood'

(3) 'Poems relating to natural objects and their influence on the mind either as growing or in an advanced state'

(4) 'Naming of Places'

(5) 'Poems relating to human life'

(6) 'those relating to the social and civic duties'

(7) 'those relating to Maternal feeling, connubial or parental'

(8) 'the class of old age'

The partial order of 1807 is to be superseded by a thoroughgoing order. There is to be order between *and* within groups: 'The principle of the arrangement is that there should be a scale in each class and in the whole. . .' The tours are the only rubrics conceived of in terms of time in *Poems, in Two Volumes*, in 1809 everything is in a rough chronological sequence. The whole is the poet's life from childhood to maturity to old age with each stage of development expressed in terms of the emotions relating to that stage. Each category represents the moods of his own mind. After writing to Coleridge, Wordsworth had to wait six years before he could practise his ideas of order, but his belief that all his works form a single structure is made clear in the 'Preface' to *The Excursion* (1814). For their author, he writes, the autobiographical poem has 'the same kind of relation' to *The Excursion*:

> as the ante-chapel has to the body of a gothic church. Continuing this allusion, he may be permitted to add, that his minor Pieces, which have been long before the Public, when they shall be properly arranged, will be found by the attentive reader to have such connection with the main Work as may give them claim to be likened to the little cells, oratories, and sepulchral recesses, ordinarily included in those edifices.[15]

In the edition of 1815 the poems are grouped as follows:

> Poems Referring to the Period of Childhood
> Juvenile Pieces
> Poems Founded on the Affections
> Poems of the Fancy
> Poems of the Imagination
> Poems of the Imagination Continued
> Poems Proceeding from Sentiment and Reflection
> Miscellaneous Sonnets
> Sonnets Dedicated to Liberty. First Part. Published in 1807
> Sonnets Dedicated to Liberty. Second Part. From the year 1807 to
>   1813
> Poems on the Naming of Places
> Inscriptions
> Poems Referring to the Period of Old Age
> Epitaphs and Elegiac Poems
> Ode

and Wordsworth explains this division at length in his 'Preface.' It is his fullest account of the scheme. The urge to classify is present from the start and he writes in the formalistic, syllogistic style to which he often reverts when he tries in prose to give laws to the imagination. He begins: 'The powers requisite for the production of poetry are. . .' and he lists six: Observation and Description, Sensibility, Reflection, Imagination and Fancy, Invention and Judgement. The next paragraph begins: 'The materials of Poetry, by these powers collected and produced, are cast by means of various moulds, into divers forms,' and he then enumerates six 'moulds' and their related forms. He continues:

> It is deducible from the above, that poems, apparently miscellaneous, may with propriety be arranged either with reference to the powers of mind *predominant* in the production of them; or to the mould in which they are cast; or, lastly, to the subjects to which they relate. From each of these considerations, the following Poems have been divided into classes; which, that the work may more obviously correspond with the course of human life, and for the sake of exhibiting it in the three requisites of a legitimate whole, a beginning, a middle, and an end, have been also arranged, as far as it was possible, according to an order of time, commencing with Childhood, and terminating with Old Age, Death and Immortality. My guiding wish was, that the small pieces of which these volumes consist, thus discriminated, might be regarded under a two-fold view; as composing an entire work within themselves, and as adjuncts to the philosophical Poem, 'The Recluse.' This arrangement has long presented itself habitually to my own mind.[16]

The short poems are only 'apparently miscellaneous,' they 'correspond with the course of human life.' The arrangement is to make that correspondence *more* obvious — and to fulfil Aristotle's requirements that a plot be a whole. Perhaps Wordsworth feels the very individuality of the short poems as divisive. As he wanted the 'Moods of My Own Mind' to stand together, he wants the 'small pieces' assembled. He goes further than in the 'Preface' to *The Excursion* in saying that they are 'an entire work within themselves.' Wordsworth's plot differs from Aristotle's form in that it assumes historical development, it is 'an order of time'. His beginning, middle and end are childhood, maturity and old age, and the effect of Wordsworth's arrangement is to give the whole of his poetic production the form of an autobiography.

One of the most common criticisms of Wordsworth's classification is that it is impossible for anyone else to decide in most cases why a poem is in one group and not another. This criticism does not take account of the inward-looking nature of Wordsworth's order. It is not his purpose that anyone other than the author should be able to determine the position of a poem, and he, in fact, warns the reader that his order is such that poems *can* be moved:

> But, as I wish to guard against the possibility of misleading by this classification, it is proper first to remind the Reader, that certain poems are placed according to the powers of mind, in the Author's conception, predominant in the production of them; *predominant*, which implies the exertion of other faculties in less degree. Where there is more imagination than fancy in a poem, it is placed under the head of imagination, and *vice versâ*. Both the above classes might without impropriety have been enlarged from that consisting of 'Poems founded on the Affections;' as might this latter from those, and from the class 'proceeding from Sentiment and Reflection.' The most striking characteristics of each piece, mutual illustration, variety, and proportion, have governed me throughout.

He specifically says 'that certain poems are placed according to the powers of the mind, *in the Author's conception*, predominant *in the production* of them' (my italics). The poet alone possesses this knowledge. Wordsworth's hope is only that 'for him who reads with reflection, the arrangement will serve as a commentary unostentatiously directing his attention to my purposes, both particular and general.'[17]

The arrangement of the poems in the edition of 1849–1850, the last collected edition that Wordsworth supervised, is more elaborate than that of 1815:

Poems Written in Youth
Poems Referring to Childhood
Poems Founded on the Affections
Poems on the Naming of Places
Poems of the Fancy
Poems of the Imagination
Miscellaneous Sonnets
Memories of a Tour in Scotland, 1803

Memories of a Tour in Scotland, 1814
Poems Dedicated to National Independence and Liberty
Memorials of a Tour on the Continent, 1820
Memorials of a Tour in Italy, 1837
The Egyptian Maid
The River Duddon
Yarrow Revisited, and Other Poems. Composed (two excepted)
    during a Tour in Scotland, and on the English Border, in the
    Autumn of 1831.
The White Doe of Rylstone
Ecclesiastical Sonnets. In Series
Evening Voluntaries
Poems Composed or Suggested During a Tour, in the Summer of
1833
Poems of Sentiment and Reflection
Sonnets Dedicated to Liberty and Order
Sonnets Upon the Punishment of Death: In Series
Miscellaneous Poems
Inscriptions
Selections from Chaucer. Modernised
Poems Referring to the Period of Old Age
Epitaphs and Elegiac Pieces
Ode

The arrangement is asymmetrical. The titles of 'Miscellaneous Sonnets' and 'Miscellaneous Poems' indicate that they were difficult to fit in, and 'Selections from Chaucer Modernised' is another grouping that does not appear to have an obvious place in Wordsworth's plan. The part played by the exigencies of printing is not known and it is not possible to explain in every case the poet's decision; nevertheless, the overall logic of the scheme is clear. There are two principal ideas, one historical, the other psychological. The first is the 'order of time,' of 'the course of human life' from childhood to old age, the underlying form of all Wordsworth's arrangements of his poetry from 1815 to 1850. The second is a conception of the mind in terms of its various powers and sentiments. The substance of each of these orders when expressed in the first person is autobiography.

These two ideas can be said to be complementary, but they are also opposites in that the first sees man as developing and the second sees the mind as more or less static. Only once do the static notions appear to disturb the 'order of time': the Italian tour of 1837 is the one item that is not in chronological order. Since the tour could have been fitted in either before or after 'Miscellaneous Poems,' perhaps this is because Wordsworth believed that all the European poems were best together. Certainly his journeys appear to have had for him an independent value. They are the only dated items on the list. It is almost as if Wordsworth had to measure with special care any movement off his home ground.

The last word is of permanence. In the 'Preface' of 1815 Wordsworth specified that his chronological sequence terminated 'with Old Age, Death and Immortality.' Death is not named in any of these rubrics (except as a punishment), but the poems of old age are followed by those of the ceremonies of death: 'Epitaphs and Elegiac Pieces.' The *Ode, Intimations of Immortality from Recollections of Early Childhood* is placed last, as it was in every collected edition from 1807. This is the mind's triumph over time.

Wordsworth's image of the mind as composed of fixed powers appears an act of will, a wish for stillness and peace. The classification of his poems is another act of will, and to the same end: to bring his developing feelings and changing self under control. He seeks to put his mind in order by arranging the productions of his mind. It is, along with the poems themselves, all part of his effort to form moments of feeling into a continuum of being. The classification is a map of the mind on which he has plotted the journey of his life.

*

Wordsworth's conception of all his creations as a single work and of that work corresponding to his own life is not unique. Other authors have arranged individual works so as to form a whole comprehending in different ways their own real or imaginary history. They all share the same notion of experience as Wordsworth and their work, like his, involves a reconstruction of the past. Although, to the best of my knowledge, no such arrangements exist earlier than the 1815 edition of Wordsworth's poems, there is no evidence that any of the subsequent plans derive from his classification of his poetry. Rather these arrangements are indications of a desire for new order growing out of a greater awareness of the world and the self. They are the enabling forms of an increased consciousness, sketches of new interpretations.

Scott (1771 – 1832) published all his novels as a set — the Waverley Novels — between 1829 and 1832. He wrote a preface and notes for each one and referred to the edition in the singular as his *Magnum Opus*.[18] This work was for Scott the start of a new life. He named not only all his subsequent novels but also himself after his first hero: the

Author of *Waverley* was his new identity. The order of the novels in the 1829 – 1832 edition is (with one exception) the order of their composition and the prefaces convert this chronological series into a history of Scott's imagination. He is aware that presenting his works in this way is an act of self-revelation. He begins the 'General Preface':

> Having undertaken to give an Introductory Account of the compositions which are here offered to the public with Notes and Illustrations, the Author, under whose name they are now for the first time collected, feels that he has the delicate task of speaking more of himself and his personal concern than may perhaps be either graceful or prudent.[19]

He states in the 'Advertisement' which precedes the 'General Preface' that he intends to describe the 'circumstances attending the first publication of the Novels and Tales' and to publish 'the various legends, family traditions, or obscure historical facts which have formed the groundwork of these Novels.'[20] The prefaces that he wrote as a result constitute a radically new departure in the history of the European novel. The emphasis is on his sources, the raw materials of his compositions and seeking to explain the genesis of each work he becomes, like Wordsworth, the historian of his own genius.

Scott's 'theory,' as he calls it, was to derive from his personal past a comprehensive picture of Scotland:

> I thought. . .that much of what I wanted in talent might be made up by the intimate acquaintance with the subject which I could lay claim to possess, as having travelled through most parts of Scotland, both Highland and Lowland; having been familiar with the elder, as well as more modern race; and having from my infancy free and unrestrained communication with all ranks of my countrymen, from the Scottish peer to the Scottish ploughman.[21]

He was very concerned to take the measure of the whole range of Scottish life: highland and lowland, old and new, peer and ploughman, and yet knew that the scheme rested on his 'intimate acquaintance,' that it was a structure made of his experience. Moreover, Scott understood that this experience included a world of events of which he was unaware. To Lady Abercorn, he compares himself to the spider who 'must spend many days of inactivity till he has assembled within his person the materials necessary to weave' a web and, describing the reading that he did from an Edinburgh circulating library during the long illness of his boyhood, he writes in the 'General Preface:'

> I believe I read almost all the romances, old plays, and epic poetry
> in that formidable collection, and no doubt was unconsciously
> amassing materials for the task in which it has been my lot to be so
> much employed.[22]

This is a very early use (1829) of *unconscious* by an artist about his own
creative processes. Scott is aware that the preface and notes to the
Waverley Novels offer a glimpse of this inner world:

> It remains to be tried whether the public (like a child to whom a
> watch is shown) will, after having been satiated with looking at the
> outside, acquire some new interest in the object when it is opened,
> and the internal machinery displayed to them.[23]

Obviously he wrote them regardless of the public's response, because
he himself wanted to look at the workings of his own mind and to
demonstrate that all the novels together form a single time-machine.

La Comédie humaine is the most thoroughgoing order devised by
any of Wordsworth's contemporaries for their own works. Balzac had
the idea of a vast work — and a rage for order — at least as early as
1828.[24] He sets out his plan in detail in the Catalogue of 1845. This is
the most complete map of *La Comédie humaine*. Balzac enumerates
the 137 works that he envisages as making up the whole (and of this
total he completed 93, including five that were added after 1845). He
divides them into three parts, of which the first is subdivided into six
sections (the numbers in parentheses are the number of works projected for each part):

    I Études de moeurs (105)
    1) Scènes de la vie privée
    2) Scènes de la vie de province
    3) Scènes de la vie parisienne
    4) Scènes de la vie politique
    5) Scènes de la vie militaire
    6) Scènes de la vie de compagne
    II Études philosophiques (27)
    III Études analytiques (5)[25]

The order has a meaning that Balzac interprets in four major texts:

the letter to Madame Hanska (20 October 1834); two introductions (1835), one to the 'Études de moeurs au XIXᵉ siecle,' the other to the 'Études philosophiques,' signed by his friend, Felix Davin, but essentially the work of Balzac; and the 'Avant-propos' to *La Comédie humaine* that he wrote in 1842.

Balzac's order is formed, like Wordsworth's, by combining an idea of human development and an abstract, theoretic image of the mind. He states that each of the six sections of the 'Études de moeurs' represents a stage of development: 'Each one of them has its meaning, its significance, and formulates an epoch of the human life.'[26] Sections one to three are 'pictures of the individual life,' sections four to six are pictures of men in the mass, 'the social machine.' The first three sections are in chronological order and show us the individual as 'young, mature and old,' although there is nothing in the section titles to suggest this and the reader would probably not be able to guess it from the novels.[27]

Again, as with Wordsworth, there is an emphasis on feeling — *La Comédie humaine* is a 'history of the human heart' — and each phase of development is associated with a particular set of feelings.[28] The 'Scènes de la vie privée' concentrate on 'the last developments of a puberty that is ending, and the first calculations of a virility that is beginning. . .principally emotions, unconsidered sensations. . .' while the 'Scènes de la vie de province' are intended to represent that phase of life between twenty and thirty 'in which passions, calculations and ideas take the place of sensations, of unconsidered movements, of images accepted as realities.' The stories of the third section had to be located in Paris, because they treat 'the age that reaches decrepitude. A capital was the only setting possible for scenes of a climacteric epoch in which the infirmities do not afflict the heart of man any less than the body.' The 'Scènes de la vie militaire' show man at his most violent. The 'Scènes de la vie de compagne' are intended as a contrast, bringing 'rest after movement, landscapes after interriors' (Blazac sees the military scenes as set in garrison towns) and 'scars after wounds.'

That last part of the work will be like the evening after a well-filled day, the evening of a hot day, the evening with its solemn tints, its brown reflections, its coloured clouds. . . Everywhere the white hairs of experienced old age are mingled with the blond curls of childhood.[29]

These elegiac tones suggest that this section corresponds to

Wordsworth's final sections on old age and death.

The clearest and most concise statement of the relation of the three major parts of *La Comédie humaine* is in Balzac's letter to Madame Hanska (26.10.1834):

> The *Études de moeurs* will represent all the social effects without any situation in life, any physiognomy, any male or female character, any way of life, any profession, any social zone, any French region, or anything whatever of childhood, old age, maturity, politics, justice or war, having been forgotten.
>
> That said, the history of the human heart traced item by item, social history covered in all its aspects, these are the base. . .
>
> Then, the second layer is the *Études philosophiques*, for after the *effects* will come the *causes*. I will have painted for you in the *É[tudes] de moeurs* the feelings and their play, life and its pace. In the *É[tudes] philosoph[iques]* I will say why the feelings, wherefore life; what is the part, what are the conditions beyond which neither society nor man can exist; and after having run through (society) in order to describe it, I will run through it in order to judge it. . . Thus, everywhere I will have given life — to the type, in individualising it, to the individual, in typifying it. I will have given thought to the fragment, I will have given to thought the life of the individual.
>
> Next. . .will come the *Études analytiques*. . .for after the *effects* and the *causes*, one ought to look for the *principles*. The *manners* are the *spectacle*, the causes are the *flats and machinery*. The *principles* are the *author*. . .[30]

The work, he tells Madame Hanska, will be the demonstration of a whole system, an analysis of the mind and a consideration of the nature of thought. Like Wordsworth, Balzac saw himself as an explorer:

> We have attained the *era of intelligence*. The material kings, brutal force, are disappearing. There are intellectual worlds and one may encounter in them Pizarroes, Corteses and Columbuses. There will be kings in the universal kingdoms of thought.[31]

Balzac compares *La Comédie humaine* to an immense, Gothic building and, as with Wordsworth, this metaphor is the one used to explain how the smaller works are integral parts of the larger whole:

But are not these so-called small things exactly like the squared stones, the scattered capitals, the metopes half-covered with flowers and dragons, that, seen in the yard, between the workman's saw and chisel, seem insignificant and small, and that the architect, in his design, has intended to ornament some rich entablature, to make arches, to run the length of the great ogival transepts of his cathedral, his château, his chapel and his country house?[32]

The individual is the basic unit for both writers — as it is for every major novelist and poet after Wordsworth. Balzac states that his novels will contain: 'in a word all the *individualities*.'[33] *La Comédie humaine* is to be a kind of census. He suggests in the 'Avant-Propos' that it will 'compete with the État-Civil,' the official register of births, adoptions, legitimisations, marriages, divorces and deaths, and he compares his work to Buffon's description of animal species.[34] Again the desire to classify is a concomitant of an interest in the smallest details. Full life histories mean for Balzac, as they do for Wordsworth, concentrating on the mundane facts of everyday life:

In grasping the meaning of this composition, one will recognise that I accord to constant, everyday facts, secret or obvious, to the acts of the individual life, to their causes and to their principles as much importance as, until now, historians have attached to the events in the public life of nations.[35]

The emphasis on the private instead of the public life is part of the growing interest in the inner world of consciousness and a new conception of society results from a new understanding of the individual. As Balzac puts it: 'Before arriving at a society composed of men, the author has had to apply himself to de-composing man, who is, so to speak, its fundamental *unit*.'[36] This is a society of individuals held together by the complex bonds of feeling that have developed out of a new self-awareness and its consequent world-awareness.

For Balzac, like Wordsworth, historicity of setting alone does not provide sufficient order for his experiences. He sees all his creations as an interpretation of the meaning of his own character. The Waverley Novels are his example, but they are not sufficiently interconnected:

Although great, the Scotch bard has only exposed a certain number of skilfully sculptured stones where one can see admirable figures, where the genius of each epoch comes to life again, and of whom nearly all are sublime, but where is the monument? if one encounters in his work the seductive effects of a marvelous analysis, a synthesis is lacking. His work resembles the museum in the rue des Petits-Augustins where each object, magnificent in itself, adheres to nothing, forms no part of any edifice. Genius is only complete when it combines the faculty of creation with the power of co-ordinating its creations.[37]

Epochs (and moments) demand to be synthesised as a whole. His metaphors of sculptured stones and of the museum in the rue des Petits-Augustins show him treating individual lives as objects, as artifacts, He repeats his criticism of Scott in the 'Avant-propos':

But having less imagined a system than having found his manner in the fire of work or by the logic of this work, he had not dreamed of linking his compositions one to another so as to co-ordinate a complete history, of which each chapter would have been a novel and each novel an epoch. Perceiving this absence of connection, which, nevertheless, does not make the Scotchman less great, I envisaged both the system favourable to the execution of my work and the possibility of executing it.[38]

It is apropos of Scott that Balzac declares to Davin that to be a great writer: 'It is not enough to be a man, it is necessary to be a system.'[39]

The desire for order is one way of denoting the poet's emotions in the majority of Wordsworth's best poems. He stands on the bank of the Wye or on the summit of Snowdon and looks — outward and inward — until he believes that he apprehends the form of the world, which he is partially aware is the form of his own mind. He enumerates what he perceives so as to abstract some encompassing form from his perception. This abstraction is an interpretation, a creation of meaning. His poems represent not a single definition of the experience, but a series of definitions or transformations. 'It is not enough to be a man' is like the statement of his motive, his inner need. Both Wordsworth and Balzac, however, like all poets and novelists, stop short of attempting to create complete and totally abstract systems. Wordsworth was unable to write a philosophical poem. Balzac was only able to complete two of the 'Études analytiques,' and, during the last eleven years of his life, he composed only one of the 'Études philosophiques' *and* 'Études analytiques,' while the 'Études de moeurs' furnished subjects for over thirty novels. Their theory-making is subordinated to metaphor-making. They abstract to make a language of experience.

European philosophy since Descartes, and particularly since Hegel, has been increasingly a matter of style. From about 1903 the main effort by practitioners of what Russell calls 'the philosophy of logical analysis' has been to make philosophy as impersonal as possible.[40] They have attempted to devise a philosophical language that is like mathematics and in the process have dismissed the work of most of their predecessors as so much *literature*. The desire to abstract, with Wordsworth as with them, seems to be a need to make things that are different fit together, and to cope with threatening repressed thoughts. The greater the perception of the uniqueness of each object, the greater the abstraction needed to combine objects. Abstraction removes a threatening object sufficiently from its fearful context to enable us to think about it. Consequently, abstraction and theory-making are among the primary processes of sublimation. English poetry from Crashaw to Blake is a poetry dominated by philosophic abstractions in which abstract words are commonly used in impersonal contexts. There is no English poet who uses abstract words to greater effect than Wordsworth, but he employs this newly purified vocabulary in order to describe the most private feelings in the most personal contexts.

The system is the man: this is certainly what we find when we examine the various classifications of their work by Wordsworth, Scott, Balzac and others. These orders mark the emergence in their makers's minds of their awareness that their works define them. The thought is clearly formulated by Valéry: 'there is no theory that is not the fragment, carefully prepared, of some autobiography.'[41] The idea that each man's life can be expressed as the history of his experience appears in each of these classifications like a ghost. The classifications of Wordsworth, Balzac, Whitman and Baudelaire (see below) are informed (in varying degrees) by a dynamic notion of human development and a more or less set image of the human mind. Each of these theories can be stated in terms of the other — and this is precisely how Wordsworth exploits their possibilities in his poetry. The stages of human development are shown to have their particular mind, or states of mind, and the powers of the mind, such as imagination, and the mind as a whole, are shown as changing, growing. Wordsworth wanted to be Archimedes. 'Who,' he asks, 'has not felt the same aspirations as regards the world of his own mind?' Each of these ideas provided him with a point 'whereon he could rest his machine' so as to work on the other. The mind when it is apprehended as a whole then can become a metaphor. The consciousness of a thing enables that thing to be used as a sign, so the day's events become the night's dreams, so literature creates language.

Balzac's 'It is not enough to be a man, it is necessary to be a system' points the way to metaphysics, but it is remarkable that the acceptance of the individual as the unit of experience has been accompanied by a loss of faith in metaphysics and religion, as if the strengthening of the notions of the self created the capacity to be tentative about the world. The need of the individual to feel part of some larger unity is increasingly satisfied by a feeling of belonging *in* the world and *to* a society of individuals. Balzac's aphorism can be understood as a re-statement of Montaigne's 'every man carries in himself the entire form of the human condition.'

Of the great poets contemporary with Wordsworth it is Whitman (1819 – 1892), acutely self-conscious, and probably the most radical innovator, whose arrangement of his poems most resembles Wordsworth's. He published all his poetry as a single book, *Leaves of Grass*, that he continuously revised and re-arranged in an effort to establish an inner order among the poems. The first edition appears in 1855, the last edition that he saw through the press was published in 1891 – 1892. A note made in 1857 suggests that Whitman was at that time projecting 365 poems, one for every day of the year. Soon he began arranging the poems in what he called 'clusters'.[42] The edition of 1891 – 1892 put the clusters in the following order (the asterisks indicate poems not included in the clusters):

Inscriptions
*
Children of Adam
Calamus
*
Birds of Passage
*
Sea-Drift
By the Roadside
Drum-Taps
Memories of President Lincoln
*
Autumn Rivulets
*

Whispers of Heavenly Death
*
From Noon to Starry Night
Songs of Parting
Sands at Seventy
Good-Bye My Fancy
[Old Age Echoes]

This, like Wordsworth's plan, is essentially a chronological order and clearly autobiographical. The 'Inscriptions' are mostly very short, the equivalent of a group of epigraphs, a proem. Next comes *Starting from Paumanok* that announces Whitman's desire to begin at the beginning:

Starting from fish-shape Paumanok where I was born. . .[43]

This is followed by *Song of Myself*, his attempt to comprehend himself as a whole, and two clusters on his sexuality. The juxaposition marks Whitman's intuition of the relation of sexuality to personality. For him as for Wordsworth, there are some topics that interrupt the unfolding of the chronological order. He is neither so interested in childhood as Wordsworth nor as concerned with his own development; the self he discovers is fully grown, but both poets are keenly aware of the self as existing in time. They seem to long for immortality as a way of never losing their memory and to be defining moments in order to counter dissolution. Even when he appears to surrender to the tide, Whitman resists ebbing 'with the Ocean of Life.' Several clusters of poems of drift are followed by those on the American Civil War. From here on the poet knows that he is no longer drifting. His course is set on leaving the world. His subjects are: autumn, death, night, parting, being seventy and goodbye.

Although 'Old Age Echoes' is technically not part of *Leaves of Grass*, it exists in order to preserve that work's integrity. The category was devised by Whitman for all the poems that he wrote after having arranged *Leaves of Grass* for the last time. Such poems would, in the nature of things, be echoes of former sounds, 'reverberant, an aftermath.' He instructed his executor:

I place upon you the injunction that whatever may be added to the 'Leaves' shall be supplementary, avowed as such, leaving the book complete as I left it, consecutive to the point I left off, marking always an unmistakable, deep down, unobliteratable division line. In the long run the world will do as it pleases with the book. I am determined to have the world know what I was pleased to do.[44]

Like Wordsworth, Whitman hoped that his poems would be read in his order, because that order was his image of himself. As he declares in *So Long*:

Camerado, this is no book,
Who touches this touches a man. . .[45]

Baudelaire (1821 – 1867), like Whitman, is a poet of a single book. He appears to have found in *Les Fleurs du mal*, as Whitman did in *Leaves of Grass*, a form for his entire life. He declares the unity of his work in the notes he prepared for his lawyer in 1857: 'The book ought to be judged *as a whole* and then there issues from it a terrible morality,' and in the letter he sent to Alfred de Vigny (about 16.12.1861), along with a copy of the second edition:

The only praise that I solicit for this book is that one recognises that it is not a simple album and that it has a beginning and an end. All the new poems were composed so as to be adapted to the particular framework that I had chosen.[46]

The table of contents is simple: Spleen et idéal; Tableaux parisiens; Le Vin; Fleurs du mal; Révolte; La Mort. Although not chronological or autobiographical in any obvious way (except that the poems on death come at the end), the plan shows Baudelaire choosing categories that order his strongest emotions. They represent the major moods of his mind.

Hugo's inscription on Balzac's tomb in Père-Lachaise reads: 'All his books form only a single book. . .'[47] Mallarmé takes the idea to one extreme: 'everything in the world exists to end in a book;' Crane to another:

It is as though the poem gave the reader as he left it a single, new *word*, never before spoken and impossible to actually enunciate, but self-evident as an active principle in the reader's consciousness henceforward.[48]

Extremes meet. The power of noticing the smallest details and discriminating the finest nuances of feeling are, in Wordsworth, and in the poets who succeed him, related to a capacity for encompassing thought. The awareness of the infinitely large and infinitely small translates itself into a sense of worlds within worlds and makes possible a new type of very short lyric, and a new density of style in poems of all types.

Wordsworth's classification of his poems rests on the same assumptions as the poetry itself. The plan is a way of ordering every poem as the record of a moment of his development. His poetical works are presented as the ongoing inventory of his mind. The classification is not merely an eccentricity of Wordsworth's but a form adopted by a number of the greatest European writers who share many, if not all, of the assumptions of his idea of order. They are the inventors of a self that is continuously changing, historians of identity, psychologists in search of lost time.

7
After Wordsworth

Wordsworth told Arnold 'that, for he knew not how many years, his poetry had never brought him in enough to buy his shoestrings.'[1] Although he tended to exaggerate the failure of his works to sell, after *Lyrical Ballads* he had to wait nearly twenty years, until the publication of *Peter Bell* in 1819, for anything approximating a comparable success, and only with the 1827 edition of his *Poetical Works* did he start to see steady and substantial sales of his poetry; even then he never came close to the sales of popular poets such as Scott and Byron.[2]

During the twenty-odd years that Wordsworth laboured for recognition, he had to bear not the indifference, but the 'unremitting hostility' — the phrase is his — of most, if not all, the established literary journals.[3] He was constantly attacked, notably by Jeffrey in the *Edinburgh Review*, who was 'more influential than any other reviewer, often carrying the others with him,' and these attacks, especially those on *Poems, in Two Volumes* (1807), appear to have discouraged the reading public from buying Wordsworth's books.[4] De Quincey is more or less correct when he says that 'up to 1820, the name of Wordsworth was trampled underfoot; from 1820 to 1830 it was militant; from 1830 to 1835 it has been triumphant.' Writing in 1835, he declares: 'At this day. . .no journal can be taken up which does not habitually speak of Mr Wordsworth as of *a* great poet if not *the* great poet of the age.'[5] This was the fame that brought the public honours: D.C.L., Durham (1838); D.C.L., Oxford (1839); a Civil List pension (1842) and the Poet Laureateship (1843). Arnold believed that the high point of Wordsworth's popularity was between 1830 and 1840, and that after 1842 he gradually lost readers to Tennyson. 'The diminution has continued,' he writes in 1879.[6] After this period of relative neglect, Wordsworth's work was more widely read, in part as a result of Arnold's essay and his selection of Wordsworth's poems which has gone through forty-seven editions since 1879.[7]

These fluctuations made very little difference to the effect of Wordsworth's work upon his fellow craftsmen. There was, at an early date, a remarkable consensus among other English writers (and not only poets) that Wordsworth was to be ranked with the very greatest authors. His poetry engaged their attention from the beginning. For most of them it was a life-long interest and their early enthusiasm survives in their later judgements. The young Coleridge (age 24) hailed Wordsworth as 'the best poet of the age' in 1796.[8] 'Since Milton,' he writes to Poole (21.3.1800), 'no man has *manifested* himself equal to him.' His comparisons in *Biographia Literaria* show his view of the magnitude of Wordsworth's achievement: '[Wordsworth's] diction, next to that of Shakespeare and Milton, appears to me of all others the most *individualized* and characteristic. . .in imaginative power, he stands nearest of all modern writers to Shakespeare and Milton.'[9] When in 1798 the young Hazlitt (age 20) heard Coleridge read some of Wordsworth's poems intended for *Lyrical Ballads*, he says that 'the sense of a new style and a new spirit in poetry came over me. It had to me something of the effect that arises from the turning up of the fresh soil. . .'[10] The young De Quincey (age 21) was so overwhelmed by Wordsworth's poetry that twice in 1806 he journeyed from Oxford to Church Coniston (once to within sight of Dove Cottage) in order to meet the poet, although on both occasions he lacked the courage to present himself to Wordsworth.[11] He, too recognised that what Wordsworth was doing was new and comments in his essay 'On Wordsworth's Poetry' (1845):

> It is astonishing how large a harvest of new truths would be reaped simply through the accident of a man's feeling, or being made to feel, more *deeply* than other men. He sees the same objects, neither more nor fewer, but he sees them engraved in lines far stronger and more determinate: and the difference in strength makes the whole difference between consciousness and subconsciousness.[12]

He believes that 'Meditative poetry is perhaps that province of literature which will ultimately maintain most power amongst the generations which are coming' and that in this 'there is little competition to be apprehended by Wordsworth from anything that has appeared since the death of Shakespere.'[13]

Every major English poet after Wordsworth has had to come to terms, one way or another, with his poetry, and its new mode of interpreting reality. Byron, Shelley, Keats, Tennyson, Browning, Hardy, Hopkins, Yeats and Stevens so absorbed his work into the substance of their verse, and thus into the forms of English poetry and into the language, that one can say that it was (and is) impossible for any English writer not to encounter Wordsworth, at secondhand if not at firsthand.[14] Wordsworth's poetic revolution is part of a great change in sensibility. John Stuart Mill and George Eliot are representative witnesses who testify to his share in that change. Mill explains that Wordsworth's poetry taught him how to feel:

> What made Wordsworth's poems a medicine for my state of mind, was that they expressed, not mere outward beauty, but states of feeling. . . They seemed to be the very culture of the feelings, which I was in quest of. In them I seemed to draw from a source of inward joy, of sympathetic and imaginative pleasure, which could be shared in by all human beings,. . . . I needed to be made to feel that there was real, permanent happiness in tranquil contemplation. Wordsworth taught me this, not only without turning away from, but with a greatly increased interest in, the common feelings and common destiny of human beings. And the delight which these poems gave me, proved that with culture of this sort, there was nothing to dread from the most confirmed habit of analysis.[15]

and George Eliot writes, in the midst of reading Wordsworth's collected poems, to Maria Lewis (22.11.1839): 'I never before met with so many of my own feelings expressed just as I could < wish > like them.'[16]

Wordsworth never seems to have found many readers on the continent of Europe. Galignani's foreman told him that they had printed in Paris 3,000 copies of their 1828 edition, but Wordsworth believed, probably correctly, that most of them were sold to his countrymen.[17] Certainly among the French, whose poets contributed so much to the making of modern poetry, the few writers who were interested in English literature were not very interested in Wordsworth. Chateaubriand (who lived in England from 1792 to 1800), writing in 1822, mentions him only in passing. He sees Beattie as the founder of what he calls the 'new poetry,' and for him Byron is 'the greatest poet that England has had since Milton.'[18] Sainte-Beuve recognises Wordsworth as the chief of 'les lakistes,' but discusses his work only briefly in one of his *Causeries du lundi* (25.10.1825).[19] Taine, in his *Histoire de la littérature anglaise* (first published in 1864), also calls Byron the greatest English author of 'the modern age.' The few pages that he devotes to Wordsworth contain some shrewd remarks and a measure of praise, but are on the whole unsympathetic and mocking.[20]

Arnold observes in 1879: 'On the Continent he is almost unknown,' and this state of affairs has continued to the present.[21] That the effect of Wordsworth's poetry on European literatures other than English has been mostly indirect makes it difficult to trace and generally problematic, but not negligible, especially when we consider how much of Wordsworth there is in Scott and Byron whose work was known and imitated from one end of Europe to the other.[22]

The great change in sensibility of which Wordsworth was a part was European. Auerbach sees it as growing out of the French Revolution — 'the first of the great movements of modern times in which large masses of men consciously took part' — and as the most profound change in European culture after the Reformation. The 'modern consciousness of reality,' in his view, is a response to the disorder spread throughout Europe with new speed by the Revolution and the many consequent alterations in everyday life. The improvements in transportation, communication and elementary education meant that 'everyone was reached by the same ideas and events far more quickly, more consciously, more uniformly.'

> For Europe there began that process of temporal concentration, both of historical events themselves and of everyone's knowledge of them, which has since made tremendous progress and which not only permits us to prophesy a unification of human life throughout the world but has in a certain sense already achieved it. Such a development abrogates or renders powerless the entire social structure of orders and categories previously held valid; the tempo of the changes demands a perpetual and extremely difficult effort toward inner adaptation and produces intense concomitant crises. He who would account to himself for his real life and his place in human society is obliged to do so upon a far wider practical foundation and in a far larger context than before, and to be continually conscious that the social base upon which he lives is not constant for a moment but is perpetually changing through convulsions of the most various kinds.[23]

Wordsworth is the first great poet of 'inner adaptation.' This demands a new language. 'The matter,' he tells Emerson, 'always comes out of the manner,'[24] He wants to strip away everything artificial in favour of 'a more naked and single style.' The 'Preface' (1800) to *Lyrical Ballads* shows him rejecting the poetic language that he had inherited: 'a large portion of phrases and figures of speech which from father to son have long been regarded as the common inheritance of Poets'[25] and discloses the new standards to which he works. The 'Preface' is not a description of Wordsworth's style, but of his stylistic ideals. He has attempted in *Lyrical Ballads* 'to bring my language near to the language of men,' and he recognises that any success can only be an approximation. He has tried 'to imitate and, as far as is possible, to adopt the very language of men.'[26] Eliot's comment (in a generally disapproving essay on Wordsworth) that here he is 'saying what no serious critic could disapprove' indicates how Wordsworth's goals have remained those of the poets who have followed him.[27]

Wordsworth makes honesty a principle of style:

> I do not know how without being culpably particular I can give my Reader a more exact notion of the style in which I wished these poems to be written than by informing him that I have at all times endeavoured to look steadily at my subject, consequently I hope it will be found that there is in these Poems little falsehood of description. . .[28]

The endeavour to look steadily at what and how he feels results in some extremely complex poetry and it is to this end Wordsworth studies 'low and rustic life':

> because in that situation the essential passions of the heart find a better soil in which they can attain their maturity,. . .our elementary feelings exist in a state of greater simplicity and consequently may be more accurately contemplated and. . .the passions of men are incorporated with the beautiful and permanent forms of nature.[29]

It is as if low life is a metaphor for the life of the unconscious and rustic life for our earliest and most primitive emotions.

Wordsworth is not the only great writer of this time who believed that nakedness and simplicity were necessary for any accurate description of feeling and who found the directness that he was looking for in prose. Stendhal criticises poetic diction for the same reasons:

> Poetry, with its obligatory comparisons, its mythologies in which the poet does not believe, its dignity of style *à la Louis XIV*, and all the apparatus of its ornaments called *poetic*, is well below prose as soon as it is a matter of giving a clear and precise idea of the movements of the heart; now, in this, one only moves by clarity.[30]

Wordsworth declares 'that some of the most interesting parts of the best poems will be found to be strictly the language of prose when prose is well written' and asserts 'that there neither is nor can be any essential difference' between the language of prose and poetry.[31] These comments mark the beginnings of what can be called, in Pound's phrase, 'the prose tradition in verse,' which, in his example, means trying to say, 'Send me the kind of Rembrandt I like' in terms of 'Send me four pounds of ten-penny nails.'[32] Among his contemporaries only Wordsworth undertakes to represent with such clarity anything as complex as the growth of a poet's mind. Arnold states that Wordsworth's 'expression may often be called bald. . ., but it is bald as the bare mountain tops are bald, with a baldness which is full of grandeur.' He recognises that 'the profound sincereness with which Wordsworth feels his subject' is a source of his 'most plain, first-hand, almost austere naturalness.'[33]

Whitman, too, proclaims the simplicity of honesty. He writes in the 'Preface' to the first edition of *Leaves of Grass* (1855):

Nothing is better than simplicity. . . .nothing can make up for excess or the lack of definiteness. . .I will not have in my writing any elegance or effect or originality to hang in the way between me and the rest like curtains. I will have nothing hang in the way, not the richest curtains. What I tell I tell for precisely what it is.[34]

As in the case of Wordsworth, this credo causes him to write some very complex (and difficult) poems. Whitman in rejecting metre and regular forms may be said to come even closer to prose in his poetry than Wordsworth. Free verse originates in the desire for greater precision in the representation of feeling and its irregularity suggests a lack of order in the world, a perception of our minds and lives as chaotic. Wordsworth's view of the uniqueness of every experience, every moment, strengthens the desire for irregular forms. Free verse is a logical consequence of applying the prose standard to poetry, of feeling that there is 'no essential difference between the language of prose and metrical composition.' This is the same logic that leads to the prose poem. The first book of prose poems, Aloysius Bertrand's *Gaspard de la nuit*, was published (posthumously) in Wordsworth's lifetime, in 1842, although it is Baudelaire who, with his *Le Spleen de Paris* (published 1855 – 1869), establishes the prose poem as a form.[35] Since 1869 some of the best poems of virtually every great French poet: Baudelaire, Rimbaud, Mallarmé, Valéry, have been in this form — as is all of Ponge's best work, and from about the same time an ever-increasing amount of the best European poetry has been free verse.

The main advocate and theoretician of free verse in English is Pound and his essay 'The Serious Artist' (1913), which he describes as an attempt 'to re-write Sidney's *Defense of Poesy*,' is rather a re-statement of the standards of the 'Preface' to *Lyrical Ballads*.[36] Good art, says Pound, is 'the art that is most precise.' 'The arts give us our data of psychology, of man as to his interiors. . .'[37] He employs the passage from Stendhal cited above and urges poets to work for the clarity of the best prose. Pound does not acknowledge any debt to Wordsworth, but then he appears wilfully to bypass many great poets and his praise of minor poets sometimes seems as much an act of defiance as of love. He glosses over Ronsard, Baudelaire and Mallarmé. He ignores Spenser, speaks of 'the donkey-eared Milton' and prefers Crabbe to Wordsworth.[38] Like Eliot, he appears ill at ease with the two great predecessors to whom he owes so much: Wordsworth and Whitman. They are too close for comfort. Pound makes his peace with Whitman in his poem 'A Pact,' but is never able to accord the same recognition to Wordsworth, although he intermittently feels the need to come to terms with him. He does recommend (1918): 'Read as much of Wordsworth as does not seem too unutterably dull,' and concedes (1934) that 'Wordsworth got rid of a lot of trimmings.'[39]

'The Serious Artist' was written at the time when Yeats asked Pound to go through his poems and point out the abstractions, and when Hueffer convinced Pound 'that Wordsworth was so intent on the ordinary or plain word that he never thought of hunting for *le mot juste*.'[40] Pound's dislike of abstractions, his difficulty in believing that an abstract word could be *le mot juste* and his impatience with involved sentences helped to prevent his appreciation of Wordsworth. He knew that 'You can be wholly precise in representing a vagueness;' he did not see that this is what Wordsworth is doing.[41]

Eliot tersely summarises Pound's views on 'the prose tradition in verse' in the dictum that poetry should be at least as well written as prose, but, like Wordsworth, he does not feel that abstractions are dishonest. There is no major English poet after Wordsworth who uses abstract words more effectively than Eliot, and the poems in which he employs the greatest number most successfully, *Four Quartets*, are an autobiography. The structure that generates the poems is that of moment and interpretation, the basic structure of most of Wordsworth's poetry. Eliot has his own 'spots of time':

> For most of us, there is only the unattended
> Moment, the moment in and out of time,
> The distraction fit, lost in a shaft of sunlight,
> The wild thyme unseen, or the winter lightning
> Or the waterfall, or music heard so deeply
> That it is not heard at all, but you are the music
> While the music lasts. These are only hints and guesses,
> Hints followed by guesses; and the rest
> Is prayer, observance, discipline, thought and action.
> The hint half guessed, the gift half understood, is Incarnation.
> Here the impossible union
> Of spheres of existence is actual,
> Here the past and future
> Are conquered, and reconciled,
> Where action were otherwise movement
> Of that which is only moved
> And has in it no source of movement —
> Driven by daemonic, chthonic
> Powers.[42]

The complex sentences, deliberately prolonged, the enjambment, the constant re-statement of the thought, the stylistic change with the movement from moment to interpretation, the musing tone and the many abstract words — they are all deployed, as in Wordsworth, to describe unusually significant moments at the edge of perception in which the poet is alone and withdrawn. These moments, moreover, are construed as intimations of another world and given a moral and religious value, even though the experience is recognised as ineffable, and the earth, with its wild thyme, winter lightning and chthonic powers, seems most powerful. Here there is even a waterfall and haunting, lingering music.

Every new poetry is a new rigour. Wordsworth's rejection of the diction of previous poets freed him from the obligation of including anything because it was *poetic* or excluding anything because it was not, and, as a result, he achieved a different and wider range than his predecessors. He could move in a few lines from the Apocalypse to insect stings, or from a dog barking at a hedgehog to the image of a mind that feeds upon infinity. Each item changes the tone of the other, each interprets the other. New subjects are new language. They do not only generate a particular vocabulary, but are symbols in their own right, whatever words are used to describe them.

Wordsworth, however, recognises that even his new rigour is inadequate for his purposes. He writes poems on the clear assumption that experience is indeterminate, that his subject 'in the main. . .lies far hidden from the reach of words.' It is because he feels his subject to be nebulous that he uses so many abstract words and why his descriptions are a succession of synonyms, near synonyms and metaphors. The constant décollage of language from the world makes him aware of language as an object so that his poetry is often about language. He makes one of his poems on the daisy out of his awareness of himself using language:

Oft on the dappled turf at ease
I sit, and play with similes,
Loose types of things through all degrees,
     Thoughts of thy raising:
And many a fond and idle name
I give to thee, for praise or blame,
As is the humour of the game,
     While I am gazing.

A nun demure of lowly port:
Or sprightly maiden, of Love's court,
In thy simplicity the sport
     Of all temptations;
A queen in crown of rubies drest;
A starveling in a scanty vest;
Are all, as seems to suit thee best,
     Thy appellations.

A little Cyclops with one eye
Staring to threaten and defy,
That thought comes next — and instantly
     The freak is over,
The shape will vanish — and behold
A silver shield with boss of gold,
That spreads itself, some faery bold
     In fight to cover!

I see thee glittering from afar —
And then thou art a pretty star;
Not quite so fair as many are

> In heaven above thee!
> Yet like a star, with glittering crest,
> Self-poised in air thou seem'st to rest; —
> May peace come never to his nest,
>   Who shall reprove thee!
>
> Bright *Flower!* for by that name at last,
> When all my reveries are past,
> I call thee, and to that cleave fast,
>   Sweet silent creature!
> That breath'st with me in sun and air,
> Do thou, as thou art wont, repair
> My heart with gladness, and a share
>   Of thy meek nature!

The poet sees himself playing with similes as with toys. He knows that his words are no more than 'Loose types of things.' The stanzas represent a series of transformations: nun, maiden, queen, starveling, cyclops, shield, star, which leave the daisy unchanged but the poet somehow altered. These metaphors are not traditional. They are unrelated except as stages in the process of the poet's thoughts. They define his consciousness, his being.

To Wordsworth consciousness is a changing unity composed of a vast number of sensations, each virtually an entity in itself, yet merging with other sensations whose origins are beyond memory:

> Hard task to analyse a soul, in which,
> Not only general habits and desires,
> But each most obvious and particular thought,
> Not in a mystical and idle sense,
> But in the words of reason deeply weigh'd,
> Hath no beginning.

(II.232 – 237)

He conceives, nevertheless, both the problem and its solution in historical terms: this passage introduces the discussion of the relation between the mother and the baby. The search for origins always leads Wordsworth back to childhood.

There is no writer before Wordsworth who has such a complete understanding of the significance of childhood in human development. This is because he saw that it was a matter of inner states of feeling and because he saw that development as beginning with 'the infant Babe. . .Nurs'd in his Mother's arms' (see I.237 – 280), if not before birth. He calls 'the infant sensibility' the 'Great birthright of Being' (II.286). As Garlitz has demonstrated, Wordsworth's contemporaries perceived this as a major characteristic of his poetry: 'From 1807 to the 1820's it was the unusual critic who did not call Wordsworth a nursery bard or compare his poems to Mother Goose rhymes.' Byron, in his review of *Poems, in Two Volumes* (1807) asks:

> What will any reader. . .out of the nursery say to such namby-pamby as 'Lines written at the Foot of "Brother's Bridge" '. . . This appears to us neither more nor less than an imitation of such minstrelsy as soothed our cries in the cradle, with the shrill ditty of 'Hey de diddle / The cat and the fiddle. . .'

Jeffrey refers to Wordsworth's 'infantine' language (1807) and 'nursery stammering' (1812). Hunt regrets (1811) Wordsworth's lapse into 'second childhood.' Scott laments 'that Wordsworth should exhibit himself "crawling on all fours, when God has given him so noble a countenance to lift to heaven." ' Haydon, comparing Scott and Wordsworth, writes (7.3.1821): 'Wordsworth must always be eloquent and profound, because he knows that he is considered childish and puerile.' 'After the 1830's the nursery comparison became extremely rare,' but it was never quite forgotten. Bulwer-Lytton, in 1846, mocks Tennyson for 'out-babying Wordsworth.'[43]

Wordsworth's concern with childhood not only produced poems about children, but a new view of adults: 'The Child is father of the Man' is a revolution in psychology. The increasing significance attributed to childhood meant that a greater value came to be placed on returning to this past, and more and more poems became deliberate acts of memory. Wordsworth's concern was not the interest of an old man in his youth, but that of a young man starting his career. He was 28 when he wrote the *Lines Composed a Few Miles above Tintern Abbey* and began his first draft of the poem on his own life. He was looking back to the near and recent past. He introduces a notion of human development which sees the development of childhood as decisive and a notion of childhood which emphasises the intensity and complexity of the child's mental life, and which makes the child as worthy as the man to be the subject of great poetry.

Wordsworth pauses near the middle of Book III of the autobiographical poem to analyse what he has thus far accomplished:

> Of Genius, Power,
> Creation and Divinity itself
> I have been speaking, for my theme has been
> What pass'd within me. Not of outward things
> Done visibly for other minds, words, signs,
> Symbols or actions; but of my own heart
> Have I been speaking, and my youthful mind.
>
> (III.171 – 177)

The pursuit of 'what pass'd within' causes him to seek at the beginnings of memory a form-giving centre to his fleeting moods. He turns inward to the past:

> O Heavens! how awful is the might of Souls,
> And what they do within themselves, while yet
> The yoke of earth is new to them, the world
> Nothing but a wild field where they were sown.
> This is, in truth, heroic argument,
> And genuine prowess; which I wish'd to touch
> With hand however weak; but in the main
> It lies far hidden from the reach of words.
> Points have we all of us within our souls,
> Where all stand single; this I feel, and make
> Breathings for incommunicable powers.
> Yet each man is a memory to himself,
> And, therefore, now that I must quit this theme,
> I am not heartless; for there's not a man
> That lives who hath not had his godlike hours,
> And knows not what majestic sway we have,
> As natural beings in the strength of nature.
>
> (III.178 – 194)

The poet, in a curious phrase, makes 'Breathings for incommunicable powers.' Breathings are utterances. The powers are the unsayable sources of the self, kept alive by poetry. The whole passage reveals Wordsworth trying to find words to express 'the sentiment of Being' (II.420). His poetry shows that no single formulation was adequate. The creation of a language of being in poem after poem is perhaps his greatest achievement. Wordsworth's successors elaborate this notion of a residual centre of identity to which all language is asymptotic.

They wrestle with it like Jacob with the angel. Hopkins describes his feeling of his ineffable singleness in *Comments on the Spiritual Exercises of St. Ignatius Loyola* (1880) in language that was later employed in some of his greatest poems:

> I find myself both as man and as myself something most determined and distinctive, at pitch, more distinctive and higher pitched than anything else I see;. . . And this is much more true when we consider the mind; when I consider my selfbeing, my consciousness and feeling of myself, that taste of myself, of *I* and *me* above and in all things, which is more distinctive than the taste of ale or alum, more distinctive than the smell of walnutleaf or camphor, and is incommunicable by any means to another man (as when I was a child I used to ask myself: What must it be to be someone else?). Nothing else in nature comes near this unspeakable stress of pitch, distinctiveness, and selving, this selfbeing of my own. Nothing explains it or resembles it, except so far as this, that other men to themselves have the same feeling.[44]

Similarly, the notes that Valéry made almost every morning from 1894 to 1945 were exercises in self-definition and the 261 notebooks that resulted are his autobiographical poem. As in his poems, his principal subject is consciousness, and although he is more self-aware than either Wordsworth or Hopkins, he shares their assumptions about the nature of the self: 'It is that within me unknown to myself that makes me, me' and:

> Our history, our moment, our body, our hopes, our fears, our hands, our thoughts — all is *foreign* to us.
> Everything is exterior (in brusque meditation) to the indescribable something that is *me*, — and that is a myth — for there is no quality, sensation, passion, remembrance,. . .of which it does not feel itself independent when its life might depend upon it.[45]

The whole of the above passage containing Wordsworth's rudimentary definition of the self (the 'Points. . .within our souls, / Where all stand single') is pervaded by his awareness of using language: 'Have I been speaking,' 'heroic argument,' 'the reach of words,' 'incommunicable powers.' He reduces every event that occurs in the world to language: 'words, signs, / Symbols or actions.' He uses the paradigm of language to define the location of his material: 'far hidden from the reach of words' and to make perception meaningful: 'the language of the sense.' The conclusion to crossing the Alps is linguistic:

> *Characters* of the great Apocalypse,
> The *types* and *symbols* of Eternity. . .

Wordsworth derives poetry from the idea of language, as if much of the feeling that he knows is beyond the reach of words is concealed in the processes of symbol-making, and his descriptions of these early events suggest that the self is the communication upon which all other communications depend.

The deeper communion that all poets (and all artists) seek is with themselves, but starting between about 1785 — 1805 poets begin to seek it deliberately and explicitly, knowing what they are doing. Every subsequent major European poet repeats Wordsworth's search for his deepest feelings, for the feeling of his own individuality and the diversity of styles is a consequence of each one attempting to devise a language appropriate to his own being.

Wordsworth interprets his life as a process working according to its own laws, with its own pathology (imagination can be impaired and restored). His sense of each moment as an entity made him vividly aware of time passing and he writes that when he tries to recollect his past:

> so wide appears
> The vacancy between me and those days,
> Which yet have such self-presence in my mind
> That, sometimes, when I think of it, I seem
> Two consciousnesses, conscious of myself
> And of some other Being.
>
> (II.28 – 33)

To describe the power of memory he finds it necessary to invent a new word. *Self-presence* (which is not in the *OED*) suggests that the self inheres in every moment of perception. The autobiographical poem is composed of such moments whose *self-presence* makes for a certain shapelessness of structure. This is marked by the verse paragraphs and the space between sections. (There is authority for both in the five major MSS, although the printed editions do not always follow the MSS.) Even arguments, such as the discussion of the education of children (V.193 – 389), are built up of more or less independent units.

The poem's task is to trace the relations between these separate moments and to connect them as the moods of a single, developing consciousness. Poe declares in 'The Poetic Principle' (published a month after *The Prelude*): 'I hold that a long poem does not exist. I maintain that the phrase "a long poem", is simply a flat contradiction in terms.'[46] Wordsworth constructs his autobiographical poem as if he shared Poe's feelings without sharing his conclusions.

From Wordsworth to the present a profound sense of the individuality — and, therefore, formlessness — of every sensation shapes the creation of literary form. Poe's description of a long poem as 'a series of lyrics' can be applied to most of the long poems written after Wordsworth.[47] The long poem composed of 'spots of time' achieves, as a result, the texture of the lyric. *Song of Myself, In Memoriam* and *La Légende des siècles* exhibit this lyric quality as do *The Waste Land, Notes Toward a Supreme Fiction* and *Canto general*. The feeling of the fragmentation of perception also changes the nature of the short poem. Modern poetry, starting with Blake, Burns and Wordsworth, is characterised by the production of innumerable short lyrics — and of *very short* lyrics (and lines). There are, before *Songs of Innocence and Experience* (1794), few poems as short and as serious as *The Sick Rose* (8 lines), *Ah! Sun Flower* (8 lines), *Mock on Mock on Voltaire Rousseau* (12 lines), *A slumber did my spirit seal* (8 lines), *My heart leaps up when I behold* (9 lines) and *She dwelt among the untrodden ways* (12 lines). Blake is the first to write a number of great poems shorter than a sonnet (and all with lines shorter than pentameters), but it is with Wordsworth that a new kind of lyric emerges, personal and introspective, neither song nor epigram.[48] Perhaps it is no accident that there are more very short poems among the *Songs of Experience* than the *Songs of Innocence*, as this new lyric is a result of assuming the moment of experience as a unit of form.

The seriousness of a short poem is a function of its symbolic power. For a short poem to have the weight of a longer poem, the very small needs to be able to contain the very large — the butterfly to hold the history of childhood. The idea is not new. Shakespeare has Hamlet declare:

O God, I could be bounded in a nut-shell, and count myself a king of infinite space, were it not that I have bad dreams.[49]

Donne sees the flea as: 'you and I. . .mariage bed, and mariage temple.'[50] It is Blake, however, who uses the capacity:

To see a World in a Grain of Sand
And a Heaven in a Wild Flower
Hold Infinity in the palm of your hand
And Eternity in an hour[51]

to create very short poems. Apparently small things can be charged with significance only when there is an awareness of the nature of metaphor (such as Blake exhibits here) and when they *can be* described in some detail. Wordsworth is able to go beyond the conceits of Donne by representing objects in greater detail. After Wordsworth objects are left more and more to be their own interpretation, are expected to be self-evident in their contexts. Even bad dreams are put into a nutshell.

If every present moment contains the entire past, then its riches are virtually infinite. If experience is ineffable, if language can never be identical with feeling, then the possibilities of modifying any statement are infinite. Valéry states that poems have no end:

that a work is never completed except by some accident, like fatigue, satisfaction, a deadline or death; for a work, from the viewpoint of whoever of whatever makes it, is only a single state in a series of interior transformations. How many times one would like to begin what one has just decided was finished!. . .How many times have I looked on what I was going to show to the eyes of others as the necessary preparation for the desired work, that I only then was beginning to *see* in its possible maturity, and as the very probable and very desirable fruit of a new wait and of an act already outlined within my powers. The work actually done then appeared to me as the mortal body to which the transfigured and glorious body should succeed.[52]

This was Wordsworth's experience with his 'Poem, Title not yet fixed upon.' Valéry said that he only stopped working on *La Cimetière marin* because of the intervention of Jacques Rivière, who happened to visit him when he was revising the poem, read it and took the MS away to publish in the review that he edited.[53] Death intervened to put an end to Wordsworth's revision of the poem on his own life and his executors arranged its publication.

The belief in the tentative nature of literary form grows out of a turning away from anything that is felt as external form and a desire for inner form. Crane writing to Sherwood Anderson (10.1.1922)

about Donne's *Of the Progresse of the Soule, The Second Anniversarie*
says:

> What I want to get is just what is so beautifully done in this
> poem, — an 'interior' form, a form that is so thorough and intense
> as to dye the words themselves with a peculiarity of meaning,
> slightly different maybe from the ordinary definition of them
> separate from the poem.[54]

Poets seek a new idea of form through the complication, twisting and
dislocation of syntax, idiosyncratic styles and private languages. They
find new meaning by altering the structure of language itself in an
attempt to master from within the shapelessness of perception.

To Wordsworth every moment in the history of his life had its own
landscape. He was aware as a boy of seeing the world in a new way and
decided to make this the basis of his originality as a poet. Talking to
Isabella Fenwick about *An Evening Walk*, he comments on the two
lines describing the sunset entwined in the boughs of an oak
(214–215; see Chapter 2, 47–8):

> This is feebly and imperfectly expressed, but I recollect distinctly
> the very spot where this first struck me. It was in the way between
> Hawkshead and Ambleside, and gave me extreme pleasure. The
> moment was important in my poetical history; for I date from it my
> consciousness of the infinite variety of natural appearances which
> had been unnoticed by the poets of any age or country, so far as I
> was acquainted with them; and I made a resolution to supply, in
> some degree, the deficiency. I could not have been at that time
> above 14 years of age.[55]

The contemplation of 'the infinite variety of natural appearances' produced a realisation of the infinite number of moods of the mind —
and the emotion of identity.

Rousseau writes in *Les Confessions*:

> Although that sensibility of heart that makes us truly enjoy our-
> selves (*qui nous fait vraiment jouir de nous*) is the work of nature
> and perhaps a product of its structure, it has a need of situations
> that develop it. Without these occasions a man born extremely
> sensitive would feel nothing and would die without having known
> his being (*sans avoir connu son être*).

Rousseau says that he would have been without this knowledge if he had not met Madame de Warens, whom he called *Maman*, and if he had not 'lived close to her long enough to contract the sweet habit of affectionate sentiments.'[56] What Rousseau found in his life with Madame de Warens, Wordsworth found in his residence in the vale of Grasmere, and in his life-long communion with nature. He could not *vraiment jouir de lui* except in feeling part of a landscape. His reports of these experiences reveal him as simultaneously withdrawn and attached. He withdraws *into himself*, into memory. The contemplation of nature returns him to the past. The act of perceiving a landscape is like submerging an exposed negative in developer, only the slowly forming image is of a scene other than the one upon which he gazes.

There is in European art before Wordsworth only an intermittent interest in landscape for its own sake. Pictures of actual places without any people — like Dürer's *View of Arco* (about 1496) — are rare. The capacity to see the landscape as a self-contained entity seems to belong to those who are capable of enough self-detachment to view themselves realistically. The landscapes of Dürer, Leonardo and Rembrandt are the work of men who are responsible for remarkable self-portraits. The only sustained period of landscape painting before Turner in which natural phenomena are, in Ruskin's phrase, 'the exclusive subject of reverent contemplation' is that of the Dutch painters: Cuyp (1605 – 1691), van Ruysdael (1628 – 1682), Hobbema (1638 – 1701) and van der Velde (1663 – 1707).[57] Dispensing with Christian or Classical subjects, even as pretexts, they come face to face with their native countryside. Although Greek and Roman subjects continue to engage artists' attention, this sudden scrutiny of the world by the Dutch painters coincides with a gradual fading away of interest in religious subjects. The publication of *Cooper's Hill* (1642), which Dryden declared would ever be 'the exact standard of good writing' and which is accepted as the first English topographic poem, falls within this period, as does the introduction of the word *landscape*.[58] Derived from the Dutch, *landschap,* and originally a painter's term, it appears to have established itself against competing forms in Wordsworth's lifetime. The first recorded occurrence of *landscape*, according to the *OED*, is in 1603; *landskip* is recorded in 1598, and both are employed by Wordsworth.

The idea that artists might devote themselves to the detailed representation of nature (like the idea of autobiography) was not accepted without considerable resistance. Johnson states in *The History of*

Rasselas (1759) that

> [t]he business of a poet. . .is to examine, not the individual, but the species; to remark general properties and large appearances: he does not number the streaks on the tulip, or describe the different shades in the verdure of the forest.[59]

Gainsborough, when asked (about 1763) to paint a picture of a patron's park, replies:

> Mr Gainsborough presents his humble respects to Lord Hardwicke, and shall always think it an honour to be employ'd in anything for His Lordship; but with regard to *real views* from Nature in this country, he has never seen a place that affords a subject equal to the poorest imitations of Gaspar or Claude. Paul San[d]by is the only Man of Genius, he believes, who has employ'd his pencil that way. Mr G. hopes that Lord Hardwicke will not mistake his meaning, but if His Lordship wishes to have anything tollerable of the name of G., the subject altogether. . .must be of his own Brain; otherwise Lord Hardwicke will only pay for encouraging a man out of his way, and had much better buy a picture of some of the good Old Masters.[60]

And a few years later in a lecture the keeper of the Royal Academy speaks of 'the last branch of uninteresting subjects, that kind of landscape which is entirely occupied with the tame delineation of a given spot.'[61]

Moreover, Ruskin could still write in 1856 'Of the Novelty of Landscape.' He maintains that the existence of landscape painting means that a radical change has taken place in European sensibility. We are, he tells his contemporaries, 'under the influence of feelings with which neither Miltiades nor the Black Prince, neither Homer nor Dante, neither Socrates nor St. Francis, could for an instant have sympathized.'[62] The new attention to nature is not just a matter of mere realism: 'the first thing that will strike us, or that ought to strike us' in modern landscapes 'is their *cloudiness*.'

> . . .we are expected to rejoice in darkness, and triumph in mutability; to lay the foundations of happiness in things which momentarily change or fade; and to expect the utmost satisfaction and instruction from what it is impossible to arrest, and difficult to comprehend.

Where previously 'no one ever thought of drawing anything, but as well *as he could*,. . .now our ingenuity is all "concerning smoke". Nothing is truly drawn but that; all else is vague, slight, imperfect. . .'[63] Ruskin only partially understood that this cloudiness was the beginning of a new accuracy.

Wordsworth, like Turner (1775 – 1851) and Monet (1840 – 1926) whose careers span the major period of landscape painting in European art, glosses over and omits details so that a given scene represents a single mood and can be apprehended as a whole. They all de-form objects in the interest of unity as well as to suggest the precariousness of that unity, the readiness of one mood to change into another. Cloudiness is a method of portraying mutability and the continuity of infinite change. The human spirit, in this view, is, as Stevens put it, 'a permanence composed of impermanence.'[64]

The language of light is the language of mental processes. Wordsworth offers us a conception of the growth of a poet's mind as a constant play of light and shadow — a succession of unique events. The degree to which this conception has become a habit of mind is demonstrated by one of Lévi-Strauss's pastimes on his first voyage to Brazil in 1934. He recalls in *Tristes tropiques* his intense study of the sunrises and sunsets: 'those feverish instants when, notebook in hand, I noted, second by second, the expression that would perhaps allow me to immobilise those evanescent and always-renewed forms,' at which he, too, looked in order to understand the nature of human behaviour:

> I observed passionately, on the deserted bridge, those supernatural cataclysms whose birth, evolution and end were represented, for a few instants each day, to the four corners of an horizon vaster than I had ever contemplated by the rising and setting of the sun. If I were to find a language to fix these appearances, at once unstable and resistant to any effort of description, if it were given to me to communicate to others the phrases and articulations of an event that was unique and that would never reproduce itself in the same terms, then it seemed to me, I would have penetrated at a stroke the arcana of my metier: there would not be any bizarre or peculiar experience to which ethnographic research would expose me, which I would not be able one day to grasp in all its meaning and extent.[65]

If knowledge is illumination, then the knowledge *of* illumination is — metaphorically — knowledge of the mind's agency. Meaning is created by one ineffable process being equated with another.

The landscape, as the background to our existence, the encompassing matrix in which we have our being, is an image of every unity, a manageable world. Scott, who introduces the landscape into the novel, explains in a letter to Anna Seward (29.6.1802), twelve years before *Waverley*, the appeal of the popular poetry of the Border as follows:

> Much of its peculiar charm is indeed, I believe, to be attributed solely to its *locality*. A very commonplace and obvious epithet, when applied to a scene which we have been accustomed to view with pleasure, recalls to us not merely the local scenery, but a thousand little nameless associations, which we are unable to separate or define.[66]

The description of a landscape communicates what is amorphous – that which a writer can neither distinguish nor specify — gathering together the nuances of innumerable intimacies, and the effect of a more precise use of words is very much greater, more evocative, in this respect, than that of the 'commonplace and obvious epithet.' Before Wordsworth poetic landscapes are usually moral and general, in some sense allegorical. For Wordsworth (and Scott) unique events can only be truly apprehended in terms of specific locations.

The sense of place is symbiotic with that of time. Perhaps Wordsworth's feeling of being unintegrated strengthened his awareness of himself as changing; certainly he envisaged his existence as a succession of scenes, each charged with a different mood. The sense of time may begin in the pulsing of the varying intensities of perception. Thinking historically involves the grasping of these changing scenes as a whole. The innovations of Wordsworth flow from his capacity to write as a historian. He gives to 'airy nothingness a local habitation and a name' in a way undreamed of by Shakespeare. His appreciation of the 'thousand nameless associations' of every locality and his ability to find names for so many of them is part of a profound feeling of the world as existing in time.

Wordsworth's assumptions, his hard-won discoveries and poetic modes are shared by virtually every European poet who comes after him, down to the present day. His poems are the types of their poems. His search is theirs. This continuity is expressed by Stevens in *Of*

Modern Poetry (1940), his attempt to define the tradition in which he works. Modern poetry is a response to a change in world-view:

> The poem of the mind in the act of finding
> What will suffice. It has not always had
> To find: the scene was set; it repeated what
> Was in the script.
>   Then the theatre was changed
> To something else. Its past was a souvenir.

Out of his immediate surroundings the poet needs to make a new theatre. As for the new poetry:

> It has to be living, to learn the speech of the place.
> It has to face the men of the time and to meet
> The women of the time. It has to think about war
> And it has to find what will suffice. It has
> To construct a new stage. It has to be on that stage
> And, like an insatiable actor, slowly and
> With meditation, speak words that in the ear,
> In the delicatest ear of the mind, repeat,
> Exactly, that which it wants to hear, at the sound
> Of which, an invisible audience listens,
> Not to the play, but to itself, expressed
> In an emotion as of two people, as of two
> Emotions becoming one. The actor is
> A metaphysician in the dark, twanging
> An instrument, twanging a wiry string that gives
> Sounds passing through sudden rightnesses, wholly
> Containing the mind, below which it cannot descend,
> Beyond which it has no will to rise.
>   It must
> Be the finding of a satisfaction, and may
> Be of a man skating, a woman dancing, a woman
> Combing. The poem of the act of the mind.[67]

The poem satisfies the poet's desire to be: in it the audience (which includes the poet) listens to itself. The moment is one of fundamental feeling, 'an emotion as of two people,' like that of the mother and 'the infant babe.' Stevens, like Wordsworth, uses sounds — slow, meditative speech in which the words almost do not seem to matter and the abrupt, resonant chords of a guitar, music verging on speech — to stand for this elusive sense of self. The poet's playing concerns the nature of things, but is not philosophy: 'The actor is / A metaphysician in the dark,' not philosophising, but twanging a musical instrument.

'The poem of the mind in the act of finding / What will suffice;' 'the poem of the act of the mind:' this is Wordsworth's achievement.

Notes

1 Self-consciousness and English Poetry

1. Memoirs, I, 313; P, xxiv.

2. Marc Bloch, 'Pour une histoire comparées des sociétés européenes,' *Mélanges historiques* (1963), I, 20. For another, not necessarily contradictory, view, compare Alan Macfarlane, *The Origins of English Individualism* (Oxford, 1978).

3. J.-J. Rousseau, 'Discours sur l'origine et les fondements de l'inegalité' (1775), *Oeuvres complètes*, ed. Bernard Gagnebin and Marcel Raymond, III (1964), 164. This is sixteen years after Voltaire declared (1759) that 'one must cultivate one's garden (*il faut cultiver nôtre jardin*),' *Candide*, ed. Andre Morize (1957), 223. Peter Jimack suggests to me that in the context of the work as a whole the garden should be understood as the world. Even if this is the case it can still be argued that the capacity to make such an inclusive metaphor — such a domestication of the world — indicates a change in consciousness.

4. Lewis Namier, 'Basic Factors in Nineteenth-Century European History,' *Vanished Supremacies* (Harmondsworth, 1962), 203.

5. Emmanuel Le Roy Ladurie emphasises the household or *domus* as the fundamental social unit throughout *Montaillou, village occitan de 1294 à 1324* (1975), but see especially 51–87, and also Peter Laslett, *The World we have Lost* (1968).

6. H.C. Lea, *A History of Auricular Confession and Indulgences in the Latin Church* (1896), I, 168–273, 347–523; E. L. van Becelaere, 'Penance (Roman Catholic),' *Encyclopaedia of Religion and Ethics*, IX (1917), 711–15; E. Mangenot, E. Vacandard, P. Bernard and others, 'Confession,' *Dictionnaire de théologie catholique*, III (1908), 828–974, and E. Amann and A. Michel, 'Penitence-Sacrement,' XIII (1933), 748–1127.

7. Lea I, 394–396; van Becelaere IX, 714.

8. Sigmund Freud, 'On Beginning the Treatment' (1913), trans. J. Riviere and J. Strachey, *The Standard Edition of the Complete Psychological Works of Sigmund Freud* (1975), XII, 133.

9. Erich Auerbach, 'Dante's Addresses to the Reader,' *Romance Philology*, VII (1954), 268–78.

10. Erich Auerbach, *Dante, Poet of the Secular World*, trans. Ralph Manheim (Chicago, 1961); 'Figura,' trans. Ralph Manheim, *Scenes from the Drama of European Literature* (New York, 1959) 11–76.

11. Dante, *Inferno*, ed. J.D. Sinclair (New York, 1961), XV. 20–1; XII.4–9; XIII.40–5; X.45; XXVI.28.

12. MS B, f 4a. There is a photograph in P.

13. Georges Gusdorf, 'Conditions et limites de l'autobiographie,' *Formen der Selbstdarstellung*, ed. G. Reichenkron and E. Hasse (Berlin, 1956), 109; *The New Encyclopaedia Britannica: Micropaedia* (Chicago, 1974), VI, 931.

14. W. Waetzoldt, *Dürer and His Times*, trans. R.H. Boothroyd (1955), 16–20; Erwin Panofsky, *The Life and Writings of Albrecht Dürer* (Princeton, 1955), 42. Dürer's inscriptions on these works are another indication of his self-consciousness.

15. Gusdorf, 118.

16. *The Autobiography of Thomas Whythorne*, ed. James Osborn (1962), xii, Paul Delany, *British Autobiography in the Seventeenth Century* (1969), 13 n 18; James

Osborn, *The Beginnings of Autobiography in England* (Los Angeles, 1959).

17. Owen Barfield, *History in English Words* (1962), 165−6.

18. W.K. Ferguson, *The Renaissance in Historical Thought* (Cambridge, Mass., 1948), 3−13.

19. Ernst Cassirer, *The Individual and the Cosmos in Renaissance Philosophy*, trans. Mario Domandi (New York, 1964). 143.

20. Theodore E. Mommsen, 'Petrarch's Conception of "The Dark Ages",' *Speculum*, XVII (1942), 226−242; Erwin Panofsky, *Renaissance and Renascences in Western Art* (New York, 1969), 1−41; for the letter to G. Colonna, *Epistolae Familiares*, VI, 2 (ed. Rossi, II, 55−60), see Mommsen, 232; for *Africa* IX.455−457, see Mommsen, 242 and Panofsky, *Renaissance*, 10 n 1.

21. Panofsky, *Renaissance*, 16; Johan Huizinga, 'The Problem of the Renaissance,' *Men and Ideas*, trans. J.S. Holmes and H. van Marle (New York, 1959), 245−6.

22. Panofsky, *Renaissance*, 30−1; Dürer uses *Wiedererwachsung* in a draft of the preface to his *Vier Bücher von Menschlichler Proportion*. F. Rabelais, *Oeuvres complètes*, ed. J. Boulenger and L. Scheler (1955), I, ix, 32.

23. Huizinga, 246−7; Panofsky, *Renaissance*, 30−1.

24. Pierre Belon, *Observation de plusieurs singularitez et choses memorables, trouvées en Grece, Asie, Iudée, Egypte, Arabe & autres pays estranges* (1553), as cited by Panofsky, *Renaissance*, 17 n 4, my translation.

25. James Hall, *Dictionary of Subjects and Symbols in Art* (1974), 328−9. Some similar comments are made by E.H. Erikson in *Young Man Luther* (New York, 1962), 191−5. I would like to thank Rosemary Harris Muir Wright for discussing the history of the images of Madonna and Child with me. She suggested Murillo as the approximate terminal date.

26. G.R. Elton, *Reformation Europe 1517−1559* (1963), 275. On the idea of conversion, see A.D. Nock, *Conversion* (Oxford, 1965), 1−16.

27. R.H. Bainton, *Here I Stand, A Life of Martin Luther* (New York, 1950), 41.

28. Paul Valéry, *Oeuvres*, ed. Jean Hytier, I (1957), 991−3.

29. *Make It New* is the title that Ezra Pound chose for the retrospective selection of his prose published by Faber and Faber in 1934.

30. R.P. Blackmur, *The Lion and the Honeycomb* (New York, 1955), 210. The novels of Hardy are, I believe, an exception to this statement; see my 'The Form of Hardy's Novels,' *Thomas Hardy After Fifty Years*, ed. L.St.J. Butler (1977), 23−5.

31. Jules Michelet, *Histoire de France*, IX−X (1855), 6.

32. Jacob Burckhardt, *Die Kultur der Renaissance in Italien* (Berlin, 1928), 131−2; trans. S.G.C. Middlemore, *The Civilization of the Renaissance in Italy* (New York, 1954), 100. I have corrected the translation.

33. Memoirs, II, 470; compare WL, V, 159.

34. *The Letters of John Keats*, ed. M.B. Forman (1947), 489; W.B. Yeats, 'Edmund Spenser,' *Essays and Introductions* (1961), 379.

35. Otto Jespersen, *Growth and Structure of the English Language* (New York, 1955), 243. Admiration of Spenser was not limited to Britain. Friedrich Schlegel told Henry Crabb Robinson that he held Spenser to be the greatest English poet 'in respect to the melody of the verse. "When I read him," says he, "I can hardly think it is a northern language, much less English." ' *Diary, Reminiscences, and Correspondence of Henry Crabb Robinson*, ed. Thomas Sadler, second edition (1869), I, 122−3; diary entry for 6 June 1802.

36. *The Letters of Hart Crane*, ed. Brom Weber (Berkeley, 1965), 77.

37. All the citations from this letter, *Epistolae Familiares*, IV, 1 (ed. Rossi I, 153−61) are from the translation by H. Nachod in *The Renaissance Philosophy of Man*, ed. Ernst Cassier, P.O. Kristeller and J.H. Randall, Jr. (Chicago, 1948), 36−46.

38. Kenneth Clark, *Civilisation* (1969), 271; see Gray's letters to his mother, 13 October and 7 November 1739 and to Richard West, 16 November 1739, *Letters of Thomas Gray*, ed. John Beresford (Oxford, 1925), 38−40, 42−6). An edition of his

letters was published in 1775.

39. *Petrarch's Secret*, trans. W.H. Draper (1911).

40. J.R. MacGillivray, 'The Three Forms of *The Prelude* 1798–1805,' *Wordsworth: The Prelude*, ed. W.J. Harvey and Richard Gravil (1972), 111–12.

41. CP, I, 376–80; CL, II, 834–45, 853–4, 864–5.

42. *The Complete Poetical Works of Percy Bysshe Shelley*, ed. Neville Rogers (Oxford), II (1975), 75–80.

43. John Keats, *The Complete Poems*, ed. John Barnard (Harmondsworth, 1973), 72.

44. Fernand Braudel, 'Positions de l'histoire en 1950,' *Écrits sur l'histoire* (1969), 31.

45. Michel de Montaigne, *Essais*, ed. Albert Thibaudet (1950), III.ii.899. The translations of Montaigne follow, for the most part, the version of Jacob Zeitlen, *The Essays of Michel de Montaigne*, 3 vols. (New York, 1936), but I have not hesitated to make changes.

46. Montaigne, III.v.981; II.xvii.735; III.xiii.1236; III.viii.1051; III.xiii.1219; III.v.986.

47. Montaigne, I, 25.

48. Ernst Cassirer, 'Some Remarks on the Question of the Originality of the Renaissance,' *Journal of the History of Ideas*, IV (1943), 55.

49. Montaigne, III.ii.899–900.

50. F.P. Wilson, *Marlowe and the Early Shakespeare* (Oxford, 1953), 104–8.

51. Louis Martz, *The Poetry of Meditation* (New Haven, 1965), 5–6; Henry Kamen, *The Iron Century, Social Change in Europe 1550–1660* (1976), 256–8.

52. The case is argued in Martz's *The Poetry of Meditation*.

53. *Selected Writings of Francis Bacon*, ed. H.G. Dick (New York, 1955), 236–9.

54. Donald Stauffer, *English Biography Before 1700* (Cambridge, Mass., 1930), 35; R.W. Chambers, *On the Continuity of English Prose from Alfred to More and his School* (1932) xlv–xlix.

55. Douglas Bush, *English Literature in the Earlier Seventeenth Century 1600–1660* (New York, 1952), 197–208; D.N. Smith, *Characters from the Histories & Memoirs of the Seventeenth Century* (Oxford, 1963), xi–xiv; *The Diary of John Evelyn*, ed. E.S. de Beer (Oxford), III (1955), 520.

56. Stauffer, *English Biography Before 1700*, 31, 75.

57. See the 'Check-list of Seventeenth-Century Autobiographies' in Delany, 175–85 and the list of 'Puritan Spiritual Autobiographies written before 1725' in Owen Watkins, *The Puritain Experience* (1972), 241–59.

58. J.H. Plumb, *The Growth of Political Stability in England 1675–1725* (Harmondsworth, 1969), 15.

59. CS, 117.

60. S.T. Coleridge, 'On Poesy or Art,' *Biographia Literaria*, ed. J. Shawcross (Oxford, 1907), II, 262. Note that in order to describe his notion of form Coleridge needs two words with the prefix *self*.

61. The dream of the Arab (V.49–139) is based on the account of a dream dreamed by Descartes on the night of 10 November 1619 in Adrien Baillet's *Vie de Descartes* (1699); see *Oeuvres de Descartes*, ed. Charles Adam and Paul Tannery, X (1908), 184–5 and Jane Worthington Smyser, 'Wordsworth's Dream of Poetry and Science: The Prelude, V,' PMLA, LXXI (1956), 269–75.

2   Wordsworth Chooses Himself

1.   Reed I, 15, 18, 21, 24–5, 27–8, 29–31. Unless otherwise noted, I have relied on Reed for the chronology of Wordsworth's life and work.

2. As '1000' is written in the margin against 1.235 (de Selincourt; 1.241, Hayden) in one MS, the poem may have been much longer. The MSS are described in PW, I, 367 – 8 and Poems, I, 923 – 4. I have cited de Selincourt's text because Hayden has modernised Wordsworth's spelling.

3. See 1.466 – 477; 536 – 545.

4. PW, I, 318 – 19.

5. *Salisbury Plain* (1793 – 1794) and *Adventures on Salisbury Plain* (1795 – c.1799); see SP for the texts and the poem's history.

6. PW, I, 318 – 19.

7. PW, I, 317 – 18, 368.

8. On the transfer and re-working of passages, see, for example, PW, I, 368 – 9, 323, 327 – 8; Reed I, 27 – 8, 29 – 31; P, 557, 560; and Music 3 – 28, 50 – 67, 157 – 68.

9. The 1798 text is printed in LB, 57 – 60.

10. J.R. MacGillivray, 'The Three Forms of *The Prelude* 1798 – 1805.'

11. MS JJ (DC MS 19). There are photographs and a transcription of the MS in PP. For this passage see PP, 114 – 15.

12. PP, 116 – 17.

13. T.S. Eliot, *The Use of Poetry and the Use of Criticism* (1964), 69.

14. John Dryden, *Of Dramatic Poesy*, ed. George Watson (1962), II, 90.

15. P, 622 – 3.

16. There are several copies of *The Seasons* that belonged to Wordsworth in the Wordsworth Library, including a copy of the 1778 edition with many passages marked in pencil, especially the section 'Spring.' He possessed in 1841 a copy of the first edition (1730) interlined with the later alterations (1744); J.P. Muirhead, 'A Day with Wordsworth,' *Blackwood's Magazine*, CCXXI (1927), 737, as cited by Mary Jacobus, *Tradition and Experiment in Wordsworth's Lyrical Ballads (1798)* (Oxford, 1976), 42 n 2. Jacobus also discusses Wordsworth's relation to Thomson, Akenside and Cowper, 33, 38 – 58, 105 – 18. Other examples of specific debts can be found in de Selincourt's notes to *The Vale of Esthwaite, An Evening Walk* and *Descriptive Sketches*; PW, I, 320 – 9, 367 – 9. Glossing 1.586 – 588 in the autobiographical poem, he remarks that: 'Wordsworth's feeling for the seasons is often expressed in language that recalls the poet Thomson;' P, 519. Dorothy Wordsworth writes to Jane Pollard (10 and 12.7.1793) that 'indeed the whole character' of Beattie's minstrel 'resembles much what William was when I first knew him after my leaving Halifax. . .' Beattie's account of his minstrel's childhood might easily have suggested to Wordsworth the idea of writing about his childhood, the very title, *The Minstrel or The Progress of Genius* might have suggested a poem on the *Growth of a Poet's Mind*. Mary Moorman states that 'the strongest contemporary influence on the young Wordsworth was Beattie;' Moorman, I, 60. Dorothy records receiving a copy of Akenside's *The Pleasures of the Imagination* in September 1795; WL, I, 151.

17. *Paradise Lost*, IX.1 – 47; John Milton, *Complete Poems and Major Prose*, ed. M.Y. Hughes (New York, 1957).

18. The discussion of these subjects, unless otherwise indicated, is based on de Selincourt's glossing of this passage, P, 513 – 15.

19. There is a possibility that this was the case. De Selincourt notes that the Milton MS at Trinity College, Cambridge, contains 'a list of subjects for a projected epic, in which the history of Britain before the Conquest is divided into thirty-three heads,' and that Milton mentions a project for a poem on King Arthur in *Epitaphium Damonis*; P, 513. Dryden in his dedication to *Aureng-Zebe* (1676) speaks of his design for a heroic poem on 'the story English, and neither too far distant from the present age, nor too near approaching it;' Dryden, I, 191.

20. The history of the *locus amoenus* in European literature is discussed by E.R. Curtius, *European Literature and the Latin Middle Ages*, trans. W.R. Trask (New York, 1953), 183 – 202.

21. Compare Edmund Spenser, *The Faerie Queene*, ed. T.P. Roche, Jr. with C.P.

O'Donnell, Jr. (Harmondsworth, 1978), I.1.4, 9.

22. The story of Mithridates is told in the lives of Caius Marius, Sylla, Lucullus, Sertorius and Pompey.

23. Plutarch, *The Lives of the Noble Greeks and Romans*, trans. John Dryden and revised by A.H. Clough (New York, Modern Library, n.d.), 762 – 79.

24. Edward Gibbon, *The Decline and Fall of the Roman Empire* (New York, Modern Library, n.d.) I, 211.

25. Gibbon, I, 211, n 12.

26. Plutarch, 768 – 9.

27. Gibbon, I, 211.

28. Prose, III, 80.

29. Plutarch, 683.

30. T.S. Eliot, 'Hamlet and His Problems,' *Selected Essays*, new edition (New York, 1950), 123 – 4.

31. Compare X.441 – 567 with X.1 – 23, 41 – 44. Louis XVI's death is not mentioned.

32. LB, 156.

33. *The Somersetshire Tragedy* also belongs to this time. This was another story poem (in nine-line stanzas) similar in many ways to *Salisbury Plain* and *The Ruined Cottage*, and potentially a long poem. The MS that Gordon Wordsworth destroyed consisted of seven pages; Jonathan Wordsworth, 'A Wordsworth Tragedy,' *The Times Literary Supplement*, 21 July 1966, 642; Reed I, 29.

34. The best discussion of *The Ruined Cottage* is Jonathan Wordsworth's *The Music of Humanity*; see also: PW, V, 362 – 415; John Finch, 'The Ruined Cottage Restored: Three Stages of Composition,' BWS, 29 – 49; Reed I, 27 – 8; Jacobus, 55 – 62, 93 – 95, 125 – 131, 157 – 177 — and Butler's edition (RCP) which has appeared since this was written.

35. Reed I, 30.

36. Music, 157; on the transition to the autobiographical poem, now see RCP.

37. Wordsworth told Isabella Fenwick: 'had I been born in a class which would have deprived me of what is called a liberal education, it is not unlikely that, being strong in body, I should have taken to a way of life such as that in which my Pedlar passed the greater part of his days. At all events, I am here called upon freely to acknowledge that the character I have represented in his person is chiefly an idea of what I fancied my own character might have become in his circumstances;' PW, V, 373 – 4. On passages transferred, see Reed I, 28, 29 – 31; Music, 16 – 17, 158; Finch, 'The Ruined Cottage Restored,' 45 – 6; RCP, 23 – 35.

38. Stendhal, *Vie de Henry Brulard, Oeuvres intimes*, ed. Henri Martineau (1955), 160.

39. CLRM, 67; item 639: 'Rousseau (J.J.) Emile ou de l'Education, 2 tomes, 8 vo. calf, a Franckfort, 1762;. . .Rousseau, Confessions, 2 tomes, 8 vo. calf; Geneve, 1782.' John Carter's 'A Catalogue of Wordsworth's Library' dated 1829 (?) records a copy of 'Du Contract Socio': *Du Contrat social* (Amsterdam, 1762); Shaver, 220. Wordsworth's reference to Rousseau in the 'Preface' to *The Borderers* (1797) is apparently to *Émile*; Prose, I; 76 – 7, 82. He mentions 'the paradoxical reveries of Rousseau' in *The Convention of Cintra* (1809); Prose, I, 332. There is a citation (in French) from *Du Contrat social* in 'A Letter to the Bishop of Llandaff' (1793) and Wordsworth draws on this work in several other places in the letter as well; Prose, I, 36, 56, 57, 59, 60. De Selincourt discusses (P, 542 – 3) Rousseau's possible influence on Wordsworth's comments on the education of children in Book V of the autobiographical poem. The relation of Wordsworth and Rousseau is considered by Emile Legouis, *The Early Life of William Wordsworth*, trans. J.W. Matthews (1897), 54 – 67; Henri Roddier, *J. – J. Rousseau en Angleterre au XVIIIe siècle* (1950), 104, 174 – 7, 377 – 80; Jacques Voisine, *J. – J. Rousseau en Angleterre a l'époque romantique* (1956), 6, 202 – 22; Herbert Lindenberger, *On Wordsworth's Prelude* (Princeton, 1963), 80 – 1, 95, 138 – 42,

251−2.

40. See Donald Stauffer's 'Chronological Table of the Most Important Biographical Works in England 1700−1800' in *The Art of Biography in Eighteenth Century England* (1941), II, 285−93; *The Autobiography of Edward Gibbon*, ed. Dero Saunders (New York, 1961), 7−8.

41. *Boswell's Life of Johnson*, ed. R.W. Chapman (1960), 301; Stauffer, I, 411. This point is made by Johnson in *The Idler* (24 November 1759); Samuel Johnson, *The Idler and The Adventurer*, ed. W.J. Bate, J.M. Bullitt and L.F. Powell (New Haven, 1963), 261−4.

42. *Boswell's Life*, 19.

43. *Boswell's Life*, 359 (15 February 1766).

44. *Boswell's Life*, 443; John Morris, *Versions of the Self* (New York, 1966), 20−1.

45. *Boswell's Life*, 853.

46. James Boswell, 'On Diaries,' *The London Magazine* (March 1783), *Boswell's Column*, ed. Margery Bailey (1951), 331, 332. Sterne discovers in 1761 that he can live more than he can record. Tristram Shandy, seeing (IV.13) that it has taken him more than three volumes to describe the first day of his life, declares: 'at this I should just live 364 times faster than I should write − It must follow, an' please your worships, that the more I write, the more I shall have to write − . . .' He, moreover, recognises this as something new: 'an observation never applicable before to any one biographical writer since the creation of the world, but to myself − . . .'; Lawrence Sterne, *The Life and Opinions of Tristram Shandy, Gentleman*, ed. S.H. Monk (New York, 1950), 252.

47. Sir Joshua Reynolds, *Discourses on Art* (New York, 1961), 90.

48. I have lost this reference.

49. W.H. Bruford, *Culture and Society in Classical Weimar 1775−1806* (Cambridge, 1962), 254−62, 418−25; *Goethes Werke* (Hamburger Ausgabe), VII (ed. Erich Trunz, 1965), 290. The translation is Bruford's (257). Martin Swales claims in *The German Bildungsroman from Wieland to Hesse* (Princeton, 1978) that Wieland's *Agathon* (1767) is the first *Bildungsroman*. He states, however, that the word was coined to describe *Wilhelm Meisters Lehrjahren* (12−13) and observes: 'It is no accident that most nineteenth-century novel theory in Germany seems to be a running commentary on the Bildungsroman, and, more specifically, on Goethe's *Wilhelm Meister*' (28).

50. Sterne, 465.

51. Ian Jack, *English Literature 1815−1832* (Oxford, 1964), 361.

52. The term *Bildungsroman* was first used by Karl Morgenstern to describe *Wilhelm Meisters Lehrjahren*; Fritz Martini, 'Der Bildungsroman,' *Deutsche Vierteljahrsschrift für Literaturwissenschaft und Geistesgeschichte*, XXXV (1961), 44 ff and Lothar Köhn, *Entwicklung- und Bildungsroman* (Stuttgart, 1969), 5, as cited by Swales, 12−13.

53. Rousseau, I (1959), 3; compare 5 and Montaigne, II.viii.422: 'me trovant entierement despourveu et vuide de toute autre matiere, je me suis presenté moy-mesmes à moy, pour argument et pour subject. C'est le seul livre au monde de son espece. . .'

54. E.A. Poe, 'Marginalia,' *Graham's Magazine*, January 1848, *The Complete Works of Edgar Allan Poe*, ed. J.A. Harrison (New York, 1965), XVI, 128.

55. There is a critical edition in Charles Baudelaire, *Journaux intimes*, ed. Jacques Crépet and Georges Blin (1949), 51−104, 327−406.

56. Arnaldo Momigliano, *The Development of Greek Biography* (Cambridge, Mass., 1971), 14.

57. CN, I.1801.16.185.

58. Ian Jack, 365. Southey's usage is the earliest listed in the OED. The *Wörterbuch* of the brothers Grimm does not register the word in German until 1853 and the *Grand Dictionnaire Larousse* (1866) states: 'ce mot, quoique d'origine grecque, est de fabrique anglaise;' Momigliano, 14.

59. Jack, 366.

60. J.S. Mill, as cited by Derek Bowman in the introduction to his translation of Ulrich Bräker's *The Life Story and Real Adventures of the Poor Man of Toggenburg* (Edinburgh, 1970), 10.

61. J.S. Mill, *Autobiography*, ed. Jack Stillinger (1971), 89–90.

62. *The Autobiography of Edward, Lord Herbert of Cherbury*, ed. S.L. Lee (New York, 1886), lxv, 2; Charles Ryskamp, *William Cowper of the Inner Temple* (Cambridge, 1959), 174.

63. Rousseau, I, 18.

3 Wordsworth's Long Sentences

1. W.B. Yeats, *The Autobiography of William Butler Yeats* (New York, 1953), 323.

2. T.S. Eliot, 'Philip Massinger,' *Selected Essays*, 185.

3. MSS A, B, C and E read: *Winander! many*; D: *Winander!* — *many*. MSS A, B, C and D read: *answer him.* — *And*; E: *answer him. And.* MSS A, B and C read: *jocund din! And*; D: *jocund din; and*; E: *jocund din* — *&*. MSS A, B and C read: *torrents, or*; D and E: *torrents; or.*
The earliest surviving draft, MS JJ, reads: *Winander & ye green; answer him. And*; *jocund din. And*; *torrents: or.* There is no full stop after *steady lake* (PP, 86–87).
The passage is published as an independent poem in *Lyrical Ballads* (1800) and reprinted in many collected editions. The text in the seventh collected edition of the *Poems* (1849), the last edition supervised by Wordsworth, reads: *Winander!* — *many; answer him.* — *And; jocund din! And; torrents; or.*

4. Milton, 210.

5. Paul Verlaine, 'Art poétique,' *Oeuvres poétiques complètes*, ed. Y.–G. Le Dantec (1948), 206–7.

6. Ezra Pound, 'Imagisme,' and 'A Few Don'ts by an Imagiste,' *Poetry* (March 1913), as cited by Noel Stock, *The Life of Ezra Pound* (Harmondsworth, 1974), 166–7.

7. Milton, 210.

8. Montaigne, III.ii.900.

9. De Quincey, *Recollections of the Lakes and the Lake Poets*, ed. David Wright (Harmondsworth, 1970), 159–61.

10. PP, 221–313.

11. WL, I, 285–8.

12. For some examples, see WL, II, 147–50; III, 174–5, 187–90; IV, 282–3; VI, 1094–5. Wordsworth may not have considered himself an 'adept' at punctuation but the MS that he sent to the printers of *Poems, in Two Volumes* (British Library, Add. MS 47864), like MS V(DC MS 23), demonstrates the painstaking attention that he gave to the matter. He meticulously corrected the fair copies (mostly in the hand of Sara Hutchinson), imposing generally a heavier and more elaborate punctuation. This is especially remarkable in his corrections of the *Ode* (ff 105–113) where he has added many commas and semi-colons to make the sentence structure as clear as possible. This same care and preference for a heavier and more elaborate punctuation is exhibited in the revisions he made for a new edition of *Yarrow Revisited, And Other Poems* in his own copy (London, 1835); British Library, Ashley 2262, A 2262 — over twenty-five years later; see also his comments to John Peace (23.2.1842) on the necessity of punctuation to 'the harmony of blank verse, when skillfully written.'

13. PW, I, 272.

14. PW, I, 32, 34.

15. Compare HG, 103, lines 781–794.

16. *The Letters of John Keats*, ed. M.B. Forman, third edition with revisions (1947), 141–4.

17. Milton, 403 – 4.
18. Prose, III, 372.
19. PP, 96 – 7.
20. PP, 240 – 3, 108 – 9.
21. PP, 114 – 15.
22. Lane Cooper, *A Concordance to the Poems of Wordsworth* (1911).
23. Prose, III, 31.
24. Henry James, 'Preface to *The Princess Casamassima,*' *The Art of the Novel*, ed. R.P. Blackmur (New York, 1950), 62.
25. James, 'Preface to *The Spoils of Poynton,*' *The Art of the Novel*, 119, 120.
26. Henry James, 'The Art of Fiction,' *The Future of the Novel*, ed. Leon Edel (New York, 1956), 12.
27. Henry James, *The Wings of the Dove*, New York edition (New York, reprint, n.d.), II, 132.
28. Marcel Proust, *À la Recherche du temps perdu*, ed. Pierre Clarac and André Ferré (1954), I, 169 – 70.
29. Proust, III, 868 – 9.
30. Proust, I, 45.
31. Paul Valéry, *Cahier B 1910, Oeuvres*, ed. Jean Hytier (1960), II, 579.
32. Nietzsche, as cited by Roland Barthes, *Le Plaisir du texte* (1973), 96.

4 The Meaning of Feeling

1. PW, V. 367 – 8.
2. PW, V. 363.
3. CS, 234.
4. Leopold von Ranke, *Aus Werk und Nachlass* (Munich, 1964 – 1975), I, 233 – 5, as cited by Leonard Krieger, *Ranke, The Meaning of History* (Chicago, 1977), 97.
5. CS, 179; compare 188 n 35, 246, 261 and CL, IV, 589 – 90, 591 – 2.
6. On the date of composition of the philosophical sections, see CL, IV, 579, 585 – 6.
7. CS, 361.
8. S.T. Coleridge, *The Table Talk and Omniana*, ed. T. Ashe (London, 1923), 171. Wordsworth's letters to Francis Wrangham (20.11.1795, 7.3.1796 and c.25.2.1797), show that he was composing imitations of Juvenal *before* he proposes the idea of *The Recluse* to James Tobin (6.3.1798). There are some interesting comments on *The Excursion* as an attempt to fulfil Coleridge's plan in J.S. Lyon, *The Excursion, A Study* (New Haven, 1950), 61 – 121.
9. CS, 207.
10. The nature of Coleridge's male friendships is well discussed in Geoffrey Yarlott, *Coleridge and the Abyssinian Maid* (London, 1971), 1 – 31.
11. Coleridge to William Godwin (25.3.1801): 'If I die, and the Booksellers will give you any thing for my Life, be sure to say — 'Wordsworth descended on him, like the Γνῶθι σεαυτόν from Heaven; by shewing to him what true Poetry was, he made him know, that he himself was no Poet.'
12. Coleridge says much the same thing to Daniel Stuart (7.10.1815).
13. DC MS 16, f 39a; PP, 144 – 5.
14. Two folios are numbered *304* in pencil in MS A; the second is my *305*. The revised text of f 304b is transcribed in P, p.450. Coleridge is 'Philosopher and Poet' in the unpublished *Home at Grasmere* (HG.660).
15. *The Prose Works of William Wordsworth*, ed. A.B. Grosart (London, 1876), III, 469.
16. *The Correspondence of Henry Crabb Robinson with the Wordsworth Circle*,

ed. E.J. Morley (Oxford, 1927), I, 401, as cited by Melvin Rader, *Wordsworth, A Philosophical Approach* (Oxford, 1967), 67. Compare Robinson's diary entry for 10 September 1816: 'He [Wordsworth] represented, however, *much as, unknown to him*, the German philosophers have done, that by the imagination the mere fact is exhibited as connected with that infinity without which there is no poetry;' *Diary, Reminiscences, and Correspondence of Henry Crabb Robinson*, II, 22 (my italics), and Caroline Fox's report in her journal for 1844 of Wordsworth's somewhat dismissive and sceptical remarks on German thought; *Memories of Old Friends*, ed. H.N. Pym, second edition (London, 1882), II, 40 – 1.

17. *The Prose Works of William Wordsworth*, ed. Grosart, III, 424.

18. De Quincey, *Recollections*, 190 – 1.

19. 'Inventory of the Books. Prints and Pictures of the late Wm. Wordsworth Esq of Rydal Mount taken by me; this 7th day of May 1850. John Hudson.' There are two copies of this inventory in similar notebooks, one with brown marbled boards and black binding, the other with blue marbled boards and red binding. The second is a fair copy of the first.

20. CLRM: I have used the British Library copy found in *Bibliographical Tracts* 1859 – 1912 (011908. ff 24). There is a facsimile in A.N.L. Munby, *Sale Catalogues of Libraries of Eminent Persons*, IX, ed. Roy Park (London, 1974).

21. Hudson does note 'Dialogues of Plato' (item 540); however, I would guess that this is one of the books listed as item 409 in the sale catalogue (CLRM): *Dialogi V* (Oxford, 1752), the Greek text. The only other work by Plato in Hudson's inventory is 'Cratyles of Plato' (item 698) (CLRM, item 409). This is probably the copy of *The Cratylus, Phaedo, Parmenides and Timaeus*, translated by Thomas Taylor (London, 1793) in the Wordsworth Library. Whether Wordsworth read it we do not know, but the marginalia in the book are in the hand of Coleridge.

22. Hudson mentions Holbach's attack on Christianity, *Système de la nature* (item 126), 'Aristotle on Poetry 2v' (item 145), 'Hobbes Tracts' (item 622) and the Plato referred to in note 21. The sale catalogue (CLRM) includes J.W. Blakesley's *Life of Aristotle* (1839) (item 103), Descartes's *Principia philosophiae* (1667) and *Geometrica* (1683) (item 106), Jacob Boehme's *De signatura rerum* (1651) (item 192), Ralph Cudworth's *The True Intellectual System of the Universe* (1678) (item 220) and George Berkeley's *Alciphron* (1775) (item 258). There are only two minor works by Locke, *A Letter to the Right Reverend Lord Bishop of Worcester* (1697) and *Mr Locke's Reply to the Right Reverend the Lord Bishop of Worcester's Answer to his Letter* (1699) (item 266). Hume's *History of England* (1793) (item 45) and his *Political Discourses* (1782) (item 46) were on Wordsworth's shelves but none of his philosophical works.

Since this was written Chester and Alice Shaver have published a list of Wordsworth's books (Shaver) from these two sources and: (1) a 'notebook recording loans made from Wordsworth's library at Rydal Mount between 1824 and 1858' (Harvard, Widener Collection 12.11.14), (2) 'A Catalogue of Wordsworth's Library' made by Wordsworth's secretary, John Carter, dated 1829 (but probably compiled earlier, possibly before 1824? — the date will be discussed, they say, in George Whalley's edition of Coleridge's *Marginalia*) and including books 'stored for Coleridge' from about 1810 to about 1830 (Harvard MS English 880, Houghton Library), and (3) what they could glean 'by correspondence with libraries and private owners;' Shaver, ix-xxxii. Their work confirms what is said in the text about Wordsworth's reading habits and the books that he owned. Their list of the books identified as belonging to Coleridge (Shaver, 313 – 63) shows that Wordsworth had available to him Augustine's *Omnium operum*, Scotus Erigena, *De divisione naturae libri*, assorted volumes of Aquinas's *Opera omnia*, Malebranche's *De la Recherche de la vérité*, Leibnitz's *Essais de théodicée sur la bonté de Dieu, la liberté de l'homme, et l'origine du mal* (1710), some Locke (exactly what is uncertain), Hartley's *Observations on Man* and Anthony Willich's book on Kant (1798).

23. Prose, I, 174, 177, 179.

24. Hudson, item 145; Prose I, 139, 179.

25. Prose, I, 139.

26. Prose, I, 180. Note Wordsworth's reference to *inoperative* truths in his letter to Coleridge of 22 May 1815.

27. Prose, I, 179, 169.

28. Prose, III, 81, 102.

29. See for example: WL, I, 454, 594−5, 650; II, 2.

30. John Finch, 'On the Dating of *Home at Grasmere*: A New Approach,' BWS, 14−15; Reed, I, 223−4.

31. Alexander Pope, 'The Design' (prefixed to all editions beginning with 1734a), *An Essay on Man*, ed. Maynard Mack (The Twickenham Edition, IIIi), (London, 1964), 7.

32. PW, IV, 463.

33. Prose, III, 5.

34. Prose, III, 6.

35. Prose, III, 5−6.

36. HG, 412. Because of the way that Wordsworth composed and because it is a question of an unfinished work, it is not absolutely certain that Wordsworth considered all three pieces — 'Pressed with conflicting thoughts of love and fear,' *The Tuft of Primroses* and *To the Clouds* — as fragments of *The Recluse*, although it is probable that this is the case, as is indicated by his statement to Samuel Rogers (29.9.1808) that: 'I have written since I saw you about 500 miles of my long Poem, which is all I have done.' He had seen Rogers in London in the spring of 1808 and these three pieces do seem to be all that he composed during the spring and summer that could form part of *The Recluse*, despite the fact that together they total 716 lines. Moorman's statement that Wordsworth may be referring to *The Excursion* seems to be disproved by Reed's evidence (II, 22−25) that Wordsworth did not compose any of *The Excursion* in this period (except as part of *The Tuft of Primroses*), and by the fact that, unlike *The Excursion*, these are meditations in the author's own person. Moorman suggests that the *Tuft of Primroses* and *To The Clouds* might be considered as intended for *The Recluse*; II, 130−2; compare Reed, II, 382 n 28, who appears to ignore Wordsworth's assertion in his letter to John Kenyon (25.7.1826) that *To The Clouds* is 'a fragment of *The Recluse*' (see note 42). Reed (II. 397) shows that the date of the letter to Rogers is probably 27 October 1808. The letter is cited from Sotheby's Catalogue, 28 July 1964, by Moorman, II, 131. The three pieces are not only continuous with *Home at Grasmere*, but also with the autobiographical poem and The Excursion. This affinity is further demonstrated by the fact that Wordsworth transfers three passages from *The Tuft of Primroses* to these poems: the analysis of the motives for withdrawing from the world is incorporated into a speech by the Solitary (E, III.367−405), some of the story of old Mr Sympson is incorporated into the account of the churchyard among the mountains (E, VII.242−291) and the description of the Grand Chartreuse becomes part of the revised version of Wordsworth's journey through France (VI.420−471; 1850); Poems, I, 1032.

37. Finch, 'On the Dating of *Home at Grasmere*,' 14−28; HG, 10−30.

38. Reed, II, 45.

39. All the references to *Home at Grasmere* are to Beth Darlington's 'reading text' of MS D, HG, 39−107 (the odd numbered pages).

40. JDW, 164−5.

41. The events are described in Dorothy Wordsworth's letter to Catherine Clarkson (19.7.1807) from which the phrases on the cutting of the trees are taken; see also: PW, V, 482−483, 467.

42. PW, II, 524.

43. PW, IV, 463.

44. Carl Jung, *Memories, Dreams, Reflections*, trans. Richard and Clara Winston (New York, 1963), 358.

45. Jung, 340.

5   The Poetry of Consciousness

1. PW, IV, 463.
2. Memoirs, II, 480.
3. PW, IV, 467.
4. P, 619.
5. P, 623 – 8. Whitman also compares himself to Columbus (see, for example, *Passage to India, Prayer for Columbus*, and the poem that he chose to conclude his last collection of poems, *A Thought of Columbus*) and Eliot, with himself in mind, affirms in *East Coker* that 'Old men ought to be explorers.'
6. MS A reads: *underpresence* and MS B: *under-presence*; this is changed to *under consciousness* in A and *underconsciousness* in B.
7. Martin Heidigger, 'Wozu Dichter' ('What Are Poets For?'), *Poetry, Language, Thought*, trans. Albert Hofstadter (New York, 1971), 101.
8. CS, 44 – 5.
9. PW, IV, 463 – 4. Compare 'Not in a mystical and idle sense' (II.232 – 237).
10. Valéry, I, 1160.
11. R.D. Laing, *Self and Others* (Harmondsworth, 1969), 86.
12. Wallace Stevens, *The Necessary Angel* (New York, 1951), 164.
13. Stevens, *Angel*, 23.
14. Stevens, *Angel*, 66 – 7.
15. The phrases are from Wordsworth's *The Thorn*; Coleridge's *Dejection: An Ode* (CS, 79); Keat's *Ode to Melancholy* (*The Complete Poems*, 349); and Whitman's *Song of Myself* (*Leaves of Grass*, 41). Wordsworth is the first great poet to write a detailed guide to looking at a particular and very limited area of countryside. This was originally published as *Topographical Description of the Country of the Lakes in the North of England* (1820) and then as *A Description of the Scenery of the Lakes in the North of England* (1822, 1823) — titles that reveal the specialised nature of the enterprise.
16. See the entries under *inscape* in the index to *The Note-Books and Papers of Gerard Manley Hopkins*, ed. Humphrey House (1937).
17. Stevens, *Angel*, 65 – 6.
18. Adrian Stokes, 'The Art of Turner (1775 – 1851)', *The Critical Writings of Adrian Stokes* (1978), III, 237.
19. PW, IV, 463.
20. John Lowes, *The Road to Xanadu* (New York, 1959), 338 – 43.
21. Prose, I, 7, 9.
22. PW, I, 270.
23. Compare also *Descriptive Sketches* (1793), 494 – 509, that with its 'solemn sea' of mist, 'gulf of gloomy blue' and 'hollow roar profound' of 'unnumbered streams' is a rehearsal for the Snowdon description.
24. PW, IV, 463.
25. The phrase 'kindling edge' is from *Who but is pleased to watch the moon on high*, another of Wordsworth's last poems; compare 'brightening edge' in *How beautiful the Queen of Night, on high*.

6   Ideas of Order

1. LB, 158, 156.
2. PW, IV, 464.
3. LB, 140..
4. LB, 3, 153.

5. LB, 163.

6. Wallace Stevens, note (about 1939) for the *Oxford Anthology of American Literature*, as cited by S.F. Morse, *Wallace Stevens, Poetry as Life* (New York, 1970), 113–14.

7. The text of all the citations from 'Moods of My Own Mind' in this chapter is that of PTV.

8. LB, 140.

9. LB, 140.

10. William Hazlitt, 'On Imitation,' *The Complete Works of William Hazlitt*, ed. P.P. Howe (1930), IV, 76 n 1.

11. The texts are from Elsie Smith, *An Estimate of William Wordsworth, By his Contemporaries 1793–1822* (Oxford, 1932), 71, 74, 79, 84.

12. Fyodor Dostoevsky, *White Nights and Other Stories*, trans. Constance Garnett (1970), 60, 61.

13. PW, I, ix; W.J. Owen, *Wordsworth as Critic* (Toronto, 1969), 155.

14. PW, I, ix.

15. Prose, III, 5–6.

16. Prose, III, 26–8.

17. Prose, III, 28–9.

18. *The Journal of Sir Walter Scott, 1825–32*, T. Nelson and Sons, reprint of 1890 edition (n.d.), II, 183; II, 262, 263, ('the *Magnum*'); II, 167 ('the *grand opus*').

19. Walter Scott, *Waverley*, Border Edition, ed. Andrew Lang (1893), xv.

20. *Waverley*, xii, xiii.

21. *Waverley*, xxii.

22. Walter Scott, *Guy Mannering*, ed. Andrew Lang (1893), ix; *Waverley*, xviii.

23. *Waverley*, xxxiv.

24. See Robert du Pontavice de Heussey's report of Balzac's comments on his story-telling during his stay with the de Pommereul at Fougères in the autumn of 1828, Étienne Aubrée, *Balzac à Fougères* (1939), as cited by H.J. Hunt, *Balzac's Comédie Humaine* (1964), 12.

25. Honoré de Balzac, catalogue de 1845, *La Comédie humaine*, ed. Pierre-Georges Castex, I (1976), cxxiii–cxxv.

26. Balzac, 'Avant-propos,' I, 18.

27. Félix Davin, 'Introduction aux Etudes de moeurs au XIXe siècle;' Balzac, I, 1147–8, 1147. Balzac's share in the authorship of these introductions is discussed by Anne-Marie Meininger, 1143–4, and indicated in the notes to the text.

28. Balzac, I, 10.

29. Balzac, I, 1145–6, 1146, 1147, 1148, 1148–9.

30. Honoré de Balzac, *Lettres à Madame Hanaska*, ed. Roger Pierrot (1967), I, 269–70.

31. *Lettres à Madame Hanska*, I, 266.

32. Felix Davin, 'Introduction aux Etudes philosophiques,' Honoré de Balzac, *La Comédie humaine*, ed. Pierre Citron (1966), VI, 702, col. 1.

33. *La Comédie humaine*, ed. Citron, VI, 703, col. 1.

34. Balzac, I, 10, 8–9.

35. Balzac, I, 17.

36. *La Comédie humaine*, ed. Citron, VI, 704, col. 1.

37. Balzac, I, 1151–2.

38. Balzac, I, 10–11.

39. Balzac, I, 1151. Many of Balzac's protagonists are, like their creator, in the grip of an obsessive grand design — for example, Xavier Rabourdin in *Les Employés*, Louis Lambert in *Louis Lambert*, Balthazar Cläes in *La Recherche de l'absolu*, and even David Séchard in *Illusions perdues*. The desire for some larger form also manifests itself in different ways in the work of Cooper ('the series of the Leather-Stocking Tales'), Trollope (Barsetshire), Hardy (Wessex), Zola (*Les Rougon-Macquart*), James (the New

York edition) and Proust (*A la Recherche du temps perdu*), and the larger structures of the last three authors all owe something to the example of *La Comédie humaine*. Originally James projected twenty-three volumes for the New York edition because this was the number of volumes in the collected edition that he had used for his first essay on Balzac in 1875, and he attempted to group his fictions into various *scenes* like those in Balzac; Leon Edel, *The Life of Henry James* (Harmondsworth, 1977), II, 625 – 8.

40. Bertrand Russell, *A History of Western Philosophy* (New York, 1945), 828 – 36. Russell read Frege in 1901; Russell, *Portraits from Memory* (1957), 25. His *The Principles of Mathematics* and G.E. Moore's *Principia Ethica* were both published in 1903.

41. Valéry, I, 1320.

42. Fredson Bowers, *Textual and Literary Criticism* (Cambridge, 1966), 45.

43. Whitman, 12.

44. Whitman, 432.

45. Whitman, 391.

46. Charles Baudelaire, *Les Fleurs du mal*, ed. Antoine Adam (1961), 254; Charles Baudelaire, *Correspondence*, ed. Claude Pichois with Jean Ziegler (1973), II, 196. Barbey d'Aurevilly writes in his review of the first edition (*Le Pays*, 24.7.1857): 'The artists who see the lines under the luxury and efflorescence of the colour will perceive that there is here a *secret architecture*, a plan calculated by the poet, meditative and determined. *Les Fleurs du mal* do not follow each other like so many lyric pieces dispersed by inspiration and gathered up in a collection for no other motive than to bring them together. They are not so much poems as a poetic work of the strongest unity. From the point of view of art and esthetic sensation, therefore, they would lose much in not being read in the order in which the poet, who knew what he was doing, has arranged them;' as cited by Enid Starkie, *Baudelaire* (Harmondsworth, 1971), 668; my translation.

47. Balzac, I, xix.

48. Mallarmé, 'Variations sur un sujet,' *Oeuvres complètes*, ed. Henri Mondor et G. Jean-Aubry (1945), 378; Hart Crane, 'General Aims and Theories,' *The Complete Poems and Selected Letters and Prose of Hart Crane*, ed. Brom Weber (New York, 1966), 221. Compare Turner's comments on his paintings: 'Keep them together,' 'What is the use of them but together?' Lawrence Gowing, *Turner: Imagination and Reality* (New York, 1966), 31.

7   After Wordsworth

1. Matthew Arnold, 'Wordsworth,' *English Literature and Irish Politics*, ed. R.H. Super (Ann Arbor, 1973), 36, 340 – 1.

2. *Lyrical Ballads* went through four editions in eight years (1798, 1800, 1802, 1803). There were, in the three editions after 1798, a total of 1,750 copies printed of volume one and 2,000 copies of volume two. *Peter Bell* sold out the first edition of 500 copies in April 1819, another edition was printed in May and 201 more copies were sold by June. These figures may be compared with the fifteen editions of Rogers's *The Pleasures of Memory* issued between 1792 and 1806, the six editions of Moore's *Lalla Rookh* that appeared in 1817 or the 20,000 copies of Byron's *The Corsair* sold on the day of its publication in 1814. The first two paragraphs are based on Thomas Raysor, 'The Establishment of Wordsworth's Reputation,' *Journal of English and Germanic Philology*, LIV (1955), 61 – 71 and W.J. Owen, 'Costs, Sales, and Profits of Longman's Editions of Wordsworth,' *The Library*, XII (1957), 93 – 107.

3. Prose, III, 80.

4. Raysor, 62, 65, 71.

5. De Quincey, *Recollections* 117, 116.

6. Arnold, 'Wordsworth,' 36 – 7. Certainly for Whitman in 'Poetry Today in America — Shakespeare — the Future' (1881), Tennyson represents English poetry (*Leaves of Grass*, 531 – 533). He does not mention Wordsworth.

7. This is the number listed in my copy, *Poems of Wordsworth*, chosen and edited by Matthew Arnold (Macmillan, 1971). Arnold's essay is the preface.

8. CL, I, 127.

9. CS, 320, 357.

10. William Hazlitt, 'My First Acquaintance with Poets' (April 1823), *Selected Essays of William Hazlitt*, ed. Geoffrey Keynes (1948), 515.

11. De Quincey, *Recollections*, 122 – 3; and see his letter to Wordsworth (31.5.1803), 385 – 7.

12. Thomas De Quincey, 'On Wordsworth's Poetry,' *The Collected Writings*, ed. David Masson (Edinburgh, 1890), XI, 315.

13. De Quincey, 'On Wordsworth's Poetry,' XI, 322.

14. Documentation of this point would require a history of English poetry from Wordsworth to the present, which is , as I have said in my preface, beyond the scope of this book. There is a wealth of material to be found simply by consulting the entry on Wordsworth in the indexes to the standard biographies and editions of prose (including letters). Shelley's *To Wordsworth* and *Peter Bell III*, Keats's *Great spirits now on earth are sojourning*, and Browning's *The Lost Leader* demonstrate in their different ways Wordsworth's far-reaching effect. Arnold states that Wordsworth is the greatest European poet of the last two or three hundred years, after Shakespeare, Molière, Milton and Goethe ('Wordsworth,' 40 – 1). Tennyson told William Allingham that Wordsworth 'had produced the finest work since Milton' and when he decided to have the dining-room mantelpiece at Black Horse Copse carved with emblematic devices 'of his favourite modern poets,' he chose Chaucer, Milton, Shakespeare, Wordsworth, Goethe and Dante; Charles Tennyson, *Alfred Tennyson* (1968), 451, 372. When 'asked, "whom did you venerate as a young man, Mr Yeats?" [h]is answer came without hesitation, "Tennyson". On the question being repeated by the inquirer, who had not expected this answer, the reply was the same with the addition of "Wordsworth",' Joseph Hone, *W.B. Yeats* (Harmondsworth, 1971), 34. Hardy's debt to Wordsworth is discussed in my article 'Hardy's Lyrics: Visions of Moments,' *Cahiers d'études et de recherches victoriennes et edouardiennes* (October 1980), 201 – 10.

15. Mill, *Autobiography*, 89 – 90.

16. *The George Eliot Letters*, ed. G.S. Haight (London, 1954). She had just bought the Moxon edition (1836 – 7) in six volumes. Her husband, J.W. Cross, comments on this letter: 'The allusion to Wordsworth is interesting, as it entirely expresses the feeling she had to him up to the day of her death;' *George Eliot's Life* (Edinburgh, 1884?), I, 49 – 50.

17. British Library MS 41,325, f 34a.

18. F. – R. de Chateaubriand, *Mémoires d'outre-tombe*, ed. Maurice Levaillant and Georges Moulinier (1946), I, 412 – 13, 418.

19. Charles Sainte-Beuve, *Oeuvres*, ed. Maxime Leroy (1949), I, 134 – 8; see also 302, 439, 1043. Herbert Lindenberger, on the evidence of M.A. Smith's *L'Influence des Lakistes sur les romantiques français* (1920), 27 – 8, 100 – 1, postulates 'a probable line of descent from *Lyrical Ballads* through Sainte-Beuve's very influential poem "Les rayons jaunes" to the city poems of Baudelaire and Rimbaud' (284 – 5, n 23).

20. Hippolyte Taine, *Histoire de la littérature anglaise* (tenth edition, 1899), IV, 337, 313 – 24. He calls Wordsworth the 'new Cowper, with less talent and more ideas than the other' (313) and says, 'When I will have emptied my head of all worldly thoughts and looked at the clouds continuously for ten years in order to refine my soul, I will enjoy that poetry. . . All the poetics in the world will not reconcile us to so much boredom;' (317 – 18).

21. Arnold, 'Wordsworth,' 37. The only translation of the autobiographical poem

238   *Wordsworth and the Beginnings of Modern Poetry*

that I know is Louis Cazamian's *Le Prélude* (Aubier, 1949). The British Library Reading Room Catalogue listed (December 1979) under 'smaller collections' the following translations of Wordsworth's poetry: German (1893), Italian (1915), Spanish (1922), Finnish (1949) and Polish (1963); there were no translations in the entry under 'larger collections.'

22. This is another point whose documentation would demand an entire book. A single example will have to suffice here. Paul Van Tieghem, in his *Le Romatisme dans la littérature européenne* (1969), states: 'It is *à propos* of Byron above all and his influence that the term 'romantic revolution' is fully justified. . . So much so that one can, without abusing chronological precision in the history of the literary expression of feeling, date from Canto III of *Childe Harold* (1816) the debut in Europe of openly personal and confidential poetry' (139). This is especially significant because Canto III is probably that work of Byron in which the effect of Wordsworth is the most marked, as Wordsworth himself noted. He grumbles to Henry Taylor (26.12.1823) about Byron's 'poetical obligations to me': 'As far as I am acquainted with his works, they are most apparent in the 3rd canto of Childe Harold; not so much in particular expressions, though there is no want of these, as in the tone (*assumed* rather than natural) of enthusiastic admiration of Nature, and a sensibility to her influences.' Most of Canto III was composed at the Villa Diodati, near Geneva, in 1816, where Byron was often in conversation with Shelley, who was staying at Montalègre, a few hundred yards up the hill, and full of enthusiasm for Wordsworth; Richard Holmes, *Shelley, The Pursuit* (1974), 324 – 37. Byron later told Medwin: 'Shelley, when I was in Switzerland, used to dose me with Wordsworth physic even to nausea: and I do remember then reading some things of his with pleasure,' L.A. Marchand, *Byron* (New York, 1957), II, 624, n 8. The results of this dose were such that Van Tiegham could specify Canto III, as distinct from the other cantos, as the most personal and the one that other poets copied.

23. Erich Auerbach, *Mimesis*, trans. W.R. Trask (Princeton, 1971), 458 – 9. Braudel, working from very different data than Auerbach, also sees our world, the world that is coming into being, as the result of a revolution that started virtually in Wordsworth's lifetime: 'The present of today's civilisation is that enormous mass of time whose dawn would have been marked by the XVIIIth century and whose night is not yet near. Toward 1750, the world, with its multiple civilisations, started on a series of upheavals, of enchained catastrophes (they are not merely the attribute of the single western civilisation). We are still there today.

'This revolution, these repeated, continued, troubles, is not only the industrial revolution, it is also a scientific revolution. . .a biological revolution in fact, with multiple causes, but with the evident result, always the same: a human inundation such as the planet has never before seen. Soon three thousand million humans: there were scarcely three hundred million in 1400;' 'Histoire et temps present,' (1959), 309 – 10.

24. R.W. Emerson, *English Traits* (1893), 280.

25. Prose, I, 132.

26. Prose, I, 130.

27. T.S. Eliot, *The Use of Poetry and the Use of Criticism*, 74.

28. Prose, I, 130, 132.

29. Prose, I, 124.

30. Stendhal as cited by Ezra Pound, 'The Serious Artist,' *Literary Essays of Ezra Pound*, ed. T.S. Eliot (Norfolk, Connecticut, 1954), 54, my translation.

31. Prose, I, 132, 134.

32. Pound, 'The Serious Artist,' 50. 'The Prose Tradition in Verse' is the title of an essay published in *Poetry* in 1914 and reprinted in the *Literary Essays of Ezra Pound*, 371 – 7; compare Pound's comments in 'How to Read,' 31.

33. Arnold, 'Wordsworth,' 53 – 4.

34. Whitman, 448. The first ellipsis is his.

35. Suzanne Bernard, *Le Poème en prose de Baudelaire jusqu'a nos jours* (1959).

36. Pound, 'The Serious Artist,' 41.

37. Pound, 'The Serious Artist,' 44, 48.

38. Pound, 'Mr Housman at Little Bethel,' 72; *ABC of Reading* (New York, 1960), 73, 77, 173 – 8.

39. Pound, 'A Retrospect,' 7; *ABC of Reading*, 73.

40. A.N. Jeffares, *W.B. Yeats* (1966), 167; Richard Ellmann, *Yeats, The Man and the Masks* (New York, 1958), 212; Pound, 'A Retrospect,' 7.

41. Pound, 'The Serious Artist,' 44.

42. T.S. Eliot, *Four Quartets*, 32 – 3.

43. The citations in this paragraph are all from Barbara Garlitz, 'The Baby's Debut: The Contemporary Reaction to Wordsworth's Poetry of Childhood,' *Boston University Studies in English*, IV (1960), 85 – 94, except for those from Wordsworth and Haydon, *The Autobiography and Memoirs of Benjamin Robert Haydon*, ed. A.P. Penrose (1927), 256.

44. G.M. Hopkins, *The Note-Books and Papers of Gerard Manley Hopkins*, ed. Humphry House (1937), 309 – 10.

45. Valéry, *Cahiers*, II, 288, 302.

46. E.A. Poe, 'The Poetic Principle,' *The Home Journal*, 31 August 1850, XIV, 266 – 7.

47. Poe, XIV, 267.

48. Moreover, the idea of short poems in blank verse is, as far as I know, the invention of Coleridge and Wordsworth.

49. William Shakespeare, *Hamlet*, ed. H.H. Furness (New York, 1963): Act II, Scene ii, 249 – 251.

50. John Donne, *The Elegies and the Songs and Sonnets*, ed. Helen Gardner (Oxford, 1965), 53.

51. William Blake, *The Complete Poems*, ed. Alicia Ostriker (Harmondsworth, 1977), 506.

52. Valéry, 'Mélange,' I, 305.

53. Valéry, 'Au sujet du *Cimetière marin*,' I, 1500.

54. *The Letters of Hart Crane*, 77.

55. PW, I, 318 – 19. Constable, who was familiar with Wordsworth's poetry, shared this conviction that the world had not been *seen* before by any artist. He writes, in a note to Leslie (1833), that of the qualities he aimed at in his pictures — 'light — dews — breezes — bloom — and freshness; not one of which has yet been perfected on the canvas of any painter in the world;' C.R. Leslie, *Memoirs of the Life of John Constable* (1951), 218.

56. Rousseau, I, 104. There are remarkably few descriptions of the countryside in *Les Confessions* considering the pleasure that Rousseau takes in it and they are general when compared to Wordsworth's descriptions.

57. John Ruskin, *Modern Painters* (1906), III, 155.

58. Dryden, 'To Roger, Earl of Orrey' (1664), *Of Dramatic Poesy*, I, 7; James Sutherland, *A Preface to Eighteenth Century Poetry* (Oxford, 1963), 123; Brendan Ohehir, *Expans'd Hieroglyphicks* (Berkeley, 1969), 3 – 24.

59. Samuel Johnson, *Rasselas, Poems, and Selected Prose* (New York, 1958), 527.

60. Gainsborough to Lord Hardwicke (n.d.), as cited by Kenneth Clark, *Landscape into Art* (1956), 48; Mary Woodall, *The Letters of Thomas Gainsborough* (1963), no.42.

61. Clark, *Landscape into Art*, 49.

62. Ruskin, III, 156.

63. Ruskin, III, 264 – 6.

64. Stevens, 'An Ordinary Evening in New Haven,' X, *The Palm at the End of the Mind*, 337.

65. Claude Lévi-Strauss, *Tristes tropiques* (1955), 48. Braudel, when he wants a metaphor for the unity and diversity of the sciences of man, turns to landscape: 'let us suppose. . .that the human sciences all interest themselves in one and the same

landscape: that of the past, present and future actions of man. . . *vis à vis* this panorama the sciences of man would be no more than observation posts each with their particular view, their sketches from different perspectives, their colours, their chronicles. . .;' 'Unité et diversité des sciences de l'homme,' 85 – 6; compare 18. This landscape stands for all human history in the same way that the 'vast prospect of the world' at the end of the autobiographical poem (XIII.370 – 373) stands for the whole of Wordsworth's life.

66. Scott as cited by John Lockhart, *The Life of Sir Walter Scott* (Edinburgh, 1902), II, 79; *The Letters of Sir Walter Scott*, ed. H.J. Grierson (1932) I, 146.

67. Stevens, 'Of Modern Poetry,' *The Palm at the End of the Mind*, 174 – 5.

Index